Migrant Belongings

Migrant Belongings

Memory, Space, Identity

Anne-Marie Fortier

Oxford • New York

First published in 2000 by
Berg
Editorial offices:
150 Cowley Road, Oxford, OX4 1JJ, UK
838 Broadway, Third Floor, New York, NY 10003-4812, USA

Berg is the imprint of Oxford International Publishers Ltd.

Library of Congress Cataloging-in-Publication Data

A catalogue record for this book is available from the Library of Congress.

British Library Cataloguing-in-Publication Data

A catalogue record for this book is available from the British Library.

ISBN 1 85973 405 7 (Cloth)
1 85973 410 3 (Paper)

Typeset by JS Typesetting, Wellingborough, Northants.
Printed in the United Kingdom by Biddles Ltd, King's Lynn.

Contents

Tables, Maps and Plates

Tables

Maps

Plates

Acknowledgements

This book was produced in three stages and in three places. First, as a doctoral dissertation in sociology at Goldsmiths' College in London (England). Second, the dissertation was revised for publication during a postdoctoral researchship at the Centre for Research on Citizenship and Social Transformation, Concordia University, Montreal. And third, the last touches were completed at Lancaster University, England. Words fail to express my gratitude to all of those who, through the years, and the stages, have helped me sustain the energy to fulfil this project.

My greatest debt goes to Paul Gilroy who has guided me with immense respect, patience and sensitivity in the completion of the first stage. I appreciate the trust he put in my work, which was a vital lifeline during those moments when I lost faith in – and track of! – my project. His vision, creativity and encyclopaedic knowledge never ceased to inspire me and to challenge me, and I will always value his example.

This project is also the result of the 'field world' that surfaced from my contacts with many London Italians, especially the leaders and members of St Peter's Italian church and the Centro Scalabrini, but also others. Without their time and support, this book would never have come about. Warm thanks to Janet Fionda and her late husband Eddy, and to Elisa and Ray Fitzgerald, for providing me with an occasional 'family home' from home. Special thanks to Roberta Mutti, Padre Gaetano Parolin, and Padre Giandomenico Ziliotto, all of whom greeted my project with enthusiasm and have been most supportive throughout. I also wish to thank Padre Giuseppe Blanda, Bruno Besagni, Olive Besagni, Wolfgango Bucci, Alberto Cavalli, Bruno Cervi, Terri Colpi, Padre Carmelo di Giovanni, Remo Finaldi, Francesco Giacon, Giuseppe Giacon, Joanna Giacon, Vittorio Heissel, Lorenzo Losi, Padre Natalino Mignolli, Lucio Sponza, and Arturo Tosi.

Kate Nash and David Leahy have generously read early drafts of this book, which I discussed with each of them for hours on end. I am immensely grateful for their rigorous and constructive comments that improved the final product beyond measure. David Leahy deserves special thanks for his sustained and invaluable thoroughness, interest, and enthusiasm even after reading numerous versions of the same chapters. I shall truly miss our early morning gab sessions at *Java U*, in Montreal, which would at times extend well into the late morning. I shall also miss the incomparable *bol de café-au-lait* and muffins but, most important, the irreplaceable ambience of the place, which became a regular daytime haunt, much appreciated for the completion of various tedious and mechanical editing tasks. Thank you Nick, Roney, Christina and Ashley.

A number of friends and colleagues from both sides of the Atlantic have read or discussed parts of the book with me and I have greatly benefited from our conversations and their encouragements: I would like to thank Sara Ahmed, Les Back, Vikki Bell, John Campbell, Claudia Castañeda, Anick Druelle, Hilary Graham, Breda Gray, Danielle Juteau, Diane Lamoureux, Minoo Moallem, Mimi Sheller, Sandhya Shukla, Beverley Skeggs, Colette St-Hilaire, Fran Tonkiss, Mark Thorpe, Odile Sévigny, Nicolas van Schendel. Avtar Brah and John Solomos closely examined the first version of this account; their questions, comments and suggestions have guided me in the revision of the dissertation. My post-doctoral sojourn with the Centre for Research on Citizenship and Social Transformation at Concordia University was memorable not only because I benefited from the luxury of full-time research, but also because of the sheer pleasantness of the place. Thanks to all members of the Centre for the intellectual richness of our discussions, as well as for their warmth, generosity and good humour: Martin Allor, Reeta Chowdhari Tremblay, David Leahy, Chantal Maillé, Margie Mendell, Daniel Salée, Sherry Simon. The comments from an anonymous reader were helpful in fine tuning the final draft. Thanks also to Debra Ferreday for efficiently completing the tedious task of formatting the bibliography at the final stage. Thank you to Kathryn Earle, from Berg Publishers, for believing in my project, and to Emma Wildsmith and Sara Everett, thanks to whom the 'production' process ran as smoothly as one can hope for. Copy-editing of the doctoral dissertation was completed by Tom Gyenes, and the final version was revised by David E. Michael.

I am eternally grateful for the unabated support of my family, especially my parents, Monique and Robert, and the late Louise Audet. This book is dedicated to the three of them. I also want to thank my dear friends, 'over here' and 'elsewhere', who have provided encouragement and patiently accepted my reduced availability and obsessions over extended periods at a time. I want to express my special thanks to Jane McElhone, in Montreal, for welcoming me in her wonderful home when I 'returned', and for the memorable times we shared there. Finally but importantly, Jessica Higgs has lovingly endured my altered states throughout all these translations in space. Extending her support even at a distance, she became a close ally in this enquiry (as she knows the story inside out!), and made it the more enjoyable for all her spirit and good cheer.

Funding for this study was provided by the Association of Commonwealth Universities, the Social Sciences and Humanities Research Council of Canada, and La Fondation Desjardins. Excerpts of this book have been presented in a number of seminars and conferences. I am thankful to those who invited me to some of these seminars, as well as to all those present, on each occasion, for their interest and comments.

Acknowledgements

Some of the chapters, listed below, were published previously in different versions, and are reprinted here with the kind permission of the publishers. Chapter 3 was published in abridged form in *Diaspora. A Journal of Transnational Studies* 7(2) 1998. An abridged version of Chapter 5 was published in *Theory, Culture and Society* 16(2) 1999.

Introduction: Performative Belongings

The rhizome is not nomadic, it roots itself, even in the air

Edouard Glissant

This book traces the formation of Italian migrant belongings in Britain, and scrutinizes the identity narratives through which they are stabilized. I use identity, here, to speak of one 'for which the experience of geographical movement and resettlement [is] formative' (Jacobson 1995: xi). Against the assumed isomorphism of space, place and culture, on the one hand, and the reification of uprootedness as the paradigmatic figure of postmodern life, on the other, I raise the ways in which cultural identity is *at once* deterritorialized and reterritorialized.[1] Questions of what it means to speak of 'home', 'origins', 'continuity' and 'tradition', in the context of migration, are paramount in this project.

I am fascinated by people's tenacious investment in seeking common grounds and configuring them in terms of identity, origins, community, and tradition. Like Elspeth Probyn, I am intrigued by the ways in which the idea of having *an* identity 'circulates as a feasible goal and [an] evident fact' (Probyn 1996: 71). One of the striking aspects of the Italian organizations I observed in the course of my research, was how hard subjects had to work to create communal spaces of belonging based on the perceived *reproduction* of traditions. My aim is to excavate the cultural and historical meanings produced in an array of institutional practices that serve to connect the fragmented and dispersed Italian population of Britain. I investigate how the project of an Italian identity is signified and formulated in particular institutional sites, within particular forms of representation and enunciative strategies. More specifically, I scrutinize the ways in which the indeterminacy of the Italian presence in Britain is negotiated and resolved within different forms of representation: written renditions of Italian immigration and immigrant lives (written by Italians); political discourses of identity; and the daily life of two London-based church-cum-social clubs, the Centro Scalabrini and St Peter's church.[2] Imagining a community, here, is both about that which is created as a common history, experience or culture of a group – a group's belongings – and about how the 'community' is attached to places, imagined or real (Gupta and Ferguson 1992: 10).

The line I follow moves through 'the imaginary possessions that are created in the name of an identity project, the belongings that . . . a group, a people cobble together from the past and the present.' (Probyn 1996: 68) Belongings, here, refers to both 'possessions' and inclusion. That is, practices of group identity are about manufacturing cultural and historical belongings that mark out terrains of commonality, through which the social dynamics and politics of 'fitting in' are delineated. As will become clear in Part II, some of these terrains are physical spaces that are appropriated as Italian cultural belongings. In this respect, they are reified as Italian 'possessions', while they constitute terrains for the creation of a collective sense of belonging: in short, they are Italian *(terrains of) belongings*.

Belonging as it operates in Probyn's work is useful because it displaces identity from its foundational status. She

> slide[s] from "identity" to "belonging", in part because . . . the latter term captures more accurately the desire for some sort of attachment, be it to other people, places, or modes of being, and the ways in which individuals and groups are caught within wanting to belong, wanting to become, a process that is fuelled by yearning rather than the positing of identity as a stable state. (Probyn 1996: 19)

By considering 'the social world as a surface' (Probyn 1996: 19), Probyn manages to deliver an account that constantly emphasizes the quivery character of identity. Identity as threshold,[3] that is, a location that by definition frames the passage from one space to another; identity as transition, always producing itself through the combined processes of being and becoming. Informed by Probyn, I approach institutional narratives of identity as part of the longing to belong, as constituted by the desire for an identity, rather than surfacing from an already constituted identity. But while Probyn adopts a Deleuzian perspective that emphasizes movement – her book is replete with 'examples of various forms of locomotion: trains, plains, horses' (1996: 11) – I approach migrant belongings as constituted through both movement and attachment. Included in the formation of belonging, then, is identity as a momentary positionality (Hall 1996a) which is always already becoming.[4] Unpacking the project of identity means that I seek out the momentary points of attachment, or points of suture in Stuart Hall's words (1990: 226), as well as the points of departure. As Caren Kaplan points out, 'even theories of nomadic rhizomes include "nodes" – those sites of intersecting movements of "lines of flight"' (1996: 143). Hence without neglecting the constitutive potency of movement in the formation of physical and symbolic locations of belonging, this study examines the new formations that emerge from deterritorialization and reterritorialization, and that are rooted, even momentarily, in a place. The phrase *migrant belongings*, in this respect, is meant to capture the productive tension that results from the articulation of movement and attachment, suture and departure, outside and inside, in identity formation.

The focus of this book is on institutional practices, not individual experiences, of identity. Institutional definitions of identity are commonly understood as tantamount to the construction of boundaries, which, in turn, is accepted as a mechanism of aggregation of differences located *within* boundaries (Cohen 1985). However, it seems to me that such a view reinstates an analytical separation between identity and difference, where the former is conceived as a container of already existing differences. Without denying that boundaries are indeed part and parcel of projects of group identity, I raise here the need to think about identity in ways that do not reinstate it as a finite, smoothed out and always already coherent narrative. By positing '"difference" *inside* the logic of analysis rather than appropriating it as an inorganic addition' (di Leonardo 1991: 30; my emphasis), I understand identity formation as a process that produces *both* sameness and difference.

The relationship between identity and difference as it operates here is at times one of synonymy: constructing cultural identity is also about constructing cultural difference. At other times, the relationship relates to the tension that arises when difference is at once constitutive of, and a potentially contesting force of, identity. Insofar as identity seeks to foreclose a field of possibilities (for example being a migrant is excluded from definitions of the 'immigrant condition'; see Chapter 2; or being single is excluded from narratives of 'becoming Italian woman'; see Chapter 4), this field is nonetheless a constitutive feature of identity and as such, impedes the possibility of a full and definitive closure of identity. Yet as Judith Butler rightly points out, this postructuralist view generalizes the operation of 'difference' in the formation of '"any" and "every" identity' (1995: 441). In so doing, it ignores the historically and culturally specific ways in which difference operates. In *Migrant Belongings*, I uncover the ways in which differences (gendered, ethnic, generational) are constructed to support the formation of a stable and unified 'community'. By closely scrutinizing the location of migrant belongings, I question generalized assumptions about 'gender' and 'ethnicity': throughout the following chapters, I insist on the contingency of these categories and of their articulation, by relating them back to the historically specific project of Italian émigré identity formation. At the same time, I intend to destabilize assumptions of sameness and universality that are often enclosed within models that naturalize boundaries as mechanisms of homogenization.

Performative belongings: thinking through gendered ethnicities

An inherent feature of this study, then, is the commitment to render visible the ways in which the formation of group identity is woven through the formation of particular subjects. Moving beyond add-on models of identity, I seek to unpack how gender and ethnicity circulate, articulate, are embedded and produced in representations of collective identity and local particularity. In this regard, this study originated from a desire to qualify the generalized assumption that '[e]thnicities are always gendered in terms of both how they construct sexual difference and how they are lived' (Brah 1992: 143), by relocating it in a locally specific setting. To rephrase what I state above, the articulation of gender and ethnicity manifests itself differently in different times and places.

Feminist accounts of ethnicity, 'race' and nation have long since alerted us to the ways in which ethnicity is essentialized or rendered absolute through its intersection with gender systems of differentiation (Brah 1992; Juteau 1983; Anthias and Yuval-Davis 1992; Yuval-Davis and Anthias 1989; Yuval-Davis 1997; McClintock 1995).[5] The thesis running through these texts is that collective expressions of identity often involve the reification of family values that underscore and naturalize the different position of men and women in society. The major contribution of this argument is to illuminate how the naturalization of women's role as carers and custodians of culture is tied up with the naturalization of ethnicity, thus revealing how cultural (re)production is configured around women's bodies. However, the argument remains caught within a family-based model of ethnicity, whereby the family is the primary ground for the production and transmission of culture; the 'first ethnic network' (Juteau 1983), while it produces universalized assumptions about the patriarchal family as a space of oppression and naturalization of sexuality and gender.

A critique of family-based accounts of ethnic identity becomes highly pertinent in relation to Italian cultural formation. *La famiglia* still maintains widespread currency in textual renditions of migrant Italianness – from fictional accounts, through autobiographies, to historical or sociological monographs such as those discussed in Chapter 2 – where it is elevated as the ultimate site and expression of Italian culture. Such a view is of little use, however, if I am seeking to move beyond universalist definitions of gender or ethnicity, for it does little more than lock gender and ethnicity into each other. Moreover, the position of women as wives and mothers is overemphasized at the expense of their active part in constructing ethnicity beyond the family realm, as some feminist critiques have rightly argued (di Leonardo 1984; Gabaccia 1984, 1992, 1994; Iacovetta 1992). In my own analysis, I establish a distinction between positing the family as the primary, if not primordial ethnic network, and viewing it as a 'strategic cultural linkage . . . that [is] chronotopically specific – that is, neither generalized nor eternalized' (Boyarin 1992: xviii). On the one hand, this study focuses on other sites than the family where ethnic particularity is produced: monographs, the press, and two religious organizations. On the other hand, I look at the kinship trope as a mode of representation of Italian specificity. My interest here is how it is deployed in different representations of the Italian presence in Britain. I seek a more detailed understanding of the ways in which gender, kinship and belonging are sutured together in particular settings. How is the relationship between gender and kinship rendered ethnically specific? In turn, how does 'the family' signify, if at all, a cultural specificity/difference? Finally, I query whether the family acquires a new significance when it connects to migration and the formation of a localized specificity. How is the family trope deployed in the formation of migrant belongings?

In a manner similar to Judith Butler's analysis of Nella Larsen's fictional narrative *Passing* (Butler 1993: 167–85), my concern is to unpack how ethnic conventions and sex/gender regulations interact and articulate in the wider project of Italian identity formation. I propose to move beyond an economy of identity/difference that rests on the mathematical logic of additions and subtractions (Butler 1993: 118), but I do not want to locate all forms of social differentiation on a level playing field (as Sara Ahmed, 1998a, has pointedly argued). Simultaneity and embeddedness do not preclude differences in the ways in which particular sites of construction of 'difference' are mobilized within the formation of cultural identity.

My engagement with Butler was crucial in the initial stages of this study. More specifically, I draw from her work on performativity (namely in *Gender Troubles* and *Bodies that Matter*) to unpack the mutual construction of social categories through performative acts of gender and ethnicity.[6] I ask how gender regulations and ethnic conventions relate to each other in their simultaneous performance.

Drawing on performative theory of language, Butler argues that performativity is primarily about citationality: it is 'through the invocation of convention' (1993: 225) that 'acts' derive their binding power; it is about the 'reiteration of norms which precede, constrain, and exceed the performer' (1993: 234). The performativity of identity, then, is not merely about routine or the reiteration of practices within one individual's life. Nor are reiterations 'simply replicas of the same' (Butler 1993: 226). On the contrary: the performative act 'works' because it draws on and covers the constitutive conventions, which, through repetition, effectively produce what appears as eternally fixed and *re*producible.

Butler's main object is to explore the materiality of sex; she de-naturalizes it and locates it as a product and enforcement of regulatory discourses. Likewise, I want to de-naturalize ethnicity, for within British new racism, the naturalization of culture diffuses 'race' and racism in cultural-related discourses of differentiation wrapped in the terminology of 'ethnicity' (see Chapter 1). Consequently, some cultural practices are reified and naturalized as 'typical expressions' of an ethnic identity; they are seen as resulting from that identity, rather than performing that identity. And displays of identity such as those examined in Chapters 4 and 5 may be read as performative acts, that is, as 'statements that, in the uttering [or displaying] also perform a certain action and exercise a binding power' (Butler 1993: 225). I consider historical texts (Chapter 2) as equally performative by virtue of the fact that they produce the 'History' they claim to be retrieving and re-presenting (de Certeau 1983). In other words, the conventions of History through which such narratives are mobilized, and subsequently consumed, support the truth claims upon which a collective Italian belonging is secured.

Butler's emphasis on the effect of sedimentation that iteration provides, impacts on how to consider ethnicity, in two ways. First, ethnic identifications may stem from the 'stylized repetition of acts' (Butler 1990: 140), a repetition which produces an effect of substantialization and naturalization of cultural belonging. To put it simply, ethnicity may be lived as a deeply felt, embodied, core identity. This refers to the complex link between ethnicity and 'race', which I develop further in the next chapter. The point is that cultural ethnicity may be 'incorporated' through repeated performative acts, the result of which is to produce the imaginary effect of an internal ethnic 'essence'. In this sense, collective performances of belonging such as those examined in Chapter 5 are to be viewed as embodied. For this, I am also indebted to Paul Connerton's text on collective memory. Though he does not explore the formation of social subjects, he emphasizes the bodily work of commemorations (Connerton 1992). For Connerton, collective forms of remembrance such as commemorations are performative, and 'performative memory', he adds, 'is bodily' (Connerton 1992: 71). In other words, Connerton details the ways in which collective belonging operates through bodily incorporations of culture. Hence when I look at rituals and commemorations, in part II of the book, I am not only contemplating the (re)production of culture. There is more to the ritual than the anthropological view according to which rites of passage act as collective reminders 'of the cohesion of society, its moral values and the legitimacy of authority' (Eriksen 1995: 126). Rather, events such as the commemorations and rituals that occur at St Peter's Italian church or at the Centro Scalabrini are deeply performative. Indeed, for Butler, performative acts include 'legal sentences, baptisms, inaugurations' and other forms of 'statements which not only perform an action, but confer a binding power on the action performed' (1993: 234). The ritual consists of a set of behaviours cast within a stylized and formalized pattern that projects bodies within a structure of meaning that precedes them.[7]

Second, the acknowledgement that cultural identity may be lived as coherent, as a deeply held core, creates a space for a contemplation of the way bodies are conscripted in group identity formation as sites for the *display* of cultural identity. Conceiving identity as performative means that identities are not reducible to what is visible, to what is seen on the body, but, rather, that they are constructed by the 'very "expressions" that are said to be [their] results' (Butler, 1990: 45). Ethnicity, to be sure, cannot be reduced to a surface appearance. Yet the centrality of the visual nonetheless sustains a significant definitional status in identity formation. As I argue in the following chapter, the Italian identity project is steeped in the ideal of visibility that reveals the extent to which identity – including ethnic identity – is a matter of 'telling' and 'showing' that which cannot be seen (Bell 1996).

Such a double process became particularly clear to me as I negotiated my access to the London Italian associative life. The first person I interviewed – an Italian woman who is well known within the community – predicted that my being a woman might hinder my access to the male dominated local Italian leadership, though I could 'pass' as an Italian because of my 'dark, curly hair and dark eyes'. What concerned her was that being a non-Italian woman might be a double liability. This question of *passing* as an Italian woman captures the very movement of identity and its indeterminacy, troubling two assumptions at once.

First, it interrogates the presumption that 'race is what can be seen, ethnicity is only what is felt' (Wallman 1978: 307). Drawing from the Barthian legacy, Sandra Wallman was distinguishing between racial and cultural discourses of ethnicity. When associated with culture, as in the North American tradition (especially in Canada), ethnicity is conceived as analytically distinct from gender or 'race': ethnicity is ultimately a matter of creating common cultural backgrounds and imagining common ancestry, while gender and 'race' are viewed as products of the attribution of arbitrary meanings to physical differences. What the question of passing raises, however, is that ethnicity may be constructed along similar 'bodily' lines. Though the body may not figure as the bearer of immutable cultural or biological difference in the formation of ethnicity, it nonetheless is conscripted to render 'visible' what is not.

As it turned out, being Italian did not really matter for my integration within London Italian associative life. Initially, it did come as a surprise to the people I came in contact with that I, a non-Italian French-Canadian from Québec, was doing a research on Italians in London. But this was not a basis of exclusion. Even when I apologized for my poor knowledge of the Italian language, this was usually shrugged off by comparing me to the English-born children of immigrants: 'Bah! Just like my daughter', I was told, indicating that there is no uniform way of 'acting' that would express 'Italianness'. Some speak Italian fluently, some don't. My ethnic identity was part of negotiations between myself and the men and women I interacted with in order to 'locate' me in relation to them. The outcome was that we met on the terrain of our common status as foreigners in Britain – being from Québec, with a Catholic background, I was included within the folds of this cultural minority. And this seemed to override 'Italianness'.

My insertion as 'one of theirs' bears methodological implications for the research practice in 'ethnic studies', where studies on cultural groups are commonly conducted by presumed members of these groups. Apart from the practical aspects that may have to do with the cultural capital acquired from having grown up in a particular 'ethnic' culture, the 'ethnic' division of labour in ethnic studies is indicative of the persisting assumption that posits ethnicity as the primary ground of identity formation. It elides a number of social differences of class, sexuality, gender, even ethnicity, that exist within 'ethnic groups', as well as obscuring the very particular context that is created from the relationship between the researcher and the individuals whose lives he or she is documenting.

A second assumption of my first interlocutor was that, though I could *pass* as an Italian, I could not *avoid* being a woman; she assumed my sex and gender would determine the kind of access I would have to Italian associative life. While my 'being female' certainly directed the channel of entry to Italian social events, my gendered position was a constant source of negotiation.

After months of regular appearances at St Peter's and phone calls to the Centro Scalabrini, I finally had an interview which was crucial to the outcome of my research: I met the president of the Italian Women's Club (*Club Donne Italiane;* CDI). That day, I joined the organization and began attending their weekly meetings, where I was introduced as Anna-Maria – and thus 'italianized'. Thanks to these women, I found out about, and took part in, different community events and more importantly, grew closer to some women who became my regular companions in these outings.

Yet if my links with the CDI gave me access to the local Italian associative life, my relations with these women were not as straightforward. From the moment I entered the Women's Club, a gendered and sexualized identity was marked upon my body, just like, as Teresa de Lauretis illustrates, when women tick the F box when filling out an application form (in Moore 1994: 85). Thus I walked into a world where specific injunctions of womanhood were spelled out (I return to this in more detail in Chapter 4, where I unpack the contingency of 'Italian womanhood'). I have discussed elsewhere (Fortier 1996b; 1998a) how a number of interrelated factors connected to age, class, status, and sexuality were at play as the women tried to locate me. To be sure, some confusion arose because of the perceived discrepancy between my student, hence 'jobless' status, and my 'late' age of thirty-something. This confusion was often ruled out by assuming I was much younger, the gap sometimes reaching ten years. In Chapter 4, I pay closer attention to the ways in which my ambivalence was resolved primarily through 'sexing my self', in the phrase of Elspeth Probyn (1993).

The point I wish to make at this stage is that the double process of gendering/ethnicizing my 'self' fed into my inquiry about the intersection of gender and ethnicity in the creation of terrains of belonging. The threshold metaphor, in this respect, aptly illustrates the very mode of my enquiry, which was a significant source of knowledge in the construction of the present account. As I trod on the very thresholds of sameness and difference, I was continually negotiating my in-between positions in relation to the people I interacted with – in the dual sense of negotiating a deal and negotiating a stream (Ginsburg and Tsing 1990: 2). Neither here nor there, simultaneously included as one of them and marginalized because sexually 'unlocatable' as a single woman, I was motivated by a double desire to belong and *not* to belong. I was drawn to the churches because they provided me with a sense of place, especially at the beginning of my study. Having recently arrived in England from my native Québec, the Catholic churches (namely St Peter's) became places that I recognized as part of my cultural horizon. In this sense, they were 'habitual spaces' (see Chapter 4). However my connection with the churches was fraught with my discomfort in the face of a system of beliefs I did not share. In hindsight, it seems as if my interest in the churches was partly motivated by the necessity to return to my past in my own process of becoming; a kind of 'detour through the past', as Stuart Hall (1990; 1993) would put it. A return to a place where all referents were familiar and reminiscent of my cultural background. In spite of the discomfort these visits fostered, the church was a place that I knew too well, and that in itself became something that I treasured as I struggled to create a 'place for myself' in London.

Ethnographers are inevitably caught up in a web of demands that come from different directions at once: academia, personal interests (career oriented, the immediate requirements of the inquiry, family related, economic concerns), and the interests of the subjects (who may be sponsoring the study, or hoping for public visibility, or looking for an advocate of their 'cause', and so on). To put it crudely, deception and role-playing are part and parcel of participant observation and give the researcher a keen sense of what writers on the method have called 'marginality'. I prefer the notion of threshold (see note 3) for it denotes a position that is not quite outside or inside, and it suggests that there is always movement and change in the nature of the relationships between researcher and the research setting. Indeed, the disclosure of what I thought, believed in, how I lived, had to be negotiated on a daily basis. Overall, my position in the field was influenced by my own cultural background, personal beliefs and lifestyle, and fed into the desire for closeness *and* distance I felt towards the people I encountered. Likewise, leaders and members of the organizations negotiated their position as they got to know me better, developed a greater sense of what my project was about, and became more accustomed to my presence.

It follows that participant observation should not be read in terms of the 'I was there' version of credentialism that allows researchers to claim some form of 'insider' knowledge. A number of factors shaped the nature of my involvement in the research settings, including the contrasts between my personal politics and beliefs and the ones expressed by the different people I interacted with. As James Clifford points out (1986: 8), the ethnographer deals with 'partial truths' which are met through 'an open-ended series of contingent, power-laden encounters' that reflect personal and ideological characteristics of *both* the researcher and the researched. Encounters that I have sought to render visible, for, as feminist researchers have taught us, the 'work of knowledge' does not come from nowhere, nor is the producer of this 'situated knowledge' (Haraway 1991) hidden and invisible (Skeggs 1997). *Migrant Belongings*, then, should be read in the context of the research relationships that I developed in these Italian Catholic milieus. The account that follows, especially Part II, is the product of the 'field-world' (Harstrup 1992) that resulted from my interactions with men and women of both St Peter's church and the Centro Scalabrini, as well as from my circulation in a variety of activities.

Outline

Migrant Belongings inserts itself in a space that lies somewhere between a descriptive account that follows the rules of empiricist orthodoxy and an abstract meta-theoretical discourse. In the following chapters, I navigate the tension between the general and the particular, at once trying to search out the details of how certain meanings are encased in institutional practices of identity, to render these practices as faithfully as possible, and to relate them to broader theoretical questions.

Guided by such questions, and informed by the nature of the relationships I developed in the field-world, the narrative is edited and organized around themes and places. Within these headings (historical meta-narratives, identity politics, the daily lives of the Centro and St Peter's) different texts, events or issues are examined in order to provide a picture of various forms of representation and discourses that co-exist and compete in the project of identity formation. I am interested in how a 'we' is created out of a number of claims that exist in relationships that are not necessarily straightforward and harmonious. Identity narratives do not form a singular, unified collective subject but, rather, generate and emerge from practices and motifs that are highly dispersed. I am not concerned with creating the image of a unified 'identity', nor am I seeking to over-emphasize the coherence within the symbolic repertoire that constitutes the boundaries of belonging. In the following chapters, I examine the limits, thresholds, tensions, discontinuities, contradictions and strategies of coherence and stabilization involved in the formation of an Italian identity. As will become apparent, though I am fascinated by the quest for *an* identity as a feasible and desirable project, I do not want to re-produce identity as a finished text or transparent object.

The book includes six chapters. In Chapter 1, I locate the Italian project of identity within a broader theoretical and historical context. This chapter identifies the starting point of the study, and sketches its connection with recent theoretical discourses of diaspora. I critically assess attempts to differentiate subjects of migration (diasporas, immigrants, ethnic groups) and argue for the use of diaspora as a heuristic device rather than a descriptive category. I then discuss the Italian identity project in relation to contemporary British cultural and political life, where Italians occupy an ambivalent position as constituting a cultural minority (in linguistic and religious terms, at least) and as members of the white European majority. The indeterminacy of the Italian presence in Britain is seized by Italian leaders in the figure of 'invisible immigrants'. An image that both re-instates and challenges the invisibility of whiteness.

Subsequent chapters are divided into two parts. Part I ('Histories and Identity Politics') probes meta-narratives and explores how historical and political narratives seek to establish a distinct émigré identity and culture. In the two chapters of this section, I seek out the ways in which gender and ethnicity are worked into and deployed in these narratives. In Chapter 2, I look at textual renditions of the Italian presence in Britain and insert them within the broader project of communal memory and recovery. Written by Italians, these texts constitute specific instances in the creation of an imagined community, for they provide a partial solution to the indeterminacy of the Italian collectivity, by authorizing its existence and legitimating the actions undertaken to create an Italian group identity. I show how the literature on Italians in Britain sketches an indeterminate portrait of a collectivity whose common ground is defined in terms of the 'immigrant condition', configured in terms of settlement, sacrifice and the trope of kinship.

Chapter 3 centres on the politics of identity of current Italian emigrant leaders in London. These politics are expressed in the language of citizenship that includes political, cultural and generational concerns. Though they emerge from a multiplicity of locations – Europe, Britain, Italy – they are essentially directed at Italy, and in this respect constitute some form of return to the nation/homeland. This raises a number of issues: the articulation of the homeland with local particularity; the relationship between diasporic and nationalist consciousness and their impact on definitions of culture. Stemming from the political discourses are transnational geographies of identity through which the invention of a political constituency of 'Italians abroad' emerges in tandem with notions of the citizen as legal *and* cultural. This chapter thus examines an array of practices of the nation (political debates, state ceremonies, recollections, and beauty contests) to reveal the kind of 'community' and 'citizens' they perform.

Part II ('Spaces, Memories and Displays of Identity') focuses on the daily life of two London Italian organizations: St Peter's Italian church and the Centro Scalabrini. Focusing on the social dynamics of cultural practices in the two socio-religious centres – ceremonies, rituals, festivities, textual recollections – I explore the relationship between the construction of the identity of places and the construction of terrains of belonging. This is about the ways in which 'memory work', to borrow John Gillis's phrase (1994b: 3), may be localized and the different forms this localization may take. What I am concerned with is how the 'here' is inhabited and invested by an Italian presence; how the Italian presence manifests itself in London, and what is expressed in these displays. Temporality, spatiality, geography and genealogy articulate differently in each location, creating new 'soils of significance' (Hoffman 1989: 278) inhabited by, and variously defined by, particular kinds of subjects. I suggest that 'community' events and commemorations are not only about cultural (re)production; they are also about manufacturing bodies that inhabit the spaces that are claimed as Italian (terrains of) belongings.

I begin, in Chapter 4, with the Centro Scalabrini. Following on from the preceding chapter, I explore how the Centro positions itself in the face of the changing character of emigration. This institution is looking to broaden its mandate to become a church for emigrants rather than simply an ethnic church. This project is wrapped in the universalist discourse of Catholicism, which I assess in relation to the more immediate and regionalist forms of life that take place in the Centro's premises. Two levels of analysis emerge. First, I excavate the ways in which the 'drama of emigration' is retrieved as where Italians 'come from', but also as that which must be transcended. As such, the 'drama of emigration' grounds a distinct form of knowledge that inverts grand narratives of history and collective growth in what Kathleen Stewart has called 'unforgetting' (1996: 80). Also, by analysing the pictorial narrative of emigration found in the Centro's church, I show how it is entrenched in modern ideas of transcendence that are associated with maleness. Secondly, I look at the Italian Women's Club to explore the extent to which the Centro is a space inhabited by different forms of sociality that complicate its universalist claims, yet which operate through fixed definitions of modes of being. More specifically, I scrutinize the kind of 'Italian woman' that the Women's Club 'promotes' (sic) and performs, and reveal how is it inflected by class, race and sexuality.

The analysis of three episodes drawn from the life at St Peter's church shapes the contents of Chapter 5. Various forms of cultural practices that mark out spatial and identity boundaries for the London Italian population are discussed in connection with wider theoretical questions about the reterritorialization of identity, the invention of tradition, and the embodiment of culture. In this chapter, I engage more directly in an analysis based on a 'corporeal approach' to group identity formation; that is, an investigation of how bodies and space produce each other in both ethnically and gender specific ways. In contrast to the Centro Scalabrini, activities at St Peter's are essentially about re-membering: the formation of individual and collective bodies, which are called upon to inhabit the church and its surroundings. I return to this notion in the conclusion, where I explain how re-membering stitches together memory, location and the body in the process of 'populating' Italian (terrains of) belonging.

The closing chapter looks back at the central findings of this enquiry and examines their implications for theorizing identity and culture in migrant belongings. First, the prominence of memory work in Italian practices of identity leads me to interrogate geographically based definitions of diaspora. I explore the usefulness of Paul Gilroy's notion of the changing same as an alternative means of conceiving continuity and change, but I reconnect it with the 'lived experience of locality' (Brah 1995: 192). Questions of what it means to speak of 'here and there', 'home', and indigenousness are assessed in light of Italian migrant belongings. Second, I return to the connection between gender, generation and ethnicity and discuss the implications of the conclusion that may surface from my 'findings' whereby gender difference, in Italian migrant belongings, is the modality in which cultural specificity and authenticity are represented. I reflect on this conclusion in the light of my concern to present an account that does not reproduce a fixed image of (Italian) ethnicity as inherently family based and heterosexist. I also relate this finding back to the conditions of enduring racism that surround the Italian project of visibility. To say that gender difference is the key figure of cultural identity poses the question of the position that absolutist notions of ethnicity, or racist conceptions of culture, occupy in the definition of Italian identity. The third section is about bodily representations and performances of culture; or body-images. Without reducing identity to the body, I contemplate the analytical status of the body – the body as threshold concept – in understandings of cultural identity formation. Here, I revisit the constitutive vectors of migrant belongings – movement and attachment – through the lens of what I call the body motions of duration.

To be sure, I do not assume to tell the 'whole story': this book does not consist of a comprehensive study of a group's 'culture' as if it were a whole that one can capture and describe in detail. My effort is not to provide an answer to the 'problem' of defining the Italian presence in 1990s Britain. Rather, it is one of remembering that the practices of identity described here are themselves modes of questioning that are carried out through the location of migrant belongings.

Notes

1. Deterritorialization and reterritorialization have been coined by Gilles Deleuze and Felix Guattari (1980) in their attempt to theorize the constitution of territory through movement. In an interview with Claire Parnet, Gilles Deleuze stated that 'there is no deterritorialization without an effort for reterritorialization' (Boutang and Pamart 1995). But reterritorialization is not to be confounded with 'the return to a primitive or more ancient territoriality' (Deleuze and Guattari 1980: 214). In a manner akin to Walter Benjamin's theory of translation, or Homi Bhabha's hybridity (1990), Deleuze and Guattari suggest that elements reterritorialize themselves onto each other (Deleuze and Guattari 1980: 214). While each element maintains some of its own territoriality, their combined reterritorialization produces a new territoriality. In this respect, Deleuze and Guattari's notion of deterritorialization–reterritorialization is useful, for it refuses to seek out pure 'origins'. However, as will become clear in the remainder of this chapter, I do not follow Deleuze and Guattari in their emphasis on movement. Rather, I propose to explore both movement and attachment in the formation of migrant belongings.
2. See appendix 1 for more details about the research methods and other methodological considerations.

3. The threshold is reminiscent of Victor Turner's notion of liminality, the second stage of his three-stage 'ritual process' (1969). For Turner, the threshold is a stage of uncertainty between two clearly defined stages: the beginning (separation) and end points (reaggregation) of the ritual process. In terms of identity, this conception suggests that individuals pass *from* one identity *to* another, and that the threshold is a momentary stage of uncertainty. In contrast, I conceive identity *as* a threshold; as a momentary positionality that forecloses the fields of possibilities (Butler 1993). Identity results from the negotiation of social norms and conventions of 'being', and as such, it may potentially, but not necessarily, disturb these conventions. My theoretical orientation is further developed, and hopefully clarified, in the remainder of this chapter. See also the concluding chapter on 'duration', which, in contrast with Turner's tendency to structure rites of passage into discrete moments, offers a conception of temporality as a series of indeterminate 'moments' that feed into each other.
4. Nicolas van Schendel's notion of *identité mouvance* (1986, 1992) evocatively captures this combination of flow, continuity, as well as positionality. *Mouvance*, in French, not only means movement; it also holds a legal connotation pertaining to tenure, the holding of a property (belongings) or of a title, an 'identity'. For van Schendel, *identité mouvance* is not immobilized in belonging, but rather proceeds with and from belonging (1992): hence identity, here, is at once defined by 'possessions', the social processes of fitting in, and the claim to a name.
5. The list is long, especially if we include the recent developments in feminist theory that seek to explore the embeddedness of identity. For the purpose of the argument I put forward here, I focus on a literature that centres on the link between nationalism, ethnicity and gender and that highlights familistic discourses of gendered ethnicity.
6. Sneja Gunew (1996) also uses Butler in her exploration of performative acts of cultural ethnicity. Though she does not address questions of embeddedness (with gender or 'race' for instance), her paper is an original contribution to conceptions of the performativity of cultural ethnicity.
7. Again, references to Victor Turner might come to the reader's mind. See chapter 5 for a short discussion of his work in relation to the rituals observed at St Peter's church.

–1–

Situating the Italian Project of Visibility

> Borders and diasporas are phenomenon that blow up – both enlarge and explode – the hyphen
>
> Smadar Lavie and Ted Swedenburg

In the Chiesa del Redentore, at the Centro Scalabrini of London, a stained glass window neatly captures the *raison d'être* of the religious order that runs this Brixton-based Italian Catholic mission. The image in the window depicts John Baptist Scalabrini, the founder of the congregation, encountering emigrants at the Milan train station in 1887. This incident is said to be at the origin of the foundation of this missionary order, which caters to Italian (and other) emigrants world-wide. The railway tracks trace a central line in the scene, drawing our gaze towards a globe that covers the opening of a tunnel. The tracks and the globe meet at the centre of the image, symbolically linking Italy with the world, and the present with the unknown future. In the foreground, stands Scalabrini, and, slightly behind him, two 'pioneers' (sic)[1] of the London Mission – P. Walter Sacchetti, founder of the Centro, and P. Silvano Bartapelle. In the background, to the left of the tracks, stand two figures, a man and a woman, their luggage on the floor, looking towards the globe, their back turned against us. In this pictorial rendition of the foundational myth of the London mission, temporal and geographical differences are fused within a gesture that marks an initiating moment that extends into the present. The anachronism of joining Father Scalabrini and two founding fathers of the Brixton Centro (established in 1968) breaks down the temporal distance and emphasizes the continuity of the congregation's concerns. At the same time, the location of this event in the past is effectively interrupted by the central figure of the railway track. The railway, in Italian immigrant historicity, bridges distinct but overlapping timespaces constitutive of an Italian 'émigré' identity: here/there; now/then; present/future; Italy/elsewhere. In his account of Calabrian immigrants living in Bedford, Renato Cavallaro alludes to the railway as a hyphen linking two timespaces. He suggests that the railway between the home and the workplace acts as a hyphen that symbolically links Italy (home) and Bedford (workplace), the space of origins and the industrial space, tradition and modernity (Cavallaro 1981: 93).[2] The railway-as-hyphen runs on the border zone of sameness and difference, of identity and change. Moreover, in spite of its absence, the expected train speaks volumes of movement across and within space. The train is 'something through which one goes, it is also something by the means of which one can go from one point to another, and then it is also something that goes by' (Foucault in Probyn 1996: 11). In short, the railway track foregrounds the space of movement and the movement across space (Probyn 1996: 11). In this representation of the Scalabrini mission, the train station symbolically represents a zone between Italy and abroad, a borderzone (Anzaldùa 1987), the poles of which are linked by the tracks. It follows that the identity of the travellers standing on the platform is already shaped by movement and difference, which are located in the 'elsewhere' awaiting them somewhere on the globe. Even before they have left the platform, they are already 'emigrati'.

The aim of this book is to uncover the constitutive potency of 'betweenness' in the formation of an Italian migrant belongings. Or, as Lavie and Swedenburg suggest, I propose to 'blow up' the hyphen, that is to both enlarge and explode it (1996b: 16).[3] My approach converses with a new strand of social research that is burgeoning around 'diaspora'. An important contribution of this body of work is to mediate the relationship between the constraining local and the inflated global by conceiving of a new surface of identity formation that Avtar Brah has called the 'diaspora space' (1996: 209). Composed of genealogies of displacement and genealogies of 'staying put', diaspora space inserts itself between localism and transnationalism and proposes a conception of identity as a positionality that 'is not a process of absolute othering, but rather of entangled tensions' (Clifford 1994: 307). The space of diaspora weaves new webs of belonging that trouble spatial fields of 'nation', 'home', territory, 'community'. To be sure, 'betweenness', in discourses of diaspora, is commonly defined in terms of two territories, which does little to break down the borders of nation states and their congruence with *a* culture. Many have stressed the centrality of the homeland in definitions of diaspora (Safran 1991; Cohen 1997; Tölölyan 1996), and suggested that diaspora compels us to examine how 'there' is rearticulated 'here' (Clifford 1994). This argument has been criticized for neglecting the ways in which a number of diasporic populations or individuals negotiate new forms of belonging outside of this two-way geography (Kirshenblatt-Gimblett 1994). In the concluding chapter, I further develop this argument in light of the new geographies of identity that emerge from Italian 'émigré' identity practices.

In recent years, cultural critics have written extensively on the implications of theorizing diaspora (Clifford 1994; Marienstras 1975; Radhakrishnan 1996; Brah 1996; Gilroy 1994, 1995; Kaplan 1996); others have contributed to the debates by focusing on transnational exchanges between dispersed populations (Gilroy 1987, 1991, 1993a, 1995; Bhachu 1991; Van Hear 1998). Yet, because diaspora denotes multi-location and border crossings, it is easy to privilege notions of the multiply-positioned subject and to overemphasize hybridity, difference and diversity (Helmreich 1992) without any considerations for continuity, for what is 'persistently there' (Clifford 1994: 320) beyond the retention of food and folkways. Rather than engaging with a radically pluralist approach, I attempt to move beyond pluralism and essentialism by 'dealing equally with roots and routes' (Gilroy 1993a: 190) or, to be more accurate, by scrutinizing the social dynamics of rootings and routings in the construction of an émigré Italian identity. *Migrant Belonging,* joins a small but growing body of work that explores how a 'diasporic mode of existence' (Marienstras 1975: 184) mediates the formation of localized cultures, identities or 'communities' (Jacobson 1996; Bhatt 1997; Harney 1998; Gray 1997; Lavie and Swedenburg 1996c; van der Veer 1995). I approach Italian immigrants of London as part of a diaspora and view different versions of self-representation in connection with wider discourses and social contacts. Rather than focusing on the transnational circulation and exchange of cultural practices between dispersed Italian populations, I examine the formation of local particularity in relation to local, national and transnational connections – how here and there, migration and settlement, routes and roots are negotiated and connected in the formation of spaces of belonging. This is a world constituted by the space that brings together 'where you're from', 'where you're at' (Gilroy 1991), and where you're going, and reconfigures them into new webs of meaning.

Key to theoretical definitions of diaspora is forced dispersal, or displacement (Gilroy 1994: 207; Clifford 1994; Safran 1991; Cohen 1997; Van Hear 1998). The mass emigration of Italians over the last century is largely the outcome of severe economic conditions and drastic changes in the economic structure, joined to demographic pressures and lack of political will. Unavoidable 'push' factors forced migration as the ultimate solution to survival. To be sure, differences of class, gender, regional origin and 'kind' of emigration (political rather than economic, for instance) are to be accounted for in order to prevent generalizations that represent Italian diasporization as a homogeneous phenomenon (see below and Chapter 2). But the point is that overall, Italian emigration cannot be compared to the exile of millions of Jews, the enslavement of Africans, or the flight of thousands of Cambodians. Nor can it be assimilated to the voluntary migration of individuals – usually professionals or highly/semi-skilled workers – between countries of the overdeveloped world. Similarly, their settlement in different parts of the world, if once marked by discrimination, ostracism, ethnicism and racism, differs from slavery, indentured labour, or pervasive anti-black racism and anti-semitism. The routings and rootings of diasporas need to be located within specific maps and histories. A useful distinction can be made, for instance, between conditions of dispersal; such a distinction is found in contemporary Jewish culture, where diaspora means scattered, and exile is designated by the term *Galut* (Kirshenblatt-Gimblett 1994: 343, n5). Such a differentiation is important if we are to consider how particular forms of diasporic imagination connect with historically specific conditions of dispersal and (re)settlement. Hence the material conditions of Italian diasporization – the massive dispersal of Italian from impoverished rural areas – has fostered particular kinds of diasporic imaginations that, in turn, influence the production of locally specific cultural forms, such as those that will be examined throughout the following chapters. In contrast to many displaced people, Italians foster a narrative of return that sustains a vision of Italy as a 'spiritual possibility', as the Italo-Québécois poet Filippo Salvatore puts it (in Caccia 1985: 158). In sum, I want to emphasize the limits of elevating diaspora as the 'exemplary condition of late modernity' (Mishra in Tölölyan 1996: 4). Diaspora, as I understand it (in line with Paul Gilroy 1993a), is a heuristic device not a descriptive concept, and as such, it compels us to consider the specific conditions of dispersal and settlement that surround and shape the formation of identity. 'Thus historicised', as James Clifford pointedly argues, 'diaspora cannot become a master trope or "figure" for modern, complex, or positional identities' (Clifford 1994: 319).

In his discerning essay on diaspora as a theoretical formation, James Clifford thus warns against the universalization of diaspora. In spite of this caveat, however, he reproduces a common tendency, in contemporary cultural criticism, to expunge immigration – and immigrants such as Italians – from the theoretical horizon of diaspora. 'Diasporas are not exactly immigrant communities. The latter could be seen as temporary, a site where the canonical three generations struggled through a hard transition to ethnic American status' (Clifford 1994: 311). Though he does not reproduce the difference as absolute, Clifford nevertheless draws a distinction between migrancy and immigration, exiles and immigrants.

Clifford posits European immigrants as gradually participating 'as ethnic "whites" in multicultural America' (1994: 329, n8). In contrast, he adds, diasporic transnationalism breaks down the minority/majority structure whereby a number of 'minorities' have defined themselves in ethnically absolutist ways (1994: 329, n7). This argument reinstates the line of continuum that extends between immigrant and ethnic status, in the US and Canada. Hence Clifford's attempt to distinguish immigrants from diasporas also posits ethnic groups outside of transnationalism. Khachig Tölölyan is even more explicit in his distinction between 'the ethnic and the diasporic'. For him, 'an ethnic community differs from diaspora by the extent to which the latter's commitment to maintain connections with its homeland and its kin communities in other states is absent, weak, at best intermittent, and manifested by individuals rather than the community as a whole' (1996: 16). He cites Italian-Americans as exemplary figures of 'ethnics', but assuredly not 'diasporic', because 'they are highly unlikely to act in consistently organized ways to develop an agenda for self-identification in the political or cultural realm, either in the hostland or across national boundaries' (Tölölyan 1996: 16-17).

Tölölyan's argument is founded on two premises: firstly, that 'consistently organized protest' is the sole measure of people's commitment to self-identification and affirmation of cultural specificity. Consequently, a hierarchy is established between a 'strong' ethnic identity, expressed in mobilized action, and other forms of identification, imagined or symbolic, viewed as expressive of lesser, weaker identities; such was the implication behind Gans' (1979) 'symbolic ethnicity' or Weinfeld's (1981/1985) 'affective ethnicity'. This argument comes out of the legacy of the 'ethnic studies' tradition grounded in reified definitions of ethnicity as something that exists out there, that may be activated or disactivated. Moreover, Tölölyan raises the important question of representation. Who is speaking for whom in the 'organized protests for self-identification'? Who is represented and how?

Secondly, both Tölölyan and Clifford seem to accept that immigration is summed up in the worn-out assumption of a linear process of integration, acculturation and assimilation, whereby immigrants move *from* one culture *into* another. Echoes of melting pot discourses resonate through the image of immigrants happily shedding the clothes of the 'old' world to slip into those of the 'new' (see Sollors 1986: Chapter 3). Immigrants, in other words, are seen as sliding into the 'host culture', acquiescing in the demands of an industrial society, rather than actively engaging in shaping and negotiating their immediate circumstances to fit their various needs and projects. Consequently, as Caren Kaplan writes, 'immigrants are seen to replace one nationalist identification for another while diasporic émigrés confound territorial and essentialist nationalisms in favor of transnational subjectivities and communities' (1996: 136).

I agree with Clifford that, indeed, the assimilation trope in the US posits white Europeans as the exemplars of standards, values and experiences of minority collectivities. Yet immigrant populations experience 'diasporic moments' (Clifford 1994: 328, n3), which, to be sure, 'could be further plumbed, rather than marginalized, for links between the historical experiences of migration and displacement' (Kaplan 1996: 137). A large number of *immigrant* populations – not only *migrant* ones, as Clifford states – share 'forms of longing, memory, (dis)identification' (Clifford 1994: 304) with displaced peoples. Similarly, displaced people inevitably deploy strategies of 'dwelling' within their new living environment that are akin to those of immigrants. What needs to be called into question is the conception of immigration as an end in itself. Following on from this line of thought, I want to consider the extent to which identity in im/migration is lived and represented in terms of diaspora, and to illuminate how a diasporic consciousness manifests itself and converses with other forms of consciousness (such as nationalism). By casting im/migration in dialogue with diaspora, definitions of identity are understood as the outcome of a number of mediations that weave together multiple locations and histories.

Clifford's differential construction of subjects of displacement poses another, perhaps deeper question: that of the conditions of possibility surrounding the emergence of such constructions. Undeniably, legal and social histories of immigration in the US commonly reveal how they turn around issues of race and class. Put simply, immigration is often the site of struggle over definitions of class, race and nation. Yet Clifford's generalized notion of immigration fails to acknowledge that the ways in which these issues are played out in immigration take different forms in different parts of the world. For example, the status of immigrants as appropriate or inappropriate foreigners, in the nineteenth or early twentieth centuries, was measured up against the racialization of the domestic space in Britain (McClintock 1995), and the racialization of labour in the US (Roediger 1991, 1994). Though both historical processes share common rhetorical strategies – such as the use of dirt as the key metaphor in substantiating the boundaries of inclusion/exclusion – these were staged in different spheres of social life: the domestic sphere in Britain (hygiene and cleanliness), the labour market in the United States ('dirty work' associated with 'nigger work'; Roediger 1994: 191). Furthermore, labels of 'white ethnics' (in the US) and 'white negroes' (in the UK) attributed to some immigrant populations (such as Italians or Irish) testify to different forms of articulation of race, culture, class and nation. It also signals the variability of definitions of whiteness, indeed of the ways in which whiteness is 'seen', a point I discuss below.

It is beyond the scope of this book to engage in greater detail in the analysis of the racialization of Italians and its connection with the shaping of a British 'nation'.[4] My point is that the study of Italian immigrants in Britain is to be viewed in the context of the historical developments of ideas of race and ethnicity in relation to immigration. In the US, Canada and Britain, ethnicity is equated with immigrant; thus underpinning a notion that ethnicity is the attribute of minority populations, the 'Other's' humanity (Juteau 1983).[5] However, in contrast to the American and Canadian contexts, immigrants and ethnics, in Britain, have, from the onset, been identified as 'people of colour'. Ethnic groups, in Britain, are not perceived as 'settled' or 'integrated' immigrants, as they are in the US — the 'white ethnics' – or in Canada – the 'cultural minorities'. Ethnic groups, in Britain, are nothing but foreigners and 'Other'. Moreover, as Paul Gilroy has argued (1995: 27), with the neo-fascist groups being an everyday hazard, and the threat of 'reimmigration' or 'repatriation' being repeatedly raised by governments as a solution to the problems they see as embodied in a black presence that is deemed incompatible with the exalted standards of national culture, the presence of ethnic groups is not invested with the same legitimacy as it is in Canada or the US, even though in the latter countries they may be allocated subordinate positions.

The use of this interlocking notion of ethnicity, 'race' and immigration has developed along this line in both political and theoretical discourses in Britain. British 'ethnic' studies have, up until recently, centred on Asian and Caribbean populations, consistently ignoring other migrants such as Italians. This unequal development in research practice suggests that racisms or ethnic absolutisms have been conceived as concerning blacks and Asians, not whites. As I have argued elsewhere, the quasi absence of interest for white populations in ethnic and racial studies may be viewed as reinstating the unproblematic nature of whiteness (Fortier 1994; see also Frankenberg 1997: 1).

It is the very absence from British research practice that led me to conduct this study on a white immigrant population. This is not meant in the 'me too' spirit of balancing the scores: a kind of call to bring whites into the agenda and to refigure whiteness as injury ('whites, too, are unique; whites, too, must struggle to name their culture and retain their autonomy'; Frankenberg 1997: 19). What intrigued me from the outset was the difference between British and Canadian discourses of ethnicity, and how that manifests itself in the identity formation of Italians as émigrés. This appears particularly clear to me, as I shuttle between Canada and England, two parts of the world where ethnicity works so differently, both in the political realm and in theoretical discourses. My own understanding of ethnicity straddles British and Canadian 'traditions': bringing in the study of a white population within the British sphere of ethnic studies where ethnicity is commonly associated with blacks and South Asians ('people of colour', is the American parlance), or questioning the conceptual distinction between 'race' and ethnicity within Canadian (and Québécois) ethnic studies circles. Put simply, ethnicity, as I use it, is a 'point of suture' that may be conceived as predominantly racialized (as in the UK) or predominantly culturalized (as in Canada/Québec and the US), though it always includes both processes. Ethnicity acquires a special significance in different contexts because of the different ways it articulates with ideas of race, culture and nation. Moving beyond ethnicity, then, does not mean to erase it from the map, nor to deny its political relevance as a moment of closure. As Werner Sollors (1986) suggests, it rather requires laying bare the strategies and narratives of its construction as natural and eternal foundation of cultural groups. Moving beyond ethnicity is a step towards revealing how it articulates with broader discourses such as those of ancestry and descent; it requires paying attention to the formation of particularistic identities without entrenching absolute difference.

In this respect, this study will hopefully provide some insight into the construction of white 'normality' and universality. Similarly, I hope to destabilize generalized notions of ethnicity in Britain by positing that the London Italian identity project cannot solely be understood in racialized terms. As I explain below, the Italian project of recovery is tied in with conditions of continuing racism that interpellate Italians in historically specific ways.

Interrogating the visible

The project of identity formation for Italian émigrés is to be viewed in the context of contemporary Britain, two features of which are significant for my immediate concerns. First, narratives on the Italian presence emerged at a time of absence of effective channels of commonality and solidarity linking this dispersed and divided population. Immigration from Italy to Britain had dropped since the mid-1960s, after which the number of returns to Italy sometimes outweighed the entries in Britain. The British Italian population has diversified along generational, cultural and class lines as it has gradually blended within the British socio-economic fabric. In London, 'Little Italy' is no longer a place of residence for Italians, now dispersed in London suburbs. Hence narratives about the Italian presence in Britain first appeared in the mid 1970s, at a time when the 'identity' of Italians in Britain was highly indeterminate. As Kobena Mercer writes 'identity only becomes an issue when it is in crisis, when something assumed to be fixed, coherent and stable is displaced by the experience of doubt and uncertainty' (1990: 43).

Secondly, the integration of Britain in the European Union, in 1973, cleared a space for Italians (and other European immigrants) to claim some form of equal status in relation to Britons, on the grounds of their European identity. As will be shown in Chapter 3, the language of European citizenship provides a new vocabulary for Italian emigrant leaders and constitutes the ground for the formation of a new émigré identity.[6] By emphasizing their Europeanness, Italians represent themselves as both equal to, and distinct from, Britons.

The use of this narrative, however, is up against populist animosity towards the European Community that further fuels England's own 'identity crisis'. Issues of national autonomy and integrity are wheeled out in debates over border controls, where foreigners are represented as criminals and deceivers. Images of 'Euro-scroungers', joined by those of 'bogus asylum seekers', feed into a conception of Englishness that is enclosing itself within increasingly rigid borders. At the same time, there is much stress put on the shared cultural and historical background that unite European citizens, thus emphasizing the legacy of Eurocentric thought and imperialism in the definition of European belonging. In this context, Italian immigrants find themselves at the threshold of difference and sameness in their relation to British national culture. In Britain, they constitute an immigrant, multi-generational population, a linguistic and religious minority, which is also absorbed within the white European majority.

The indeterminacy of the Italians' presence in Britain is seized in the figure of 'invisible immigrants'. First coined in a statistical survey on Italians, Spanish and Portuguese immigrants (MacDonald and MacDonald 1972), the phrase was subsequently appropriated by Umberto Marin, author of the first monograph on Italians in the UK (discussed in Chapter 2), and by Father Graziano Tassello, a leading advocate of Italian émigré identity,[7] in a speech that he gave in 1983 and which was reprinted in Britain's leading Italian newspaper, *La Voce degli Italiani* (hereafter referred to as LV). Under the headline 'The Future of "Invisible Immigrants"', Padre Tassello explained that in the context of recent migration of 'people of colour' (sic) and of the ensuing re-configuration of a British 'multi-ethnic' society, Italian immigrants have become invisible. He then reflected on the new meaning of the Italian presence in Britain. Its economic contribution and integration (namely in the catering industry) was no longer sufficient, he argued, to represent the present experience of Italian immigrants. He concluded with these words:

> [T]here lies within you a legitimate fear about the future of Italian emigration in Great Britain: the fear of losing your own ethnic and national identity. There exists a difficulty in grasping an Italy which has deeply changed. There is a difficulty in spreading your values within English society. We need to open the debate. We need to discuss the role of the newspaper, in a changing community; the role of the associations, which are not only nostalgic returns to the past, but instruments for a new identity . . . (LV 831, October 1990: 15)[8]

'Invisibility', in the British context, is a notion caught up with 'race struggles' that makes its appropriation by Italians both arrogant and challenging. First, its meaning emerges from the very racialization of immigration and 'multicultural' politics, and its adoption by Italians may be read as a gratuitous claim for equality by a population whose invisibility is the product of its integration and acceptance within British society, rather than from conditions of marginalization and imposed silence which configure the 'invisibility' of blacks in Britain (Mercer 1994: 7). Though Italians in Britain have been subjected to discrimination and ostracism during the 1939–45 war years and before (see Sponza 1988), 'invisibility', in their current project of recovery, is not figured in terms of this past. Invisibility, rather, is deployed in discussions about multicultural Britain, and about the organic integration of Italians in the British social landscape. Italians represent themselves as 'invisible immigrants' to emphasize the political indifference they come up against in their country of settlement, as well as to describe what they view as the quiet, non-disruptive nature of their insertion within the British social fabric (see Chapter 3). Tassello's re-appropriation of the phrase is interesting precisely because it forecloses the possibility that invisibility might have been desirable for some Italians. As Terri Colpi reports (1991a: 111), and as some of those I met in the course of my study have testified, the intense Italophobia pervading public discourses during the 1939–45 war years, in Britain, compelled many to seek to hide their Italianness: avoiding speaking Italian in public, anglicizing their names, or their trade (the façade of Italian delis bearing signs stating 'This firm is entirely British'; in Colpi 1991a: 111). Thus a shift in meaning has occurred in the intervening years: from constituting a 'passing' strategy, invisibility is now perceived as the undesirable result of assimilation that causes the loss of an original 'ethnic and national identity'.

Second, the project of 'visibility' is couched in a politics of difference that both mimics and calls into question the 'invisibility' of whiteness (Dyer 1988, 1997). At one level, the label 'invisible immigrants' speaks volumes of assumptions that whiteness is, indeed, invisible; that it is not a 'colour' and that whites are not subjects of racialization (or 'ethnicization') on the basis of bodily features. Tassello's explicit racialization of others – 'people of colour' – does not necessarily mean that he is consciously racializing whiteness. Nonetheless, by casting the black 'Other' against a narrative about the role of Italians in the Europeanization of 'the English', Tassello entrenches the association of invisibility with Europeanness and consequently, racializes it as white.[9]

By seeking to move out of invisibility, Italians push against the principles of British 'new racism', or cultural racism.[10] Their project of recovery evolved in the context of populist angst over the definition of Englishness/Britishness that has been systematized in the 1960s within a neo-racist discourse of cultural identity. Within British cultural racism, the naturalization of culture diffuses 'race' and racism in ethnic-related discourses of differentiation. This is what Paul Gilroy calls 'ethnic absolutism' (1987: 59).

> [C]ulture is conceived along ethnically absolute lines, not as something intrinsically fluid, changing, unstable, and dynamic, but as a fixed property of social groups rather than a relational field in which they encounter one another and live out social, historical relationships. When culture is brought into contact with race it is transformed into a pseudo-biological property of communal life. (Gilroy 1993b: 24)

Culture is used as a measuring stick for the integration of minorities and 'foreigners' into the national culture. Ethnic absolutism constructs cultural factors as elements of differentiation, thus underlying the idea of 'ethnic groups'. Moreover, social inequality finds justifications and operates on these absolutist grounds; that is to say that the 'inherent cultural nature' of ethnic groups explains their different positions in the social strata, if not the impossibility of the insertion of minorities into mainstream national cultures (Gilroy 1987: 61). Ethnic absolutism is the process of constructing culturally essentialized groups, of reifying cultural differences as absolute differences and bases for social mobilization. What strikes me in this discourse is the role ethnicity plays in tying up culture and biology. Ethnicity is the nodal point that mediates culture and race and allows them to congeal in pseudo-biological underpinnings. As 'race' is culturalized, 'ethnicity' is essentialized. What stems from this is the notion of an invisible ethnicity as well as the idea that ethnic identification is somewhat intrinsic. Ideas that people 'naturally' socialize and group with 'those of their own kind' implies that they share a sentiment of a deeply incorporated unified identity (Duffield 1984). It is within this conception of culture as a inherent part of our beings, as a possession (we 'have' cultures) that the blurring of nature and culture occurs, and that cultural differences appear as immutable. In short, culture and difference, rather than biology and hierarchy, are the key organizing principles that distinguish cultural racism from scientific racism.[11]

The question I raise here, then, concerns the impact of such discourses on white immigrant self-representations. Though the authors and leaders discussed in Chapters 2 and 3 may not have racist intentions, it may be argued that the circumstances in which their descriptions were produced and consumed constitute 'conditions of continuing racism' that interpellate them and influence their narratives of self-representation (Lawrence 1982: 74). More to the point, it is possible to argue that the project of retrieving Italians from their invisibility became feasible when ethnic identity was re-configured around cultural rather than racial difference.[12] Their narratives, in other words, are assessed, here, in the context of the prevalent discourses of ethnicity, culture and nation. To what extent do these texts mimic absolutist discourses of culture, entitlement and authenticity? How is essentialism deployed in identity narratives? What are it's organizing principles? How does it circulate in the diaspora space of Italian émigré culture?

I use the image of invisible immigrants as the starting point of my enquiry, for it captures the complexity of the issues running through the construction of a 'new identity' for London Italians. The ambivalent cultural and political ground Italians occupy – being Italian, European, residing in Britain – pushes against the borders of identity/difference insofar as they are configured in terms of visibility. The Italian project of recovery is telling of the intense slipperiness of in/visibility and, by extension, of 'whiteness' and 'blackness'. For instance, I was puzzled when I first encountered the phrase 'invisible immigrant', because it contrasted sharply with the label 'visible minorities' that appeared in the Canadian bureaucratic jargon in the late 1970s to speak of immigrants from the Caribbean, Africa and South-East Asia. There is a fascinating play of seeing and naming that revolves around ideas of visibility and invisibility: a play that is deeply embedded in the constant displacement of bodily inscriptions of identity/difference that render the skin/body 'radically unstable' (Ahmed 1998b: 27). It is in this sense that I find the Italian project of visibility compelling. For it complicates the 'empiricism attributed to the visual field' (Fraser 1999: 111). Indeed, the indeterminacy of the Italian presence in Britain gives rise to specific negotiating strategies to solve this uncertainty. There exists a range of sites of identity formation and mobilization that Italians resort to, that cannot be understood in terms of 'ethnicity' alone. 'Invisible immigrants' compels me to proceed from the very thresholds of identity formation, to explore the very tensions and ambivalences that shape the Italian migrant belongings.

'Ethnic organizations' are commonly perceived as run by 'cultural entrepreneurs' who are nothing more than cultural integrists. By extension, the quest for an identity, for a 'habitual space' (Gaetano Parolin in LV 967, February 1997: 5), are relegated as the privileged field of middle-class intermediaries who have only their personal interests in mind. Institutional discourses of identity are conceived as unidimensional representations that fix and encase social categories within clearly drawn boundaries. Such crude models of ethnogenesis or 'entrepreneurship' are of little use when confronted with leaders' self-critical appraisal of what it means to 'construct a community'. By foregrounding the role of print journalism and organizations as 'instruments for [creating] a new identity', Graziano Tassello is expressing his clear awareness of his role and that of his organization (the Scalabrinian congregation) in constructing a new identity. Tassello's speech exemplifies much of what I have observed throughout my research: that is that the men and women I met in London have a complex view and agenda about identity formation and recognize the 'creative capacity [of their institutions] to *create* a community' (my emphasis).[13]

There are few attempts to closely scrutinize the inherent complexity of 'official discourses' of migrant leaders. As I will show throughout the next chapters, London Italian leaders develop a conception of cultural identity that combines competing definitions that straddle the tension between absolutist and pluralist notions of identity. Their project, moreover, appears at a time when Italian migration has radically changed, that is, when *im*migration has practically come to a halt. Part of the goal to 'create a community', then, is the recovery of the history of Italian immigration to the British Isles (especially Britain). This history is summarized below.

Italian migration to the British Isles: a brief overview

The Italian presence in the British isles results from a history of emigration that reached important proportions in the aftermath of the unification and proclamation of the Kingdom of Italy by Victor-Emmanuel II in 1861.[14] During the century between 1876 and 1976, 26 million Italians left Italy, 60 per cent of whom did so between 1876 and 1921 (Painchaud and Poulin 1988: 22). Emigration considerably reduced during the inter-war years, and rose again between 1946 to 1976, when up to 7.2 million Italians left their country (Painchaud and Poulin 1988: 21). Interestingly, Robert Foerster ([1919] 1968: 42) reported that up to two-thirds of the early emigration was temporary. Many Italians returned to Italy, and left again, for the same or a different destination. This situation led to the acceptance, in Italy, of an expanded definition of emigration: 'in time an emigrant became, officially, anyone not travelling for pleasure, health or business, who went abroad either for permanent settlement or temporarily, for a period often less than a year' (Foerster [1919] 1968: 4).

The important first wave of migration, then, occurred in the last decades of the nineteenth century and the beginning of the twentieth century, up to the late 1920s (reaching a peak, in 1913, of one person in every 40 leaving Italy; Mack Smith 1959: 239). Until 1880, Italians migrated mainly to Europe, especially France. During the last two decades of the nineteenth century, Argentina, Brazil, and the US became their preferred destination. The latter eventually attracted the largest numbers of Italian emigrants, up until 1921, when the Immigration Act, based on ethnic origin, restrained immigration from Italy and made France once again the preferred destination of Italian migrants during the decade between 1920–30.

A number of factors incited Italians to leave. On the one hand, the 'bourgeois' revolution instituted the principle of free circulation of persons in 1865; the principle was reasserted by law in 1873 and set in the constitution. On the other hand, the impoverishment of the Italian rural areas – resulting from a complex combination of factors such as a rapid population growth, soil erosion, unemployment, and heavy taxation – and the industrialization of many Western countries, acted concomitantly as push and pull factors in the yearly migration of hundreds of thousands of Italians (Romano 1977: 93–4; Foerster 1919/1968).

In 1861, the Italian-born population of Britain was estimated to be 4,608 (see Appendix 2). By 1891, this population had more than doubled, to reach 10,934. It had doubled once again by 1901, with 24,383 Italian-born in Britain, after which this population stabilized, the immigration being partly impeded by two British government Acts. The first was the Aliens Act. Adopted in 1905, the Act was introduced to curb the immigration of 'undesirable' aliens, and used to 'check the influx of Jews from Russia and Russian-ruled Poland.' (Sponza 1988: 13). This Act also policed 'itinerant commercial activities', and was used to expel foreign prostitutes and convicted criminals. The Act, however, only slightly affected Italian immigrants, who were less likely to be expelled than Russians/Poles, Germans or French (Sponza 1988: 237). Hence migrants from Italy continued to arrive in Britain in great numbers until 1913, through *padroni* sponsored channels (see below). In 1920, a second Act, the Aliens Order, introduced the work permit. This Act considerably obstructed the entry of Italian immigrants to Britain in the second half of the 1920s. Soon after, in 1924, Italy also began to restrict emigration from its territory. From encouraging the dispersal of 'Italian workers abroad', Mussolini shifted to a view of emigration as a harmful reduction of the pool of available labour (Colpi 1991a: 73). Immigration became illegal in 1928 (Harney 1998: 13), although travelling concessions were given to the more educated middle-class who intended to return to Italy (Colpi 1991a: 73). It is not until the late 1940s that new immigration waves from Italy were to re-appear.

Throughout this first period (1860–1930), the main European destinations were France, Switzerland, Germany and Austria-Hungary (up to 1913). Comparatively, Britain was the recipient of a very small number of Italian emigrants; for example, while only 80,843 Italians emigrated to Britain during the 49 years from 1875 to 1924 (Marin 1975: 167), over 1.5 million migrated to France from 1901 to 1930 (Romano 1977: 98; Foerster 1919/1968: 8–9). Altogether, however, the pattern of migration to Britain followed the overall migration flows in terms of 'waves' and regional provenance.

Italian immigrants to Britain, at the turn of the century, came essentially from northern Italy, mainly from Lombardia, Emilia and Toscania, with nonetheless an important contingent from Campania (southern Italy). London was their main place of settlement, although a small number went to Glasgow, Liverpool, Cardiff and, to a much lesser extent, Ireland. At the turn of the century, Italian migrants were settling predominantly in the areas known today as Soho (in the then 'district' of Westminster) and Clerkenwell ('district' of Holborn), both in central London. In the 1900s, the poorest parts of Holborn 'had been *the* area where most Italians clustered' (Sponza 1988: 20; emphasis original), attracted by cheap rents and the convenient location for their itinerant occupations (organ-grinders, chestnut sellers, costermongers) or artisan workshops (statuette makers).

Itinerant traders virtually disappeared after 1905, due firstly to restrictions spelled out by the British Aliens Act forcing foreigners to enter the formal economy, and secondly to the decline of this section of the Italian population (Sponza 1988: 13). From hawking and street entertaining activities of earlier times, Italian immigrants turned to catering services: family-run ice-cream trading, or employed in restaurants, hotels and clubs. These changes in the occupational structure, along with an increase in family-based migration networks, signalled the gradual disappearance of *padrone*-run hawking groups.

Chain migration was an important channel of emigration for Italians. In the period 1830–1930, the most prominent path was run by a system called *padronismo*.

> The *padrone* transformed the process of emigration into a business; he offered work contracts to people in Italy, sought volunteers to fulfil them, organised transport and employed people himself once at the destination. (Colpi 1991a: 34)

This type of *padrone* differed from its North American counterpart, who acted as kind of a broker by recruiting, hiring and controlling fellow Italians on behalf of a Canadian or American employer (such as the Canadian National Railway Company), often collecting a fee from the recruits apart from the commission paid by his employer (Ramirez 1984: 64, n36).[15] In Britain, however, the *padrone* was the employer and he most often recruited children, generally young boys. The early *padroni* (1830–80) controlled boys involved in itinerant commercial activities, namely organ grinders. Later (1880/90 to the late 1920s), the *padroni* employed boys in their own small businesses, following the transition from informal to formal economic activities. This new type of *padronismo* is said to have been more personal than the previous one, since most *padroni* recruited boys or young men and women from their home village in Italy. However, as mentioned above, along with the formalization of the economy came a more family-based migration of independent migrants, thus undermining the *padrone*-based channels.

The post 1945 period, when a number of countries (re)opened their borders to Italian workers, is the second period of mass migration from Italy. Between 1946 and 1976, 7.5 million Italians left their country (Painchaud and Poulin 1988: 21).

In contrast to the earlier migration, these migrants came overwhelmingly from southern parts of Italy, compelled to leave because of severe economic conditions. Two thirds of the post-war migrants went to European countries. The 1958 Treaty of Rome, creating the European Economic Community, institutionalized the European labour market where Italy, on its own request, could export its labour surplus (Painchaud and Poulin 1988: 22). From 1949 to 1962, between 6,000 and 11,000 Italians entered Britain each year (with the exception of 1950 and 1952). London remained the preferred place of settlement, but cities such as Bedford and Bristol were hosts to significant numbers of Italian immigrants recruited under volunteer worker schemes.

Post-war immigrants were mainly of three categories: 1) prisoners of war; 2) caterers; 3) industrial workers. There were approximately 1,500 POWs who stayed in Britain under 'civilian workers' contracts or, later, the European Volunteer Workers Scheme (Sponza 1995). New immigration, on the other hand, brought new workers in the flourishing catering industry. It was in the post-war years that London saw its first Italian coffee bars, and subsequently its first *trattorie*, all of which 'sold Italianness', as Terri Colpi puts it (1991a: 141).

Industrial workers, for their part, arrived in Britain under bulk recruitment schemes. The reconstruction of Britain after the war of 1939–45 required a vast amount of labour resources, which were recruited from many parts of Europe, notably Italy and Poland. The rapid growth of the Italian-born population in the 1950s is largely due to such schemes. Women were solicited for the textile, rubber and ceramics industries of central and northern England. Many were also hired as domestic servants or hospital orderlies. Men, for their part, were predominantly recruited as foundry workers, miners, tin-plate workers, and brick workers (Colpi 1991a: 145–52).

After a last peak in 1965 and 1967, Italian immigration to Britain dropped and stabilized to one or two thousand annually (Bottignolo 1985: 209). Since 1969, returnees to Italy have outnumbered those entering Britain (except for 1984). The characteristics of these migrants are unknown, but it is likely that a number of them include individuals who came to Britain on a temporary basis, in contrast to earlier migrants who 'fled' from severe economic conditions in Italy.

The Italian-born population of London in 1991 was 30,052. As for the total Italian population of the UK – including 'second' and 'third' generations – numbers are not very accurate, for they come from Italian official sources who rely on estimates calculated as multiples of the number of family or individual records in the archives of the local consulates. Nevertheless, approximations for 1981 move between 150,000 and 196,000 of residents of Italian descent in the UK – less than 1 per cent of the entire population – and between 100,000 and 150,000 for Greater London (Colpi 1991a: 169). In 1987, 34 per cent of the Italian population worked in the hotel and tourism industry (including 32 per cent that were either self employed or entrepreneurs), and 23 per cent in the industrial sector (99 per cent of which were employed labourers).

In London, the dispersal of Italian residents from Clerkenwell and Soho began in the 1920s and 1930s, though these areas remained important Italian neighbourhoods until the war years. Today the population is scattered in the Greater London area, north and south of the Thames: Islington, Westminster, Camden, Enfield, Barnet, Haringey, Wandsworth, Lambeth, to name a few of the preferred boroughs where Italians now reside (see Appendix 3). It is this dispersed population that present day Italian immigrant intellectuals (in the Gramscian sense; included here are authors, religious and political leaders) are seeking to aggregate under a 'new identity'.

The migration of industrial workers is said to be 'responsible for the change in the [organizational] structure and orientation of the Italian presence in Britain' (Colpi 1991a: 136), constituting what is known as the 'new' Italian communities, in contrast with the 'old' communities established before the 1939–45 war. The 'new communities' were more diversified in terms of geographical origin than the 'old communities': although they were predominantly from southern Italy, there were not as many village groupings as in the case of their predecessors, due mainly to the impersonal migration networks run by British recruitment schemes, rather than the earlier *padrone*-run chain migration. Also, industrial workers and professionals arrived under conditions that differed greatly from those of their forerunners who migrated outside of the chain migration route. Being employed on arrival under government schemes, new immigrants had little need for 'middle men' to arrange for personal matters. It is in this context that parish priests began acquiring a new role. The priests and the 'ethnic church' were increasingly recognized as leaders and organizers both by Italians and their employers (Colpi 1991a: 152). Today, London Italian associative life is tightly bound up with religious institutions (Parolin 1979). The social events of a large number of London Italian clubs and associations take place in St Peter's social club or at the Centro Scalabrini, and are usually preceded by a religious service. Larger 'community' outings include a pilgrimage to the Aylesford monastery of Our Lady of Mount Carmel, and the Scalabrini picnic – held on the grounds of the Scalabrini retirement home in Shenley (Hertfordshire) – which is solemnized by a Holy Mass. The churches play a significant role in 'community' life and in creating a 'community' that supersedes regional differences; an all-encompassing 'Italian community'. It is the nature of this role, and the forms of belonging it fosters, that I explore in the second part of this book. For, to paraphrase Richard Rodriguez, clearly something is going on in these churches that is not only liturgical (1995: 78).

In sum, *Migrant Belongings* is a contemplation of the ways in which Italians act upon their environment to create localized terrains of belonging. This study took place at a time when the Italian immigrant leadership was reviewing its role in the face of the need to redefine the meaning of the Italian presence in Britain. Overall, this project is located in the struggle for control over historicity – that is, the symbolic capacity of a social group 'to produce it's own social and cultural field, its own historical environment' (Touraine 1977: 16). This process includes the construction of systems of knowledge that can be used to intervene in the very creation and functioning of the Italian community (Touraine 1977: 15). It is such systems that I examine in the chapters that follow.

Notes

1. The event represented in this window is described in a booklet produced by the London Centro Scalabrini for the celebration of its 25th anniversary in 1993. In the text, the two founding fathers are identified as 'pioneers'. See Centro Scalabrini di Londra (1993).
2. More on Cavallaro's study in Chapter 2.
3. This position is drawn from the postcolonial critique according to which the hyphen of 'post-colonialism' or 'post-modernism' separates timespaces into discrete entities. Postcolonial critics have also argued that the hyphen maintains the 'other' outside of histories and geographies defined in Eurocentric and masculinist terms (Ashcroft, Griffiths and Tiffin 1989; Shohat 1992; McClintock 1992; Spivak 1990; Appiah 1992; Grewal 1996). Similarly, some have withdrawn the hyphen from 'multi-culture' in order to seize, in the term 'multiculture', the inherent hybridity of cultural forms (Back 1996).
4. As I point out in the following chapter, Lucio Sponza's analysis of representations of Italians in nineteenth-century Britain reveals how the public debate about hygiene, street noise and the degeneracy of the city was ethnicized by figuring Italians and Irish as sources of that degeneracy. This adds to Ann McClintock point that English racism used the metaphor of

   > *domestic degeneracy* . . . to mediate the manifold contradictions in imperial hierarchy – not only with respect to the Irish but also to the other 'white negroes': Jews, prostitutes, the working-class, domestic workers, and so on, where skin color as marker of power was imprecise and inadequate. (1995: 53; emphasis original)

   Italians were not immune to such discourses. Definitions of their suitability as British residents revolved around the 'barbarism' of the Italian way of life, viewed as an expression of the 'ineradicably bad' character nature of Italians, as testified in an article published in 1892.

> The Italians mostly come from Naples and the vicinity where they live in pauperism, filth and vice, with no other ambition than to get cheap food enough to keep them alive . . . They are ineradicably bad, and only the fear of the law's punishment . . . keeps them in any way disciplined. The degraded habits of this class of immigrants, innate and lasting as they are, stamp them as a most undesirable set, whose affiliation with our own people must in time work great injury. (W.H. Wilkins in Sponza 1988: 235)

5. The attribution of ethnicity to the 'Other' is in direct continuity with the anthropological approach to tribal societies and their 'modern' equivalent, ethnic groups (Jenkins 1986). A product of colonialism, this approach separates and hierarchizes cultures into discrete and coherent systems of norms, values, organizational structures, behaviours and ways of life (Bhabha 1994).
6. As well, it seems, as in the US, where a new European-American ethnicity is emerging, bringing Italians together with other Americans of European descent (Alba 1994: 21). This, however, is set against the backdrop of American racial politics, where European identity may be viewed as a response to the black Africanist discourses of identity. As I state above, the articulation of race, class and nation takes on different forms in different contexts.
7. Padre Tassello is a Scalabrinian priest living in Rome, who writes regularly in *La Voce* on issues concerning identity politics. The Scalabrinian Order runs the Centro Scalabrini studied in Part II of this book and publishes *La Voce degli Italiani.* More details on this congregation are given in Chapter 4.
8. All quotes from *La Voce degli Italiani* are my translations from Italian.
9. The very exclusion of blacks from conceptions of European citizenship and culture has led some authors to view them as 'invisible Europeans' (Back and Nayak 1993).
10. I prefer the phrase cultural racism, because 'new' racism suggests a clear move away from 'old' scientific racism. But as a number of authors have shown, past usage of 'race' was multiple, and at times cultural and biological definitions coexisted (McClintock 1995; Tonkin, Mcdonald and Chapman 1989). And today, publications such as Herrnstein's and Murray's (1996) *The Bell Curve* (and the intense debate that it provoked) remind us that scientific discourses still have some currency, alongside culturalist discourses. For details about new racism in Britain, see Barker 1981; Duffield 1984; Gilroy 1987.
11. Assuredly, difference converts swiftly into hierarchy, in cultural racism. But this is different to the systematic hierarchical classification of 'man' into 'races', which was a key principle of scientific racism after the publication of Darwin's *On the Origin of Species* in 1859, and the advent of social Darwinism (McClintock 1995).
12. The reconfiguration of ethnicity is not the doing of state regulations and discourses alone. 'New ethnicities' of the late 1970s and early 1980s challenged

notions of cultural conformity with nationalist discourses by making strong claims for the respect of difference. I strongly suspect that Italian writers were informed by these struggles, but the extent of this influence needs to be further explored. For example, Bruno Bottignolo only mentions in passing that Italians in Swindon were involved in the local Commission for Racial Equality, without providing further details about the circumstances of this involvement (1985: 59). Such cases would be worth documenting, if only to reveal how 'race struggles' and 'race politics' influence the politics of identity of white immigrant populations such as Italians.

13. Speech given by Padre Giandomenico Ziliotto on the night of the Centro Scalabrini's 25th anniversary choir recital, 4 December 1993. This event is discussed in Chapter 4.
14. Some stories about 'Italian' immigration to Britain trace the paths of migration back to the Roman Empire (Palmer [1977] 1991; Marin 1975). In the Middle Ages, an important trade industry lead to the settlement of a Venetian colony in London that minted its own currency (Palmer 1977/1991: 244). In 1581, an 'Italian' (sic) church existed in London, with a congregation of 66 (Palmer 1977/1991: 244). Finally, Terri Colpi speaks of the first 'Italian colony' in Clerkenwell, central London. It is said to have existed since the seventeenth century (Colpi 1991a: 27). The anachronism of attributing an Italian identity or nationality to these early migrants seems to escape the authors' notice. Such narratives testify to the intense malleability of the past, while it wraps Italian national identity with an aura of eternity.
15. This system of *padronismo*, which was widespread in North America at the turn of the century, was not exclusive to Italians and could take different forms.
16. Data from the Italian Foreign Ministry, compiled in *La Voce* 831, October 1990: 15.

Part I
Histories and Identity Politics

–2–

Imagining a Community: Migration, Settlement, Sacrifice and the Trope Kinship

> [E]very story that relates what is happening or what has happened constitutes something real to the extent that it pretends to be the representation of a past reality. It takes on authority by passing itself off as the witness of what is or of what has been . . . Historiography acquires this power insofar as it presents and interprets the 'facts'. How can readers resist discourse that tells them what is or what has been?
>
> Michel de Certeau

At the beginning of my fieldwork, I asked some interviewees: 'What is the Italian community?' Each paused, looked at me, perplexed, and uttered something about the impossibility of defining it, about it being an 'amorphous mass' (sic), before complying with my request and attempting to describe its configuration. Emerging from these interviews, was an image of a community characterized by diversity: differences of class, regional origins (in Italy), place of residence, generations (no one mentioned gender differences, however). As the interviewees spoke, the community's boundaries remained blurred. The 'community' described to me did not consist of a geographically confined area, or of a life of daily contacts between individuals. It was not a neighbourhood, nor a 'street corner society' such as the one they might have known in former Little Italy.

A similar picture surfaces from much of the literature on Italians in Britain: these texts also depict a collectivity characterized by a high degree of diversity *within*. The Italian population is differentiated along class and status lines, regional origins in Italy, generations, time of arrival and place of residence in England. At the same time, ideas of an Italian 'community' surface, albeit in different degrees and forms, from the written renditions of the Italian presence in Britain. Hence some kind of coherence is created from the disparate histories, social relations, social positions, of Italian migrants. What are the organizing principles of this coherence?

In examining these questions, I shall scrutinize monographs produced by Italians on Italians in Britain and unwrap what they say about the origins of the Italian presence, and how they say it. In other words, this chapter is about how written narratives cobble together elements of the past in the name of an identity project. Following on from Benedict Anderson's insights on printed language as a site for the production of national identities, I conceive these texts as specific instances in the creation of an imagined community (Anderson 1983). The question is: what *kind* of community is imagined? How is the Italian presence qualified? What discourses of communality gel together the disparate population of Italian immigrants?

These questions surround my scrutiny of textual practices that substantiate the existence of an Italian 'community' in Britain. I start from the premise that the 'problem' of naming and enclosing *an* Italian presence in Britain is partly solved by writing its history, which authorizes its existence and legitimizes the actions undertaken to produce a distinctly Italian form of belonging (de Certeau 1980/1990: 182–3). 'The story does not express a practice. It does not limit itself to telling about a movement. It *makes* it' (de Certeau 1984: 80; emphasis original). In other words, these stories *produce* what they claim to be *re*-presenting and *re*-covering. The texts are examined as a 'performative act[s] of organising what [they] enunciate' (de Certeau 1984: 155). By identifying the common threads running through these stories of 'community', I seek to unpack the organizing principles of these narratives and of the fields of belonging they delineate.

John Gillis (1994b) points out that new forms of 'memory work' appear at times when there is a break with the past. When reading the monographs written by and on Italians, it is important to bear in mind that these publications first appeared when a geographically locatable 'Little Italy', in London at least, had gradually disintegrated, and when particular lifestyles (in England and in Italy) were now merely spectres in the shadows of a distant past. The dissolution of 'pockets of Italianness' within the English social and urban landscapes goes hand in hand with a movement of distancing from Italy (both physical and metaphorical): the 'origins' of Italians in Britain are now multiple and faded as a result of the passing of time and inevitable fragmentation of the collectivity. Concurrently, the social character of the collectivity is undergoing significant transformations as 'younger generations' now constitute a significant proportion of the overall Italian population, and as new Italian migrants are viewed as disturbing the still waters of this 'established' community (see below). Finally, it bears repetition that these accounts also developed in connection with broader discourses of national integrity which, in Britain, were at the centre of populist angst over the perceived threat of both immigration and the New Europe.

The first attempt to write a general history of Italians in Britain appeared in 1975.[1] Written by Father Umberto Marin, a Scalabrinian priest who spent a number of years in England, *Italiani in Gran Bretagna* was published in the aftermath of the integration of Britain within the EC. This, according to Marin, incited politicians and sociologists to turn their attention toward *Invisible Immigrants* in Britain (Marin

1975: 5),[2] that is, immigrants from European countries. At one level, the 'invisibility' Marin wishes to uncover is located within the racialized politics of nationality in British society and neo-racist discourses of entitlement and belonging: he wrote his history of Italians immigrants in the context of debates about the social and economic incorporation of black and other ethnic minorities. At another level, Marin's project of redemption, a project of claiming the 'right to difference', is licensed by the British government's recognition of Europe as a political and economic unit. Marin intends to use this platform to rehabilitate the Italian presence in Britain (see Chapter 3).

Marin's publication appeared at a time when representations of Italian immigrants had radically changed. Images of the 'ineradicably bad' Italian migrant of the late nineteenth century (Sponza 1988: 235), of the enemy alien of the war years (see below), and of the gang-land club owners of Soho in the 1950s (Sir Harold Scott in Gilroy 1987: 80), had gradually subsided to be substituted by more positive representations. For instance, in his household survey of immigrant populations of Bedford (Indians, Pakistanis, West Indians, Italians, Polish, Ukrainian, Latvian, and Yugoslavian), John Brown (1970) praises the qualities of Italians whom he elevates as model immigrants, that is, as those who are the most likely to integrate into the British way of life. 'Here are the characteristic Italian qualities [hard work, perseverance] that have won the respect of Bedford. These, and the spotless cleanliness of their houses and shops, an irresistible recommendation to British natives [sic]. Cleanliness, after all, is next to godliness' (1970: 88).[3] Brown's conclusion is founded upon the legacies of nineteenth-century discourses of the 'home' as a space of virtue, morality and purity (Forty 1986), while it repositions Italians not as 'dirty' or 'untrustworthy' (Sponza 1998), but, rather, as presenting the perfect model of cleanliness and, by extension, virtuous morality. The re-ethnicization of home and hygiene in 1970s Britain, establishes a new hierarchy between 'ethnic minorities', placing Italians at the top. The implication was that Italians are best suited for the white British 'way of life', at least when it comes to 'home-life'. The effect was to further substantiate the formation of whiteness and 'non-whiteness' as the basis of distinct ethnic identities, and emphasizing the 'foreignness' of 'black' minorities.

The elevation of Italians as exemplars of standards and experiences of integration was not lost to authors like Umberto Marin, who recognizes the privileged position Italians occupy in contemporary British society.

> The Italian collectivity in Great Britain is considered a privileged collectivity. Favoured by a liberal immigration policy . . . it has harmoniously integrated within British society and as such, represents a kind of Eden within the troubled emigration front. For the British state, it is an exemplary immigration sediment, the best integrated, the most successful, which acts as a model for other national collectivities that are more alienated and worried. (1975: 104)

Yet in spite of this acknowledgement, Umberto Marin's goal is to further redeem Italians and give them a positive image of themselves as immigrants and 'foreigners', without, however, neglecting the daily difficulties and struggles that immigrants encounter when seeking to settle in Britain. Language differences, political indifference, labour market constraints and expectations were major stumbling blocks which Marin makes a point of emphasizing in order to dismiss the assumption that things were easy for Italian immigrants. Bruno Bottignolo holds a similar view:

> The absence of limitation and differences such as to bring about situations of open conflict alone [e.g. racism], does not create easy social interaction. An Italian in Great Britain finds no great obstacles [sic] to his insertion into the new society, but neither does he find many realities to help his insertion or to favour the active practice of the limited rights of citizenship which are conceded to him . . . The Italian immigrant's invisibility is ultimately also an expression of his limited socio-cultural relevance. (1985: 71)

The project of recovering the Italian presence in Britain is tantamount to questions of difference and 'socio cultural relevance'. What is at stake, here, is not only the recovery of Italians' political and cultural presence within both the British and Italian nation states, but also the establishment of their legitimacy as a distinct social group. One way of establishing this is through the creation of cultural and historical environments.

Umberto Marin's book instigated an interest in the Italian presence in Britain and a small catalogue of publications subsequently emerged.[4] For the purpose of this chapter, I focus my attention on three monographs about Italians in the British isles (Colpi 1991a; Marin 1975; Sponza 1988), as well as on two monographs on Italian immigrants in the Bristol region and in Bedford respectively (Bottignolo 1985; Cavallaro 1981). With the exception of Cavallaro, these books speak of an entire population of Italian immigrants, rather than focusing on only one section. They are of interest to me because, each in their own way, they attempt to solve the indeterminacy of the Italian population by identifying its common grounds beyond regionalisms. Finally, these books are all produced by Italians who have in one way or another, a personal commitment to the British Italian 'community' – with the exception of Renato Cavallaro.

Bruno Bottignolo is a priest from the diocese of Padua, who was serving in an Italian mission in Bristol at the time of his study. His book is the published version of his doctoral dissertation, which he conducted under the supervision of Mary Douglas, at Cambridge University. Umberto Marin, for his part, is a Scalabrinian priest. Though now residing in Milan, he remains to this day a prominent figure in the English Italian 'community'. He lived in Bedford from 1960 to 1966, and in London from 1966 to 1979, where he was involved in the foundation of the

Centro Scalabrini. Marin took over the editorship of *La Voce degli Italiani* in 1963, until he returned to Italy in 1979. In 1973, he was awarded the distinction of *Cavaliere* (the Italian equivalent of knighthood) for his services to the Italian Republic. As for Lucio Sponza, he arrived in England in the 1960s. An academic and historian, Sponza is dedicated to researching the Italian presence in Britain which, in his view, has a very rich history that remains to be documented (1995). Terri Colpi is a self-identified Italian Scot, '[b]orn into one of the oldest Italian business families in Scotland' (1991a: book jacket). She has produced a number of publications on Italian immigrants, but has gained some notability in the Italian community with *The Italian Factor* and *Italians Forward*. The former was the first comprehensive account about the history of the Italian 'community' and was neatly complemented by the latter, which consists of a photographic album of past and present Italian life in Britain. For these reasons, Colpi is viewed as an important contributor to the advancement of the community. She was recently rewarded for this contribution by receiving the honorary title of *Cavaliere* (LV 934, June 1995: 6).

Within this selection, as well as within the entire literature on Italians in Britain, Renato Cavallaro's *Storie senza Storia* is unique because it was clearly founded in an analytical and theoretical project.[5] Cavallaro, a sociologist attached to the Sociology Institute of the University of Rome at the time of his research, used individual life stories to reconstruct the itinerary of the collective consciousness of Calabrian[6] immigrants in Bedford. Informed by Bakhtin and Lefebvre, he scrutinized narratives about changes and displacements in the immigrants' spatio-temporal horizons, and the type of knowledge produced in these stories. Conducting an ethnographic type of study, he complemented the life stories with observations of the daily lives of the Bedford Calabrians. The freshness of this study is that it explores the constitutive effectiveness of memory and the power of enunciation in identity formation. His account captures the lived experience of migration and the creativity of peoples 'art of living' (Probyn 1996): the ways in which social change, ruptures, transition are appropriated, made sense of, and reprocessed in the collective imagery of migrant lives.

Lucio Sponza's book, for its part, aims to dispel images of Italians as a homogeneous ethnic group. He reveals the open-ended character of the emigration process by emphasizing the importance of the economic structure as an explanatory factor to the immigration and settlement of Italians in nineteenth-century Britain. The originality of Sponza's account is that he relates the attitudes of British society towards Italians to class struggles that manifested themselves in debates about poverty, hygiene, foreigners, and so on. He identifies four issues around which these concerns and debates revolved and which had a direct impact on Italians: the living conditions of the organ grinders, especially the children; the annoyance with street music; the overcrowding and alleged sanitary hazard within the Italian

Quarter; and the suspicion of the immoral practices of Italians (1988: 140). What his research reveals is the ethnicization of social or political issues, and some of the operations through which ethnic identities are given substance. In Sponza's words, Italian immigrants of the nineteenth century, popularized in the image of the organ grinders, 'acted as a sort of litmus paper [sic], revealing the degree of social and ideological polarization and antagonism of mid-Victorian London (and Britain)' (Sponza 1988: 179).

Umberto Marin and Bruno Bottignolo, for their part, emphasize the political organization of identity as a constitutive force of a 'community'. For Marin, the redemption of Italian immigrants will ultimately be political, while Bottignolo's concerns revolve around the 'nature and the meaning of the community activities of the Italians in the Bristol region, with particular reference to their political position' (1985: 38).

Finally, Terri Colpi's book provides an impressionist view of the origins and characteristics of the present day Italian community. In turn, *The Italian Factor* stands out as a highly normative and objectifying representation of the community. The Italian 'Community' (or *Comunità;* both always with a capital *c*) is given as a unified 'thing', the membership of which is policed by the degree of conformity to its cultural contents. 'This book is not directly concerned with those who have opted or drifted out of the Community; it is concerned with those who have an Italian way of life, are linked with Italy and who feel at least partly Italian' (1991a: 16). What this 'Italian way of life' means is spelled out along the lines of settlement, migration, and memory, through which Colpi asserts the undeniable presence of an *Italian Factor* within British society. For her, the actions of individuals are *expressions* of cultural-ethnic identity or identification.

> Although only around a quarter of a million people resident in Britain today are either Italian-born or of Italian origin, they are a distinct presence within British society. Their long history in this country, their specialist development of the catering industry, their continued contact with Italy, their ever evolving migration picture and finally their strong Italian 'ethnic memory', which makes them cling even after generations to aspects of their Italianness, all contribute to Community traditions . . . *The Italian Factor* in British life has truly come of age. (Colpi 1991a: 22)

Each author, to be sure, approaches the Italian presence in Britain with different agendas in mind. Without neglecting these differences, the analysis that follows focuses on how the texts trace and link up threads of histories that 'reveal' how the 'Italian factor . . . has come of age' (Colpi 1991a: 22). These textual renditions invent a community by periodizing it, stabilizing it and objectifying it: three interlocking processes that create a sense of particularity from which terrains of belonging can emerge. Periodization is about making sense of the present by dividing the past into significant moments in its construction. The remainder of this chapter is organized around three such moments: foundations (constituted around tradition), settlement (configured around continuity), and the immigrant condition (which is about identity and difference). Stabilization, for its part, is about 'points of suture' that secure the incessant movement of the 'community identity'. These will be examined in the last section of this chapter, in relation to the trope of kinship that pervades these histories. Finally, objectification is about making 'culture' and 'community' into a thing that we can stand back from and look at as an undeniable entity (Handler 1988): such practices are identified throughout the three sections.

Foundations

In contrast to the American or Canadian Italian historical landscape, British Italian historiography has allocated little space for the creation of a cultural patrimony founded on the achievements of 'patriarchal pioneers'. Such is the project of Umberto Marin, whose panorama of the earlier migration of noteworthy men is meant to create a pedigree of Italian presence in Britain. His aim is '[t]hat Italian émigrés, forced out of necessity to leave their own fatherland *(patria),* are convinced that the streets of the world are not only paved with loneliness, weariness and nostalgia, but also with an incomparable cultural patrimony. By recovering this patrimony, the émigré redeems himself [sic]' (1975: 7). Marin clearly sets out to create genealogical traces of cultural heritage to which present-day immigrants may somehow lay claim. To paraphrase Michel de Certeau (1980/1990: 162), Marin evokes respectable ghosts of the past to create a habitable, and masculinized, space for his contemporaries. Narratives of the 'right of blood' are woven through a quest for patriarchal pioneers that will secure claims of ethnic distinction. The underlying assumption is that the past accomplishments of 'great men' somehow testify to the inherent qualities of the Italian culture, of which all Italians are the natural bearers.

But Marin's account does not stop there. In a characteristic move, Marin, as do subsequent historiographers, devotes most of his book to what he calls the 'real émigrés': in the nineteenth century, he writes, 'popular emigration joined the transient emigration of élite Italians; along with the artists and political refugees arrive the first real émigrés in Great Britain' (1975: 27).

The distinction between different migrant subjects relies heavily on settlement (see below). Moreover, ideas of authenticity are configured around notions of tradition and its organic connection to the land, the figures of which are the *paesani*. Peasants are represented as bearers of an original, traditional culture, expressed, for example, in practices of *campanilismo*, *paesanismo*, *comparaggio.*[7] Though these practices are not 'typically' Italian – close-knit community relations such as *campanilismo* and *paesanismo*, that develop in small villages, have been a widespread feature of social life in most parts of the world, although conventions do vary – Terri Colpi refers to these forms of social relations only in their Italian version, thus objectifying them and ethnicizing them as particular Italian traits.[8] Aside from Colpi's objectifying practices, however, there is a common tendency among writers of British Italian history, to emphasize the bucolic origins of the Italian presence in Britain.

Tracing genealogical connections between emigration and past seasonal migration is one such instance. For Lucio Sponza, the origins of Italian immigration to Britain go back to 'an old tradition of seasonal and vagrant migration' (1988: 24) or to 'an ancient custom' (1988: 36), which took Italians to different parts of the Italian peninsula (for summer transhumance, or displacement to plains for intensive cultivation), and gradually to different parts of Europe. And it is out of this 'old tradition' of vagrancy that the 'founders of the Italian colony' (Sponza 1988: 24) set foot in Britain in the early 1800s.

The connection of past lifestyles with nature and the land are most clearly emphasized in Renato Cavallaro's work. For him, Calabrese migrants struggle with opposite forms of time: coming from rural areas, where life is regulated by cyclical time that is 'founded essentially on rhythms of nature' (1981: 62), they find themselves at odds with the 'linear' industrial time, where 'time is money'. Consequently, Cavallaro ends up reproducing a linear model of migration as a movement from one culture to another, and of immigrant identity as being caught up between two cultures that are respectively associated with tradition (rural) and modernity (urban), 'old' and 'new'. This narrative is not unique to Cavallaro. The tendency in written renditions is to obscure differences of class and background among immigrants by locating 'Italian culture' in timeless traditions that evolved in connection to agricultural lifestyles, thus establishing a particular version of a myth of origins. The insistence on the bucolic origins of the 'real' immigrants lays down the foundations for the construction of an integral culture that mimics what Lisa Lowe has called 'cultural nationalism' (1996: 34, 75): a discourse that establishes a separate purity of a culture, in this case of Italian culture, as part of a struggle against assimilation in Britain. The naturalist and realist mode in which the 'recovery' of Italian history operates, traces a link between cultural heritage, soil and identity, and lays down the foundations for the definition of an authentic Italian culture.

The emphasis on rural migration ties in with the association of emigration with rupture and discontinuity: the 'real' émigrés were *forced* to leave Italy.

> As was the case with the emigrants from Italy in the nineteenth century, few of the southern Italian immigrants to reach Britain in the 1950s actively 'chose' to come to this country . . . Southern Italians who emigrated in the 1950s tend to express the view that they 'had to emigrate' and that they had 'no choice' in the matter. (Colpi 1991a: 134)

Emigration is an event that breaks away from the traditional migration.

> Emigration constitutes the great caesura, the parting line that separates the remote past, absolute, closed and compact like a circle where all the points are equally distant from real time, from the near past, relative, tightly linked to the present by uninterrupted passages of time. Emigration is the zero moment of social growth, an individual and collective product of time, not always located in a definitive historical process, but always brought into focus by a date which signals a fundamental moment in the personal, family memory. (Cavallaro 1981: 41)

Emigration separates the remote traditional past from the nearer past of 'forced' displacement. In this respect, *e*migration is different from *mi*gration, insofar as the 'timeless tradition' of migration is interrupted by *e*migration. From a 'natural' phenomenon, migration turned *e*migration became a socio-economic obligation. The 'old tradition . . . became for many more people the only option' (Sponza 1988: 24). Emigration signals the passage from seasonal migration to an imposed diasporization of Italians, and thus opens a new page of history for Italy and for the emigrants themselves. Emigration is the zero moment of collective social growth, from which the original peasant, vagrant immigrants moved 'forward' into a 'new life'.[9] The subtle addition of the prefix indicates a break, a move out of the national borders, a change of location or position, as well as a change in times. This demarcation is most striking in Cavallaro's analysis: his argument that emigration is the zero moment of social growth rests on a linear conception of time and displacement, the initial moment being marked forever in the increasingly remote past. In this respect, emigration is conceived as static, confined to the moment of departure. Hence a distinction between migration as foundational, and emigration as zero moment is significant. Migration as foundational opens a terrain of signification upon which the meaning of *e*migration as breaking point is deployed.

The conception of emigration as the inaugural moment of growth and change suggests some kind of permanence, of no return. Paradoxically, the closure of emigration as that moment when one *leaves* Italy, also geographically *locates* it within Italy. Emigration, this 'zero moment', evokes the image of one foot still firmly set on Italian ground while the other is boarding the ship or train; it is a passing moment and the moment of passage. This 'moment', where stillness and movement collide, is evocatively captured in the Scalabrinian stained glass window discussed in Chapter 1. Emigration is a chronotope where 'temporal and spatial indicators are fused' (Bakhtin in Stewart 1996: 93), indeed where time is frozen in a static place, and where space becomes 'charged and responsive to the movement of time' (ibid.) The emigration chronotope delineates a new spatio-temporal horizon inhabited by images of dispersal and of passages *from* old times *to* new times.

While migration is rooted in Italy as an age-old tradition, *e*migration is the linchpin with Italy within British Italian remembrances of dispersal. The question now is: how is the relationship with England integrated in histories of the Italian presence in Britain? To put it differently, Italy and tradition are integrated as foundational, that is, as where Italians *come from*, through the differentiated tropes of migration and emigration. How is the space Italians *moved to* and now *live in* integrated within the project of collective identity? How is the specificity of Italians as *emigrants* sutured to Britain?

Settlement

Foundations do not rest on migration and diasporization alone. As James Clifford points out, the term 'diaspora' is a signifier not simply of transnationality, movement and forced migration, but also of settlement, dwelling and the 'struggles to define the local' (1994: 306). The turn of the century is identified as the time when Italian immigrants changed from being sojourners to settlers; the period when the community became more internally cohesive, stable and sedentary. It is at this time that the 'early community' is identified as a settler community (Colpi 1991a; Sponza 1988). In immigration literature, notions of 'settler' and 'settlement' refer to the process of establishing a new life in a country of immigration; establishing residence in the 'host' country. In this section, I shall unpack the notion of settlement and draw out its connections with colonial and gender discourses.

The stabilization of the founding community is associated with changes in the occupational structure of the Italian migrant population of nineteenth century England: the first moments of settlement appear when Italians move out of vagrant occupations organized around small working-units (some of which were family run). For example, ice-cream vendors, who were also itinerant, began working in more formalized environments. This shift meant the demise of the less formal *padrone*-run hawking groups. Thus the re-organization of labour along capitalistic lines (smaller, more formalized working units) determines another change in the patterns of mobility of Italian immigrants. Their labour is stabilized and more controlled. For both Lucio Sponza and Terri Colpi, capitalism played a significant role in creating the conditions of possibility for the settlement of the Italian 'community'. A thread running through their accounts links the formalization of labour and the emergence of Italian small catering businesses to the maintenance and reproduction of ethnic identity. It is not only a question of making a trade of one's ethnicity. It is subtly more than that.

> [T]hose families who have remained in business, ethnic or otherwise, have retained an *Italian factor* and indeed are normally extremely proud of it. Secondly, since one of the main avenues to progress in Scottish society involves entering the public sector and local government, many Italians have followed this path. This, however, has led in most cases to an *'institutionalised assimilation'*. The capitalistic drive to progress has been

> lost amongst this group but, more importantly, *so has their Italianità.* (Colpi 1991a: 197; my emphasis)

For Colpi, private enterprise favours the maintenance of ethnicity. Moreover, the journey of Italians within the market economy is represented as the slow conquest of occupational niches through which they assert and reproduce their ethnicity.

> It took a very long time for the boy of 12 or 13 arriving in the early 1900s to climb his way up the employment hierarchies from the back kitchens into the salons and the dining-rooms. But it could be done, and not only did the majority achieve this, but to such an extent that soon the best hotels sought and would employ only Italians, thereby clinching the catering niche entirely for their compatriots. (Colpi 1991a: 62)

The colonizing metaphor colouring this passage conveys and enhances the relationship between economic expansion, conquest and settlement. A metaphor Colpi also uses in her description of the movement of nineteenth century 'pioneers'.

> Gradually, pioneers began to move further and further afield, until the season was spent abroad in many different locations. Migrants thus began to spread out across Europe and indeed the world. Owing to the increasing distances involved in these migrations, it became inevitable that the communities these migrants established became more permanent and less seasonal or temporary. This became true for London as much as it did for Moscow or San Francisco in the middle of the nineteenth century. (idem: 33)

While the shift from founding to settling the community appears as the product of complex transformations that cannot be reduced to the mere transposition of original Italian practices into the British economy, the celebration of the first 'pioneers' does not escape colonial discourse. To put it differently, the reterritorialization of Italians in Britain follows a path of capitalism and colonization. As Caren Kaplan puts it, '[d]eterritorialization is always reterritorialization, an increase of territory, an imperialization.' She cites Deleuze and Guattari: '"Write, form a rhizome, increase your territory by deterritorialization, extend the line of flight to the point where it becomes an abstract machine covering the entire place of consistency"' (1996: 89). Though I hesitate to claim that reterritorialization is *always* an imperialization – insofar as I want to distinguish lived experiences from theoretical discourses of reterritorialization – Kaplan's point strikes an important warning against the imperial inflections supporting theoretical discourses of movement, displacement and travel. Moreover, it draws attention to the ways in which the colonial discourse operates as a legitimating mechanism in the effort to install an Italian identity and presence in Britain. In the above passage from Colpi, the foundations of the 'community' are stabilized, and the legitimacy of the Italian presence secured, through a narrative of historical achievements measured in terms of the 'glories' of capitalism and imperialism.

But the reproductive moment of the 'settled' community is not left to chance. The passage from foundations to settlement is also marked by changes in migration patterns where family-based networks allowed for an increased presence of women in the Italian population. In foundation narratives, the distinction between sojourners and settlers suggests a masculinist conception of mobility and movement that initially excludes the possibility of women migrants. 'As long as the majority of the Italians were street musicians and statuette vendors (by and large involving temporary migration), it is reasonable to assume that there was not much scope for women to join their men in Britain' (Sponza 1988: 59).

Narratives of settlement, for their part, make room for the possibility of women migrants, but only in a limited form. In Terri Colpi's *The Italian Factor,* a section on 'the early Community' begins as follows:

> In the 1830s and 1840s the male-female ratio of the Italian presence in this country was very imbalanced and it was not until the middle of the second half of the century, the 1860s and 1870s, that women began to arrive in sufficient numbers to balance the sex-structure of the Colony in London . . . Apart from the three groups of semi-skilled craftsmen described in the previous section, the general immigration of the poor Italians with no trades, training or skills continued to be the largest portion of the flow and in the late 1870s this began to follow a more classical pattern of chain migration where the *padrone* and others began to bring over female members of the family. The Community thus became more sedentary and stable . . . (Colpi 1991a: 41)

Colpi's way of introducing the 'early Community' suggests an equation between settlement and the immigration of women *brought in* by the men: women as cultural baggage. To be sure, Italian labour migrations in the nineteenth and twentieth centuries were overwhelmingly male due to a combination of economic and social factors.[10] Yet as is the case with the overall body of work on the Italian diaspora, British texts on Italian immigration present a masculinized version of early migration that dilutes the immigration of women within a broader settlement narrative. Women's migration, in contrast to men's, brings emigration to a halt and marks the initial moment of settlement. Already in 1919, Robert Foerster criticized what he labelled the 'law of emigration' according to which '[t]he first emigrants are nearly all men; after a while the women and children follow; emigration ceases – the cycle is complete' (1919/1968: 45). His critique points to the tendency to associate women and children with the termination of migration and the initiation of settlement. In short, definitions of settlement are grounded on a distinction between sojourners and settlers configured around masculinized definitions of mobility and movement – migrant workers – and feminized representations of stability, sedentariness and continuity – settler wives and mothers.

These gendered narratives are deeply connected to ideas of continuity, which is a key issue in the claims about the passage from 'founding' to 'settling' the community. 'Indeed, it was not until this second stage of development [between 1880–1918] that the Community was assured of a future: an Italian factor would become an enduring facet of British life' (Colpi 1991a: 47). It may well be argued that this constitutes a good example of the ways in which ethnicity (and nation) is gendered. Projects of collective identity commonly involve the location of the family as a building block in the growth of the community. In turn, the excavation of family values underscores and naturalizes the different positions of men and women in society (Anthias and Yuval-Davis 1992; Yuval-Davis and Anthias 1989; Juteau 1983, 1996; Brah 1992; McClintock 1995; Yuval-Davis 1997).

Yet it seems to me that the confinement of women within the family is disrupted by migration. Though they circulate within an emphatically patriarchal framework – men are by no means absent; they are migrant workers, soldiers and husbands who most often instigate women's migration – the migration of women is a vector of transition. As they move through historical moments and geographical spaces, they mark out the thresholds of identity and difference, being and becoming, migrancy and settlement, past times and new times. Women, here, are not simply stationary border figures who enable the male plot (McClintock 1995: 70), but move through and produce the very thresholds of belonging; a belonging grounded in both migration *and* settlement, movement *and* sedentariness. Terri Colpi makes it a point of highlighting the migration of thousands of Italian women in the 1950s, who came on their own, under bulk recruitment schemes (at times outnumbering men in a proportion of 3 to 1; Marin 1975: 93). Colpi suggests that these women were the 'pioneers' of the 'new' post-war immigration from Italy that resulted from the recruitment of workers (1991a: 145). These women, the majority of whom were single and in their twenties, were employed predominantly in the textile, rubber and ceramic industries. They went to Norwich, Coventry, Wolverhampton, Lancashire, Cheshire, Derbyshire and Yorkshire. Many women returned to Italy after having completed their work contract, but hundreds settled (Colpi 1991a: 146).

Although not necessarily family bound, the identity of these women remains represented as deeply family based. In other words, the definition of local particularity is familiarized, and its familiarization naturalizes gender differences. Indeed, the identity and modes of belonging of Italian immigrant women are assumed to result from their family ties, while male migrants' identity is defined through the unfolding, in solitude, of their individual sacrifices, heroics and the fulfilment of their obligations as dutiful fathers or sons.

> The girls [sic], who had come from all over Italy, experienced considerable homesickness and isolation at leaving their family-centred way of life behind . . . Because of the

> shortage of Italian men at that time, their search for spouses led to much inter-marriage, not with locals, by whom they were positively shunned, but with other ethnic groups [Polish, Yugoslavian, Ukrainian and Latvian]. (Colpi 1991a: 146)

> Early first-generation male migrants, single and perhaps especially married, made the most sacrifices . . . To be in this completely alien environment carrying out heavy industrial labour in adverse climatic conditions, without even the food that they were accustomed to, was for many an intolerable level of *sacrifici* . . . A further element of *sacrifici* related to the obligation of the migrant to provide financial support for his wife, children, and often parents at home in Italy . . . The women at home too made *sacrifici* since, apart from the struggle to survive, they were bereft, often for many years, of their men folk. (Colpi 1991a: 154)

Setting aside, for the moment, the significance of the trope of sacrifice in defining a distinct émigré culture (see next section), I want to reiterate how written renditions of Italian settlement in Britain reproduce a model that has long typified immigration historiography. Within these narratives, women migrants are consistently relocated within the family setting, represented as wives and mothers. Moreover, the mother figure is reified as the guardian of the family nucleus and 'the symbol of what is most sacred within a family' (Bottignolo 1985: 59; Colpi 1991a: 216). Anxieties about the digression from acceptable femininity that the single working women migrants potentially represent, are closed down through their heterosexualization. Thus normalized, women migrants are integrated as agents of cultural reproduction and stability in the formation of the 'community'. In this respect, the settler community is not only familiarized, but it is feminized insofar as the promise of continuity is configured in terms of the female presence.

In short, these narratives posit settlement, with its implicit notion of origins and gendered forms of stabilization, as an important symbolic marker, delineating the Italian immigrant collectivity and rooting it, as it were, in English territory. The settler figure emerges as the symbol marking the boundary between e/immigrants and migrants. Migrancy is yet again marginalized, defined against a time-space based on permanence and some form of rooting. In contrast to the currency of travel metaphors in contemporary social thought (Kaplan 1996), these texts suggest a cancellation of the traveller, and seek to redeem emigrants from endless wandering by establishing settlement as the defining moment in the birth of the present day 'community'. The 'real' émigrés are settlers, not migrants.

This image acquires even greater potency in the face of the growing presence of 'new' migrants from Italy: young men and women who come to England, most often on a temporary basis, to study, learn English, work in restaurants, and so on. Unlike their predecessors, these youths are not here to settle, nor, it seems, do they identify as 'immigrants' (Sodano 1995). Associated with ideas of permanence (in contrast to migration), as well as detachment from 'origins' (see Chapter 3), these youths also dissociate themselves from the institutional 'community', whose agenda does not include their immediate concerns. Moreover, the colour coding of immigration, in Britain, establishes an equation between blackness and foreignness: hence being white Italian is perceived as incompatible with being immigrant. In turn, the Italian leadership does not view these youths as immigrants, that is as 'settlers', and consequently does not consider them as part of the 'community'. Migration, in short, becomes the site of struggle between 'old' and 'new' visions about the Italian presence. Father Giuseppe Blanda, former head of St Patrick's International Centre,[11] in Soho, was very outspoken about the need to revise the notion of 'immigrant'.

> I don't think that we will have any longer, in the future, the old form of immigration. The old form of immigration is past, it is history. [The community leaders] don't want to call [the newcomers] immigrants . . . [These migrants] come here for a period of three to six months, or for two years. To learn English, to study. They want to combine study and job. This is a new phenomenon. We have to face this new situation. *Mobility is a new phenomenon everywhere.* (personal interview; my emphasis)

Within the Italian population, namely those who relate to the two churches, the new migrants are often associated with drug addiction and HIV/AIDS. During the 1990s, the popular press (both English and Italian) regularly documented young Italian drug users and abusers. The work of Padre Carmelo di Giovanni, from St Peter's church, with young drug users and people living with HIV/AIDS, has further drawn attention to a segment of the London Italian population that many would prefer to ignore. Padre Carmelo, and latterly the Centro Scalabrini,[12] have sought to educate their fellow Italians on the problems some young people face in London today. Yet the popular response was unyielding: 'We don't wanna know!' as Silvio[13] whispered when Father Carmelo was giving a sermon on the issue. For Luigi,[14] a London-Italian man brought up in the area near St Peter's church known as 'The Hill', these youths are perceived as abusing the system, as taking advantage of 'society' without contributing anything in return. Overall, they are not considered 'real' immigrants, that is, settlers who have sacrificed a lot in order to build a 'home' in Britain.

It is in the context of the changing face of Italian migration, and its representation in the popular press, that the London Italian 'community' discourse is drawing a distinction between migrants from settlers. With this new Italian presence so close to 'home', as it were – Kings Cross, the London area notorious for drugs and prostitution and the location of a shelter for homeless Italians, is only a few minutes away from St Peter's church, *the* Italian church (Chapter 5) – it may be suggested that the 'community' is seeking to enclose itself and tighten its boundaries. The project of communal recovery may be read partly as a response – de Certeau writes that memory 'responds more than it records' (1984: 88) – to the increasingly noted presence of 'new' migrants from Italy. A response drawn from notions of 'community' and continuity which are based on gendered ideals of sedentariness.

So while the foundations of the Italian presence in Britain are signified by emigration defined as a discrete moment that marks a break in time and space, settlement constitutes a gendered point of attachment from which ideas of locality and continuity can emerge. How, then, is this local particularity defined?

The 'immigrant condition'

Lying at the foundation of the Italian community, migration has been uncovered, so far, as a signifier of both tradition and vagrancy. It is simultaneously a thing of the past, belonging to a timeless tradition that accounts for the mass displacement of Italians at the turn of the century, and a thing of the present, a mode of existence deemed incompatible with the ideal of settlement and thus located on the margins of the Italian 'community'. In this section, I turn to the positioning of migration within what Bruno Bottignolo has named the 'immigrant condition' (1985: 86). For this writer, the Italian community does not emerge spontaneously from the common ground of ethnicity. It results, rather, from interactions between people sharing similar conditions of existence: 'Their common experience and shared destiny join[s] them and [makes] them feel very close to one another' (Bottignolo 1985: 87).

Multiple meanings are projected by the authors discussed here, onto the 'immigrant condition'. Wrapped in languages of deterritorialization, alienation and sacrifice, this 'condition' is paradoxically a double source of empowerment and alienation. Firstly, it is conceived as a source of alienation because of its marginalization from the politics of nationality. Secondly, stories of the 1939–45 war years in Britain are about alienation and suffering as sources of collective empowerment. Thirdly, sacrifice emerges as a recurring theme deployed within kinship narratives that guarantee the identity and difference of the 'Italian factor'. These three features, scrutinized below, weave the fabric of a new surface of belonging expressed in a teleology of suffering/redemption.

In a first instance, recovering the Italian presence comes out of a particular relationship to the nation and the norms of the nation-state. Running through the accounts of Marin, Bottignolo, and Cavallaro lies an image of the 'always-already' foreigner.

> The immigrant is in society, but for society, be it Italian or English, he is lost. Migration is not only a passage from one society to another, it is also a journey in which one goes out of a society and the practice of associated life, to find himself living in a situation of liminality . . . Once outside his own country, the individual, who is no longer recognised as a citizen but is accepted and perceived as a foreigner, finds he is in a state of isolation and 'weakness'. (Bottignolo 1985: 51 and 71)

This alienation manifests itself in the ways Italians feel they are 'in someone else's home' (Bottignolo 1985: 53; interestingly, this analogy was also used by Silviana,[15] a British-born Italian woman I had many conversations with). In addition, the perceived indifference of Britons towards the plight of Italian immigrants struggling to negotiate a different culture and way of life sustains the sense of invisibility. 'An Italian migrant who enters and lives in Great Britain can go unobserved. He is often described as an "invisible immigrant"' (Bottignolo 1985: 71).

A recurring sense of loss and alienation from both Italy and Britain marks the narrations of Italians in Britain. These authors seem uncomfortable with the idea of a serene experience of the diasporic mode of existence. Migration acquires an eschatological meaning that ties the destiny of Italian immigrants to a predetermined fate. Once the migration process is initiated, it is never ending. For Marin, for instance, it does not end when integration is seemingly achieved, nor does the physical return to the Italy bring migration to a halt: '[i]n fact, the problems of emigration are not subtracted, but they rather add up: those who re-enter the fatherland do not cancel the drama of those who will find themselves constrained to leave; and those who re-enter do not conclude their emigrant event, but reproduce in another form their interminable odyssey' (1975: 97).

Migration is equated with endless wandering; it is a state of perpetual homelessness that is conceived in pathological terms, epitomized by Bottignolo in the figure of the 'stateless person': '[t]hrough the migratory act, the Italian immigrant has lost a great deal of his political relevance and has become practically a stateless person' (1985: 49).

The pathologization of the 'immigrant condition' emerges out of the power attributed to the norms of the nation state: modern definitions of the nation establish that all ethnic groups must be mobilized to create a territorial state, thus making the nation state the last stage in the 'natural' development of peoples (Marienstras 1989). Modern ideas of the nation are typically conceived as bringing diaspora to an end, and they endure, in particular forms, in the projects of redemption designed by Marin and Bottignolo.

Bruno Bottignolo finds that the 'national myth' is the key source of empowerment for Italian immigrants. His examination of the Italian political structure in Bristol reveals that Italian immigrants entertain an ambiguous relationship with their four main institutions: the Catholic mission, the community organizations,[16] the Italian teachers and schools, and the consular agencies. In short, it seems that suspicion of anything that might smack of political activism or profit-making activities often fostered animosity and criticism against individuals in charge of local institutions, and at times led to the dissolution of the entire set up. Yet Bottignolo points out that despite the tight social control over the running of Italian organizations, Italian immigrants would preferably rely on Italian rather than English institutions, whatever the services sought. Beyond practical reasons – such as language proficiency – Bottignolo explains this preference by the sense of common nationality.

> The national consistency was particularly important when immigrants acted as a group. In these circumstances, as we have seen, Italians were mobilised and gathered above all in the myth of nationality. For the Italian immigrants, only an Italian entity as an ideal point of reference could mobilise their commitment and offer them that 'ubi consistam' by which they could escape their impotence. The national myth explains, at least partly, why immigrants tend to load their institutions, which alone would have very specific and limited functions, with meanings. On the other hand, the lack of financial means of these institutions further underlines the important role that the nationality myth has for the immigrants. (1985: 139)

Bottignolo adds that this national myth fosters somewhat of a spontaneous sense of duty between 'fellow countrymen' (1985: 139). In addition, the national myth overrides regionalisms, epitomized by the bell-tower mentality, that is, village or regional-based chauvinism. For Bottignolo, this is a move forward in the creation of a united and diverse Italian 'Community': a community 'without a bell tower'.[17]

Bottignolo resorts to the national myth as a necessary source of stabilization for Italian immigrants who may be nostalgic 'for [the] citizenship of their original mother country' (1985: 30). For the 'forever-foreigners', alienated culturally and structurally from the host society, identified first and foremost as manual labourers – 'It is not men who immigrate but machine-minders, sweepers, diggers, cement mixers, cleaners, drillers . . .' (Bottignolo, 1985: 76) – the retrieval of their humanity is only possible by returning 'home'; a home born out of the combination of images of family and nation. 'To re-become a man *(husband, father, citizen, patriot)* a migrant has to return home' (Bottignolo 1985: 76; my emphasis). In contrast to the argument put forward by Sally Westwood (1988) on the importance, for immigrant women, of having an occupational identity, Bottignolo represents the recruitment Italian male migrant labour as an emasculating experience for the men involved. The recovery of their masculinity requires a 'return' to Italy, the 'fatherland' (*patria*).

The annalists of the 'community' are literally caught up with the norms of the nation state. A sense of impasse comes out of these authors' attempts to redeem Italian immigrants from their 'condition' when they do so in nationalist terms. If the national myth is a source of power, it is not enough to bring about the full redemption of Italians in Britain. How can discourses of Italian nationality and symbolic return 'home' be viable when 'home' is in Britain for a large segment of the British Italian population? Both Bottignolo and Marin agree that the redemption of Italians from the state of perpetual vagrancy resides in the construction of a political agenda that will allow Italians to 'return home', as it were, in the form of a renewed Italo-European citizenship. As we will see in the following chapter, this emerges as a partial solution to the menace of estrangement from Italy. But problems arise when nation is used as the norm for definitions of identity. When nation and culture come together, identity becomes organically rooted in a given timespace and makes the possibility of multi-local ties difficult, if not unthinkable. Similarly, the construction of local particularity is hindered, or incomplete, if it rests solely on sustaining relations with Italy, a place Italian immigrants come from, but no longer live in. How, then, do Italian writers define the specificity of the British Italian population, over and beyond its relationship to Italy?

Terri Colpi excepted, all the authors discussed here resist the objectification of ethnicity as the primary ground for continuity, solidarity and identity within the Italian immigrant collectivity. Bottignolo's words cited earlier, according to which Italian commonality stems from shared experiences of migration and settlement that have now become the sites of memory of a large part of the Italian population, succinctly illustrates this point of view. What, then, do these memories speak of? Tales supporting a 'diasporic founding text' are usually expressed through a Christian teleology of suffering/salvation, founded on stories of exile, loss, resistance and the anticipation of redemption (Clifford 1994; Cohen 1992; Gilroy 1993a: Chapter 6). In the literature on Italians, such tales are most vividly evoked in memories of the 1939–45 war years.

On the night of Mussolini's declaration of war on the Allies (10 June 1940), Colpi reports that anti-Italian riots broke out in different parts of Britain. 'Across the country, a night of smashing, burning and looting ensued' (Colpi 1991a: 105). The extent of damage caused by these riots is a contested point. According to Lucio Sponza, a journalist went out on the early morning of the 11 June and counted only two or three broken shop windows in Soho (Sponza 1995). However, the damage is said to have been greater in Scotland (Colpi 1991a: 105). Beyond discrepancies in details, these events are nonetheless remembered as signalling the beginning of a distinct period in Italian historicity. This period, in turn, is marked by two events that have become emblematic in definitions of a specific British Italian experience: the internment of Italians and the sinking of the *Arandora Star*.

In the week following the 10 June, over 4,000 Italian men – including 300 British-born – were arrested and interned as 'enemy aliens' (Colpi 1991a: 113; also Marin 1975: 86).[18] These arrests have been the object of a host of different accounts. On the one hand, they are condemned as an injustice resulting from a hasty and unorganized response on the part of the British authorities. They caused undue hardship to separated families, many of whom lost their business and property and had to start from scratch after the war. Yet while it is deplored and marked as a breaking point in the life of the 'old community', this event is also represented as a moment of Italian 'unification'. Indeed, the internment camps are also remembered as unique terrains of encounter between diverse sections of the Italian population.

> It was here, for the first time, that all geographical and socio-economic sections of the British Italian Community met: the young, the old, the fascists, the innocuous or non-fascists, the anti-fascists, the upper crust from London, the shopkeepers, the artists, the musicians, those from the north of Italy and those from the south of Italy. It was a most extraordinary gathering. (Colpi 1991a: 113; see also Rossi 1991)

The camps were also, it seems, sites where antagonistic and hostile relationships between English and Italian were absent. Stories of life in the camps are stories of alliances and friendships rather than of division and animosity. Such alliances are further emphasized in accounts of the integration of Italian POWs in English society after the armistice between Italy and the Allies (Sponza 1995). Hence, the internment of hundreds of Italian men is remembered not only as a significant moment of solidarity within the Italian collectivity, but also as a time of alliance, rather than enmity, between Italians and Britons. One man I interviewed spoke of his time spent in the camps in such terms. Alberto Cavalli, a volunteer at St Peter's social club, was arrested at the age of seventeen, along with his father, and they eventually wound up in a camp on the Isle of Man. He recalled the arrest with no animosity against British authorities: he considered that he was a victim of circumstances and that the Britons had little choice. As for life in the camp, he reminisced how, all in all, it was rather comfortable: 'we had everything we wanted: sports grounds, canteen, swimming, walks, pictures once a week at the local cinema.'

Alongside these rather fond memories, the *Arandora Star* begets a set of radically contrasting images. The *Arandora Star* was a 1,500 ton ship that set sail to Canada on 1 July 1940, transporting 1,500 men: German POWs, German Jewish refugees, and Italian internees. On 2 July, it was torpedoed and sunk, killing over 700 men, 446 of whom were Italians.

The tragedy was a central feature of an exhibition by the Scottish-Italian photographer, Owen Logan, at London's Photographers Gallery in March 1994. Entitled *Bloodlines – Vite allo Specchio* (or 'mirrored lives'), the exhibition was constructed around a central axis stretching between two significant events, one habitual, one traumatic: the weekly draw of the Neapolitan lottery, and the sinking of the *Arandora Star*. A large photo of the ship, hanging from the ceiling, is what visitors first encountered when entering the exhibition room. It was mounted in a double-sided glass frame: on one side, the image of the *Arandora Star*; on the other, the photographs of three survivors. At the opposite end of the room, facing the survivors was a photo from the Neapolitan lottery draw. On either side of this central axis were two parallel life spans, one devoted to Italian lives in Britain, the other, to Italians in Italy. All photographs were numbered according to the same sequence on each side, producing an effect of parallelism, or a mirroring effect. A distorted effect, rather, because the photographs did not relate to similar events.

La lotteria carried the number zero – the zero moment – while the *Arandora* was numberless – unaccountable. The montage of the photographs of the ship and the Italian lottery facing each other suggests that they are not so much opposites, but mirrors of each other. For Owen Logan, both events have one key element in common: chance. How else can we explain, he seems to ask, the survival of the three men facing the *Lotteria*? Logan explores the links between personal dreams and public events in the lives of emigrants whom he likens to gamblers. Immigrants enter into a relationship with chance, placing a bet on the future; a bet which nevertheless rests on an act of faith. Like the lottery, migration is a gamble. The outcomes are unpredictable and unplanned.

> Last century many of the poor emigrants from Italy arrived in Britain on foot, having walked across Europe. The presence of their descendants in this country is the result not of a plan, but of an accord made by the first generation with fate, or its secular double, chance. A better life was envisaged in another place, but the location of these other lives and places could never be certain. Children were born during the search. Britain was one place which for many became the destination. (Logan 1994: introduction to the exhibition catalogue; unpaged.)

The significance of the *Arandora Star*, then, goes beyond its tragic fate. In his catalogue, Logan locates the story of Italian emigration within the wider context of the migration and circulation of people around the world. The catalogue opens with photographs of Algerian emigrants at the port of Algiers and on the ferry that goes to Algeciras, in Spain. Logan cites Tahar Ben Jelloun: 'I am the other who has crossed the country on a footbridge suspended between two dreams'. Ships, here, are emblems of this footbridge, suspended between spaces, leaving the familiar and leading onto the unknown Elsewhere.

The tragedy of *Arandora Star* constitutes a highly resonant event for British Italians, marking the specificity of British Italian historicity. 'The sinking of the *Arandora Star* was, and still is, the most tragic event in the history of the Italian Community. It also makes the British Italian Community unique in global terms: no other Italian Community in the world has suffered such a blow' (Colpi 1991a: 115). The tragedy is elevated as a key moment in the making of a unique British Italian identity. Through this event, suffering is remembered in all its potency; in contrast with recollections of internment camps, the death of these men speaks primarily of alienation, exclusion, discrimination, and humiliation of Italians living in Britain during the war years. In short, the British Italian community defines itself by the grief over the lives lost in the *Arandora Star*. In this respect, the sinking of the *Arandora Star* is a version of what Paul Gilroy calls the 'living memory of the changing same' (1993a: 198). This memory is 'persistently there' (Clifford 1994: 320), grounding a distinct kind of belonging in remembrances of collective alienation and suffering, and recovered in a variety of forms: on plaques, in books or periodicals, in commemorative ceremonies.[19] In addition, this version of the changing same is inscribed as an embodied memory: 'The tragedy of the *Arandora Star* will remain for many years like a scar, everlastingly painful and bloody, within the living body of the Italian collectivity' (Marin 1975: 86–7). The metaphor of the body conveys compelling images of collective suffering and further instantiates definitions of local particularity and 'community' as it gives substance to the meaning of the immigrant condition as a condition of collective suffering.

Moreover, this is a suffering that results from the sacrifices of emigration. Indeed, sacrifice is a recurring image of the plight of Italian immigrants. ' "Ho fatto tanti sacrifici all'estero" – I have made so many sacrifices abroad – is a key phrase used by the migrants in England. It is employed often and sums up their attitude, both to emigration and to their experiences (i.e. being abroad is conceptually inseparable from hardship, both material and psychological)' (Colpi 1991a: 268). Within discourses of the Italian immigrant condition, the difference between emigrants and exiles is captured in the trope of *sacrifice,* which alters the teleology of suffering, and founds a distinct form of displacement that is based on relative choice, and the possibility of return. Sacrifice, here, grounds the emergence of distinct cultural forms that result not from discontinuity and rupture, but rather from continuity (if only in relation to the homeland).

The world of the Italian *emigrato* is a world normalized by a system where sacrifice guarantees redemption, embodied in the future generations. A striking feature of this trope is that it is deeply embedded in the family, and inherently confined to it.[20] As an emblem of émigré culture, sacrifice is expressed through a teleology that charges parents with the responsibility of transmitting to their offspring this 'founding value'. A teleology that assigns the children, in turn, with a responsibility towards their parents as well as towards the community and Italy. As Renato Cavallaro puts it with regards to Calabrese immigrants in Bedford:

> the family develops a centripetal reciprocity that stems from the family head and that results from the daily imperatives founded upon 'sacrifices'. If emigration is the projection of an existence destined to sacrifice, then sacrifice must be assumed, by future generations, as a necessary condition for group cohesion . . . And sacrifice is not without an author. The father, in fact, reproduces the order-obedience relationship which – along with the father's own readiness 'to sacrifice' – lies at the basis of the stability of the hierarchy of authority. (1981: 112)

A striking feature of the ways in which sacrifice is deployed in these texts, is how it operates differently on male and female subjects. Consider the passages quoted earlier from Terri Colpi's book, where the sacrifices of migrant men and women were configured in terms of heroic achievements for men, and loss and devotion for women. Sacrifice has widely been associated with femininity, and especially motherhood, in representations of Italianness and, more broadly, of white ethnicity (see Chapter 5). But here, sacrifice also acquires a special significance in relation to men's dislocation: sacrifice serves to restore masculinity and patriarchal authority, which were perceived to have been 'weakened' in the migratory process.

Sacrifice, in short, constitutes a binding element between the generations within family groups and reinstates patriarchal authority. Sacrifice also becomes a thread of continuity, a reminder of the immigrant condition and an emblem of émigré culture. The canonical three-generation narrative of immigration-integration is more than a linear process of gradual 'de-generation' of an original culture substituted by a new, adopted culture. Stories of immigration wrapped in tales of sacrifice and relocated in the distinctly patriarchal family setting, move away from the present and look towards the future where sacrifice will deliver its cohesive and redemptive effects. In other words, the relocation of sacrifice within the family setting emphasizes kinship ties and invests them with a special significance in the context of migration.

It follows that there is more to the migrant family than an institutional site for the reproduction and naturalization of gendered differences. What are the different layers of meaning invested in the family and its relation to migration, locality and authenticity? What kind of family is being constructed? What does the centrality of the family mean in Italian historicity? How does it relate to the creation of a historical and cultural environment for Italians in Britain?

Family in migration: a post-national essentialism?

To begin with, a distinction must be made between defining the community as *based* on the family – '[a]lthough individualism is the mark of Italianism, the family is at the very core of the Community' (Colpi 1991a: 191) – and symbolically representing the Italian community *as* a family – as in representations of national communities (McClintock 1995) or 'racial' communities (Gilroy 1993a, 1993c). The picture produced in stories of Italian immigration to Britain is one of a community of families whose continuity relies heavily on the preservation of family norms and values. The reproductive moment of the 'immigrant condition' is not left to chance: it is located within gendered differences and a system of generational responsibility that summon family-based representations of cultural continuity.

Italian immigrants – and Italian ethnicity in general – are commonly represented as 'more family conscious than the population at large' (Colpi 1991a: 191). Once again, this is not specific to Italian immigration historiography: representations of 'ethnic minorities' have commonly contrasted 'host' societies and 'ethnic cultures' in terms of family lifestyles. Though differentiated along ethnic or racial lines, a common feature of these representations is that they are cast in opposition to the dominant 'host' culture.

For the authors discussed here, Italian families and kinship systems are characterized by a high degree of formalism about the obligations and social control between kin (Garigue and Firth 1956; Colpi 1991a: 194; Sponza 1988: 236-237). For Renato Cavallaro, there is no mediating space between the collectivity and the family: in other words, there is no 'institutional life' outside of family-based systems of relation because the construction of daily existence is solicited by values that are deeply rooted in this 'in-group' (Cavallaro 1981: 119). In short, he argues that the family microcosm hinders the development of institutional structures (Cavallaro 1981: 115). In this respect, Cavallaro reconstructs the 'primary' family group and the home as the ultimate familiar place for the Calabrese immigrants of Bedford; it is the supreme symbol of solidarity: '[t]he family is, in fact, the totalising experience of the solidarity system' (Cavallaro 1981: 112). The family, according to Cavallaro, acts as a 'body buffer zone' that rigidly separates one's primary group from the outside, alien world associated to the factory (1981: 102). The family is signified as the space of 'being' for the immigrants as well as for the 'second generation', whereas the 'outside' world is one of not being, of foreignness. Bruno Bottignolo goes along with this understanding of the Italian family. For him, the Italian family ethic is highly individualistic and even asocial, yet worthy of admiration (1985: 65).

> But one can talk of a family ethic in the sense too that the family is basically the only ambit and the maximum social extension of the Italian immigrant's ethical system. The Italian immigrant cares, almost exclusively, only for his own family; others' family he does not care much about, if at all. Society around him is, for the married person as it is for the single person, by itself a no-man's land, not worthy of much respect. In it one controls oneself mainly because a libertine behaviour could have disastrous effects in the family ambit. (1985: 64)

Italian 'familism' has been the subject of much debate among anthropologists and social historians, especially since the publication of Edward Banfield's (1958) study on south-Italian kinship systems, where he coins the concept of 'amoral familism' to describe a system of malevolent competition that results from backwardness and underdevelopment. In contrast, other writers have suggested that Italian 'familism' is rather a system of co-operation, responsibility and cohesion (see Harney 1998: 14). It is a system of duties and rights that reaches beyond the confines of the nuclear family, as exemplified in the practice of *comparaggio*, whereby friends are made honorary family members. Victoria Goddard (1996), for her part, rightly points out that Italian familism is at once the construction of Church and State interventions, and a central locus of identity formation and identification in individual lives.

What interests me here, however, is not the family as an institution or as the basis of a wider system of social relations. It is, rather, the family as a trope, or more broadly, the trope of kinship and its deployment within the formation of an Italian émigré culture. As such, I interrogate its significance in relation to migration, and I seek out the different meanings projected onto it. To put it simply, I examine how languages of kinship 'work', what they 'do', and in turn the meanings projected onto them within broader narratives of migration.

Seen as nurturing tight family ties, the Italian family is also associated with 'traditional' values that no longer have the same currency within the dominant 'host' culture. Such conceptions manifest themselves in representations of Italian families as offering 'more rewarding socialisation than English-style adolescent "party-going" and "pub-crawling"' (Colpi 1991a: 205). The family becomes the cradle of original, pristine forms of culture which remain uncontaminated by the 'host' society's degenerate ways of life. The Italian emigrant family appears as a protective space against adversities; Cavallaro's 'body buffer zone' (1981: 102). The location of culture within the family is further encoded in the equation between formalized, extended family structures and non-industrial, traditional ways of life. Cavallaro suggests that the family and the home are spaces that allow the re-enactment of the rural, cyclical time of 'tradition', in contrast to the urban, industrial time of modernity. By doing so, he follows the legacy of anthropological reconstructions of 'ethnic' groups, the modern version of 'tribal' societies, which Garigue and Firth (1956) have produced in their own study of 'Italianate' (sic) kinship systems. In Firth's view, the formalized and extended kinship systems he and his colleague observed among Italian immigrants in London are typical of peasant cultures, while the 'looser', nuclear system found within an English community is characteristic of Western societies (Firth 1956: 13–15). Hence, the link between a formalized, extended kinship system and 'peasant culture' is drawn from the invention of 'traditional' lifestyles, which are cast in opposition to 'modern' ways of life. This is not only how culturalist discourses of ethnicity work, but also how absolute definitions of culture become ethnically specific.

But I believe that there is more to the Italian family trope than merely a symbolic location for (re)producing ethnicity. There is this inherent paradox within the family figure: it signifies settlement, stability, continuity, and authenticity, on the one hand, and multi-local ties and displacement on the other. Consider the following observation of Garigue and Firth: '[o]ne of the main characteristics of the kinship universe of the Italianates is its geographical dispersal. Each kinship group not only links persons residing in a number of countries, but also persons living in a number of localities in each country' (1956: 88). This speaks of the 'elasticity' of kin relations and its manifestation in the context of migration (Harney 1998: 14). Transnational kinship ties characterize all diasporas, often tracing paths of belonging and displacement that span a number of different countries. In the texts on Italian immigrants in Britain, having a family in Italy is what sustains the sense of belonging to Italy.

> Apart from their families at home in Italy, the migrants had no real sense of belonging to the country of their origins – a country which they loved very much . . . It must be remembered that, in any case, the hope of many Italians was still to return to Italy one day and for these people the notion of assimilation seemed absurd. There was ever present a *nostalgia*. Perhaps mythological by this time, but no less relevant and applicable, people cherished memories of Italy. (Colpi 1991a: 86)

Colpi's inference, here, is that as time passes on, links with the land of origins take on the form of living memory that only family relations can render palpable, 'real'. Families, in emigration, are vectors of movement and displacement: people write, phone, travel or migrate between Italy and England to contact, visit or join their families. Aside from this material link, however, the sense of belonging is lived through distance, nostalgia and memories.

'Family' in migration acquires a distinctly post-national potency. For example, it becomes the beacon of emigrant struggles against nationalist, anti-immigration policies. The National Day of Migration organized by Catholic Church in Italy every year was devoted to the family in 1994.[21] On this occasion, the issue of family re-unification was raised in a critique of European countries for their failure to truly address and facilitate the greater mobility of human beings. As a Scalabrinian priest argued, '[f]amilies in migration face the increasingly rigid closure of governments and nations that raise insurmountable walls against what they label as invaders' (LV 921, November 1994: 12). Thus 'Fortress Europe' means not only the hardening of continental borders, but also of national ones. And in this context, diasporic families are viewed as pushing against national borders.

However, the family discourse of Italian emigrant intellectuals does not suggest as radical a challenge to nationalism or familyism as the one suggested by Paul Gilroy – that is, the potential of diaspora to instantiate an anti-essentialist, chaotic model of kinship that valorizes plurality and regionality rather than the 'protracted condition of social mourning over ruptures of . . . forced separation' (1994: 210–11). In the textual renditions examined earlier, the sacrificial trope places family relations at a special pitch, thus crystallizing definitions of ethnic authenticity. Kinship, here, remains emphatically based on the nuclear, patriarchal family and deeply tied to gendered images of the sacrifices and suffering of uprooting: homesickness and isolation for women migrants, and alienation, hard work and family responsibility for men. Moreover, the family is reified as an emblem of belonging for people who feel lost in a new country. It is portrayed as a safe haven within the disempowering forever-foreigner condition of (im)migration. In sum, the symbolic construction of Italian émigré belonging is projected onto an image of the ideal, patriarchal, pastoral family.

The very poignant emotions tied to being away from one's family notwithstanding, my point here is that the difficulties of migration are signified in familial terms: family signifies emigration in a very specific way; it is equated with the unnatural separation and suffering of families, and the unfair isolation of individuals from the surrounding social life. By reifying the emigrant family as emblematic of the migration experience, the different conditions of emigration are obscured and collapsed into a homogenizing fold. Discourses of emigration as a 'crisis' configured around the traumatic family separation, give a particular impetus for the recovery of the family image as a harmonious unit. Apart from obscuring the variety of experiences of migration, this rhetoric obliterates the variety of familial experiences by presenting it as a necessarily harmonious unit of self-support and emancipation. That some families are perhaps better off separated, for example, is unheard of. In a complete reversal of Banfield's 'amoral familism', the patriarchal family is a hegemonic metaphor for intimacy, for an ethics of love, for solidarity and social responsibility. The patriarchal family is the preferred institution capable of reproducing the traditional roles, cultures and sensibilities that can solve the indeterminacy of the Italian collectivity. Italian culture, relocated within family households where it is perceived as being best protected and preserved, is positioned at the centre of the narratives and of the immigrants' outlook on life in Britain. The primacy of the family thus has the dual effect of turning the Italian collectivity inwards, onto itself, and to inscribe its foreignness. As such, the family trope is a site of construction of the very boundary between self and other.

Anne McClintock (1995) writes extensively about the figuration of nation within a family iconography, arguing that it is the antithesis of national history because it constitutes a metaphor for a single genesis narrative of national origins and continuity, while at the same time, family is an institution 'devoid of history and excluded from national power' (1995: 357). Such configurations, however, are complicated by transnational family networks. In the texts examined here, the family is indeed a trope for timelessness and the location of an original, pristine culture. But it is also at once transposed and transformed by the forces of migration. Individual immigrants are systematically relocated in the family setting, yet a family which spans a number of different countries.

The paradigmatic figures of these extended family ties are migrant women, whose transnational longings speak of their multiple senses of, desires for, and responsibilities within, home and family. In her monthly chronicle of London's 'Little Italy' at the turn of the century (analysed in Chapter 5), Olive Besagni writes about transnational family ties in relation to the lives of Italian immigrant women. Here, the movement of women migrants between multiple 'homes' and 'families' spin new webs of belonging that are multilocal, plural and supra-national. '[A]lthough she enjoyed seeing everyone [in Italy], she was glad to get back to England and her sons' (*Backhill*, March 1993). Moreover, 'home', for many of these women, is not only a multilocal site of attachment, but of work as well: 'Going to Italy is like going to another home: there, I still do the cooking, cleaning, shopping. There is no difference.' This work also includes what Micaela di Leonardo has dubbed 'the work of kinship', that is, 'the conception, maintenance, and ritual celebration of cross-household kin ties, including visits, letters, telephone calls, presents, cards to send to kin; the organization of holiday gatherings', as well as decisions about the kinds of ties to be maintained (in Nardini 1999: 102). Hence transnational family ties are tributary of women's work, while at the same time, their work operates within discursive conditions of kinship.

Family is the organizing figure of a dispersed yet localized 'community'. As such, it is perhaps the organizing principle of the community's *history* (see Chapters 3 and 4), but it is also the antithesis of national (and cultural) *history* and *geography*. Within this distinctly post-national historicity, the family displaces the nation as the site and frame of memory of British-Italian émigré culture (Gillis 1994b: 17). Family in emigration acquires a particular status that combines competing ideas of settlement and displacement, stability and disruption, continuity and change. Emigration simultaneously menaces and enforces the idealized unity of the family, while the family becomes a key unifying factor that operates against the disruptive forces of emigration. In short, the family provides a vocabulary to speak of cultural identity and local particularism in terms of nurturance, fixed gender roles and generational responsibility.

Final remarks

The literature on Italians in Britain sketches an indeterminate portrait of a collectivity whose common ground is defined in terms of the shared experiences of migration. It is presented as the historical outcome of a tradition of migration, and of the living memories of settlement, suffering and sacrifice that combine in the formation of the 'immigrant condition' of existence. The 'community' is not objectified by the authors discussed above (except for Terri Colpi). It appears, rather, as a communal project being named. Community, here, is nothing but imagined, political and contingent. But it is imagined in terms that objectify particular values as foundational and guarantors of continuity. In this respect, the appeal to the family may be understood as a response to the destabilizing flux of migration and 'diasporization'.

Given the conditions of their production, I have suggested that these texts may be read as inaugural moments in the communal project of recovery. In a way, they consist of founding texts of a locally specific Italian identity. This definition of the local includes the construction of a terrain of belonging which is configured around notions of migration, settlement, alienation, sacrifice, and kinship.

Moving away from these histories, however, we need to examine how such discourses manifest themselves in the institutions whose mandate it is to (re)produce an Italian community. How pervasive are such views? Is the 'immigration condition' still at the centre of a protracted sense of alienation and foreignness? Is the family the only 'safe space' against assimilation? Is gender the modality in which cultural specificity is lived? How, in other words, is the 'new' Italian identity called for by Padre Tassello (see Chapter 1) shaped and represented within London Italian institutions?

The struggle over Italian historicity is caught up with the norms of the nation state. For most of the writers discussed here, the 'problem' of immigration is one of statelessness. For men like Marin and Bottignolo, the national mythology is the only answer to the state of endless wandering of the immigrant condition. Following on from this, I begin my exploration into Italian institutional life with a scrutiny of the identity politics of London Italian leaders. Moving away from the 'immigrant condition' to the less static symbol of 'emigration', they propose new grounds of identification that proceed from a return to the Italian nation, with a difference.

Notes

1. There is a large number of articles or small publications about Italians in Britain preceding this date and going back to the early twentieth century. Whether included in journals, books covering a broader range of issues and/or populations, or whether publications on their own, these pieces always concern a specific aspect of Italian immigrants' lives, rather than a broader description of the population. For a list of earlier publications (i.e. pre-1970), see Marin 1975 or Sponza 1988.
2. All citations from Marin (1975) are my translations from Italian.
3. Entitled *The Un-Melting Pot,* this book is about the changing face of the modern city, presented as a fragmented community, a life of co-existence rather than of communal bonding, all of which are viewed as consequences of immigration (Brown 1970: 12). Deploying a typical 'neo-racist' discourse, Brown argues that the 'integration' of immigrants is nothing but an illusion: groups keep to themselves and foster overt or covert feelings of separateness from each other, which vary from distant admiration and respect to sheer racism. Such exclusionary practices, he suggests, result from cultural differences which he represents in terms of family life and personal hygiene.
4. Three monographs cover a history of the Italian presence in Britain (Colpi 1991a; Marin 1975; Sponza 1988), one of which is limited to the nineteenth century (Sponza 1988). Other studies focus on Italians residing in particular areas in the UK and/or on a specific section of this population: Palmer 1977/

1991; Cavallaro 1970; Sarre, Phillips and Skellington 1989; Bottignolo 1985; Chistolini 1986; Rodgers 1982; Rossi 1966; Colpi 1979, 1986; Hughes 1991. Many topics are covered: social histories (Colpi 1991; Marin 1975; Sponza 1988), life stories (Cavallaro 1981), chain migration (Palmer 1977/1991), 'second generations' (Tassello and Favero 1976; Vignola, Bellisario, Bianco, Toscano 1983), Italian POWs (MacDonald 1987), Italian wartime internees (Gillman and Gillman 1980; Rossi 1991), language maintenance and education (Association of Teachers of Italian (ATI) 1982; Tosi 1991, 1984; Baldwin, Carsaniga, Lymbery Carter, Lepschy, Moys, and Powell 1980; Cervi 1991), organizations and community politics (Palmer 1981), Italian women (Chistolini 1986), spatial distribution (King and King 1977), return migration (King 1977; King, Mortimer, Strachan, and Vignola, 1984), kinship networks (Garigue and Firth 1956), religious practice (Parolin 1979), and (auto)biographies (Goffin 1979; Cavalli 1973; Rossi 1991).

5. All citations from this book are my translations from Italian.
6. From Calabria, a region in southern Italy.
7. *Campanilismo* refers to 'bell-tower' mentality (village or regionally based chauvinism), *paesanismo*, to a similar system of social relationships between co-villagers. *Comparaggio* is the principle according to which close family friends are honorary members of the family and are *compadre* (godparents) to one of the children.
8. Colpi resorts to the same strategy to identify particular trades: for example, she uses the term *figurinai* to speak of nineteenth-century Italian makers and vendors of plaster statuettes, thus suggesting that this might have been a typically Italian trade. Similarly, she writes of 'sacrifice' only in its Italian version (*sacrificio*). Further objectification is produced in Terri Colpi's suggestion that campanilismo is a thing which is active or inactive: one chapter section is entitled '*Campanilismo* in operation' (1991a: 188).
9. In this respect, Terri Colpi's photographic account the Italian presence in Britain is appropriately entitled *Italians Forward* (1991b).
10. Which is not to say that there were no women migrants who came as itinerant traders, but they remain, in British Italian historicity, severely undocumented.
11. St Patrick's International Centre is an organization that offers social and educational services to youths from different parts of the world.
12. The Centro Scalabrini's *La Voce degli Italiani* published a short article about the work of the Holy Cross Church near King's Cross which, on Thursday afternoons, offers shelter and food to homeless Italians (LV 929, April 1995: 9), as well as a series of articles on drugs and toxico-dependency among Italian youths coming to London (issues of July 1995 to February 1996).
13. Not his real name.
14. Not his real name.

15. Not her real name.
16. Known as *patronati*, these organizations were originally charitable institutions or benevolent societies. Today, they are community organizations that offer a wide range of services to Italian immigrants (information about welfare, social security, pension plans; vocational training; language classes, and so on). *Patronati* are usually associated with Italian political parties (for example, ACLI – Associazioni Cristiane Lavoratori Italiani – is affiliated with the Christian Democrat Party, which changed its name to the Popular Party in 1994).
17. Terri Colpi also seeks to move beyond regional differences, but she also views the North-South divide as a productive rather than divisive force of the Italian 'community' in Britain. 'It has been the very existence of two polarised sub-groups and the tensions between them which has often given a Community its definition' (Colpi 1991a: 178).
18. A great number of these men were members of the *fascio* (social clubs established by the Mussolini government in different parts of the world). Joining the *fascio*, however, was not necessarily a gesture of political affiliation, though it did obviously attract people who adhered to its imperialist and anti-communist politics (Cavalli 1973). For some, joining the fascist trade union was compulsory (Cliff 1995), while others joined the local *fascio* to take advantage of the social and cultural activities it organized for its members and their families. The London *fascio,* for example, sponsored a range of activities, from language classes to summer holidays in Italy for Italian children. Its premises were also used as a meeting place for other community associations, for what was known as the 'after-work club' (*dopolavoro*), and for a music school for young Italians (Colpi 1991a: 92).
19. A plaque bearing the names of all the victims has been erected in the portico of St Peter's church in 1960, and an annual commemorative ceremony has been held since that year. Terri Colpi reproduces the list of victims in an appendix to her book (1991a). A series of articles appeared in *Backhill* in 1993, tracing the stories of some victims. Italians in Glasgow also remember the event in a mosaic representing the explosion produced by the torpedo striking the ship. The plaque reads: 'We will never forget you' (Colpi 1991b: 145).
20. This differs from Richard Alba's contention that within the emerging European-American identity, the canonical three-generation integration narrative posits the sacrifices of early migrants in relation to the building of the American nation (Alba 1990: 315).
21. The title of the meeting was: 'Migrations: family, first "educative" [sic] community' *(Migrazioni: famiglia, prima comunità educante).* Past meetings also had the family as their theme: 1969, 'Man has the right to the guardianship

of the family, wherever he goes'; 1980, 'Family and Community'; 1987, 'Family, the soul of migrations'. See LV 921, November 1994: 12. The right to family re-unification is also a recurring concern for *Migrantes*, the Italian Catholic organization devoted to migration issues world wide.

–3–

The Politics of 'Italians Abroad': Nation, Diaspora and New Geographies of Identity

In diaspora, questions of identity have led intellectuals back to the nation.

María de los Angeles Torres

Toni and I were driving to his home, where I was to spend the weekend with him and Monica (not their real names). The three of us were going to the annual remembrance ceremony at the Brookwood cemetery that Sunday, and we decided to make a weekend of it. It was during the short journey between the train station and their home that Toni told me about a segment of his life in Italy: those difficult war years that shaped his memories of his place of birth. The displacement of his family from Campania (South Italy) to Sicily; his forced interruption of school at the age of ten; the difficulties of communicating with Sicilians until the young Toni finally learned the local language; and the hard work to start over again when they returned to their ransacked home and destroyed farmland. All this cast a dark shadow over his affection for Italy. At 16, he left for Scotland with his parents.

Though he maintains links in Italy through his ceramics business – he 'trades in ethnicity', as Terri Colpi would put it – Toni does not entertain a desire to return. 'Nah, I don't wanna go back. Why would I? I only remember bad things about Italy. London is like a magnet for me. Whenever I go away – in Scotland or in Italy – I'm always happy to come back; you know what I mean?' No dream of retiring to a villa back in the 'old village' for Toni. No plans to visit Italy each year. The desire to return does not inhabit Toni.

Toni's revelation struck me as going against the grain of London Italian institutional discourses of identity, where the national myth finds wide currency. Though he identifies himself as Italian, Toni has no inclination or interest in firming his ties with Italy; he is a Londoner, his family is scattered in London and Scotland, and his links with Italy are far from nostalgic or romanticized. Looking back at our journey in this south London suburb, I ponder on what becomes of the homeland in the diasporic imagination once the desire to return has left. I remember Father Tassello's speech the future on invisible immigrants, where he spoke of the changing position of Italy in Italian immigrants' horizon of belonging: what happens to the 'homeland' when it become unrecognizable? I think about Avtar Brah's distinction between 'homing desire' and 'desire for the homeland' (1996: 180) and how they may come into conflict within diasporic imaginations. During my conversation with Toni, I wondered about the Italian community leaders' concern for maintaining close ties with Italy, namely by claims for a renewed citizenship for Italians abroad. Surely, their political desire for the homeland cannot be reduced to the myth of return, nor, however, can it be read as its denial. For them, the return to the nation is deeply entwined with their resistance to assimilation in the country of residence while it is also a gesture against oblivion in, and of, the 'homeland'.

Toni's memory of Italy raises the question of how 'where you're from' is remembered and rearticulated with 'where you're at'. The 'dialectics of diasporic identification', as Gilroy (1991) puts it, are about the sometimes fraught, often equivocal relationship of immigrants to their 'homeland'. This is integral to what Richard Marienstras calls diaspora's 'transnational mode of existence' (1975: 179), characterized by the condition of being 'rooted simultaneously here and there' (Marienstras 1975: 176). For James Clifford, this constitutes the empowering paradox of diaspora, for it complicates the national ideal of culture and identity: 'dwelling *here* assumes a solidarity and connection *there*. But *there* is not necessarily a single place or an exclusivist nation' (1994: 322; italics original). By dwelling in a place where they do not 'come from', migrants potentially disrupt the 'natural' order of things in both their nation of origin and of settlement. Transnational connections and multilocal networks of belonging challenge nationalist contentions about the congruence of territory and culture. The paradox, in my view, does not stem from the double consciousness itself, but it rather surfaces when claims for cultural specificity are fashioned according to both discourses of multilocality and discourses of the 'nation'.

The nation has been widely theorized as a system of representation whereby individuals come to view themselves as part of an imagined community of people who do not come in direct contact with each other (Anderson 1983; McClintock 1995; Hall 1992). Nationalism is 'radically constitutive of peoples identities' (McClintock 1995: 353). Their shared belonging is shaped around narratives of origins and destiny that represent the nation as primordial, timeless and grounded in a mythic origin that is congruent with a delimited territory. Little has been done, however, to unpack the tension which occurs when immigrants' struggle for local particularity is 'caught up with and defined against . . . the norms of nation-state' (Clifford 1994: 307).

Ideas of nation, nationality, national belonging and nationalism are paramount in examining the way that connections 'over there' make a difference 'over here'. In line with Paul Gilroy, my concern here is not to explain the enduring appeal of nations and nationalism in identity formation (Smith 1986; Gellner 1983), but rather to critically appraise the problems that may arise when 'nation' and culture are brought together (Gilroy 1993a–b). What happens to the definition of 'national culture', for example, when emigrants rearticulate their allegiance to the homeland while refusing to physically return there? Alternatively, how is the nation written into diaspora (Gopinath 1995)?

This chapter is about the politicization of emigration by London Italians who struggle for the formalization and institutionalization of political ties with Italy, while simultaneously claiming greater authority and autonomy over the definition of the status and lives of emigrants. To be sure, the question about the relations between Italy and its diaspora is not specific to the present day emigrant political class, nor is it absent from Italian government concerns; it inserts itself within a history of discussions on the relationship between Italy and its diaspora that have been taking place since the turn of the century, although at the time, the massive emigration of Italians was met with relative indifference by the political leaders. It was when the fascists came to power in the 1920s that the politicization of emigration was systematized and institutionalized. Between 1922 and 1924, Mussolini greeted emigration as a welcome remedy to unemployment, and it fitted in with his expansionist ideals. Mussolini replaced the term *emigrante* with *Italiano all'estero* ('Italian abroad'; Mack Smith 1959: 242), and Italian emigrants' passports were stamped *lavoratore italiano all'estero* ('Italian worker abroad'; Colpi 1991a: 87). Labelling emigrants 'Ambassadors of Italy' whom he charged with 'a mission to civilize the world' (Mack Smith 1959: 242), Mussolini 'spoke openly of his mission to extend fascism "everywhere" and his propagandists began to talk about sweeping away "Protestant civilization" of Northern Europe' (Mack Smith 1983: 108). From 1924, however, the fascists began to discourage emigration, which they then viewed as reducing the much-needed labour force in Italy, and emigration became illegal in 1928.

Because of this historical link, the present project of recognition of Italian citizens living abroad is commonly associated with right-wing parties. Yet it actually finds support from all sections of the political spectrum within Italy, as testified in a vote in the Italian Senate in November 1993, on extended voting rights for Italians abroad (Appendix 5). Moreover, the project of 'representation' and 'dissemination' remains a central concern of those Italian politicians who today support the call for renewed ties between Italy and its emigrants, and who appeal to Italian emigrants as custodians of an Italian culture. As I argue below, present-day discourses of Italian identity and culture are wrapped in European discourses of citizenship, thus presented as a novelty that obscures the legacies of a not-so-new nationalism. Overall, it seems that the different views on emigration that exist between past or present Italian governments, or between Italian political parties, are a question of degree rather than of any fundamental divergence.

Italian emigrant leaders, for their part, attempt to resolve the dialectics of diasporic identification in their political demands for identity preservation and self-determination that rely on some form of 'return to the nation'. A close scrutiny of their discourse reveals its double dimension: the national myth, which secures a consistent and coherent referent of identification (Bottignolo 1985: 139) on the one hand, and migration, on the other, as a new timespace of identification, or ethnoscape (Appadurai 1990: 296–7).

Émigré politics of identity emerge from a position of 'in-betweenness', where the relations between 'here' and 'there' need to be negotiated and redefined. A distinctive feature of London Italian diaspora politics is that theirs is a three-way 'amongstness', rather than a two-way 'betweenness', connected to Europe, Britain and Italy at once. Within this 'diaspora space' (Brah 1996), the 'invisibility' of the Italian presence emerges as something that is both praised and a source of concern. It is praised insofar as it stems from the identification of Italians as Europeans, and their concurrent affirmation of their shared cultural heritage with Britons. Invisibility also speaks of the discreteness of the Italian immigrants who ploughed through the rough times of early settlement and the 1939–45 war years, 'without making a din' (LV 898, November 1993: 1). Indeed, the integration within the British social and economic landscape has grown deeper as the years have passed and as generations succeed each other. In turn, this integration is perceived as a source of concern insofar as one of the consequences of invisibility may be cultural assimilation. The central political issue, then, is the preservation of an Italian identity, which emigrant leaders propose to rescue by consolidating political and cultural links with Italy. It follows that Italian politicians (not the British) are challenged for their lack of political will to protect Italian emigrants from assimilating in British (or any other) culture. What emigrant leaders of London want is to enter the public debate in Italy about the nature of their relationship with the Italian state. But the issue of securing institutional ties with Italy goes hand in hand with the affirmation of local particularism. The politics of Italian emigrant identity are about achieving greater control over the decisions shaping Italian emigrants' lives and destinies. This was summarized by Lorenzo Losi, a leading figure in London Italian political life, in a speech he gave in 1993:

> [o]ne demand is obvious and has become explosive in the last years: that of [Italians abroad] being craftsmen of their own future, that of determinedly contributing to decisions regarding the community itself, that of being constantly interpellated through the representatives legally elected, on the decisions which directly concerns each and everyone's daily life: consular services, the school, information, etc . . . The separation between those who decide and those subjected to the decisions seems too obvious. (LV 898, November 1993: 2)

Running through these identity politics is a tension *within* practices of citizenship that, as Lauren Berlant indicates, surfaces between 'public-sphere narratives and the concrete experience of quotidian life that do not cohere or harmonize' (1997: 10). Nonetheless, London Italian political demands are expressed in a language of citizenship that 'provides important definitional frames for the ways people see themselves as public, when they do' (Berlant 1997: 10) The discourse of Italian emigrant leaders includes concerns that are political (voting rights), cultural (language tuition) and generational ('young Italians'). The first three sections of this chapter are structured around these three types of claims. In probing their organizing principles, I analyse how the experience of emigration and the promise of Italian national allegiance, are stitched together by a complex definition of culture. In other words, the focus here is on the creation of cultural meanings in the political expression of identity. It is often assumed that politics of identity based on ideas of cultural integrity and preservation emerge out of a fully formed culture.[1] It is precisely this assumption, as it lies at the basis of the 'Italians abroad' political identity, that I propose to unpack because the invention of a new political constituency of 'Italians abroad' emerges in tandem with the notion of the citizen as 'legal' *and* 'cultural' subject.

My principle source of information is *La Voce degli Italiani* (LV hereafter),[2] published by the Scalabrinian fathers of the Centro Scalabrini in Brixton (South London). Founded in 1948 by Father D. Valente of the San Paolo Society, *La Voce* has been run by the Scalibrinians since 1963. It is published fortnightly and reaches a readership of approximately 25,000, including over 5,000 subscriptions, making it the most widely read British Italian newspaper. It is written almost exclusively in Italian, apart from the occasional English article. Although it claims to be the paper for Italians in Great Britain (sic), *La Voce* is quite predominantly centred on London affairs. It does include, however, a few pages on 'Italian life in Great Britain' that recount social gatherings and activities of various organizations or *prominenti* in different locations around the UK. In contrast to the more parish-oriented *Backhill* (from St Peter's church; see Chapter 5), *La Voce* adopts a distinctly political direction.[3] This newspaper is the main public platform where the discussion on the relationship between Italy and Italian emigrants in Britain takes place. The voices we will read are those of London-based Scalabrinian priests and 'community leaders' (elected and non-elected) who join forces to struggle for official recognition within the Italian state apparatus.

As Anne McClintock rightly points out, imagined communities 'are not simply phantasmagoria of the mind but are historical practices through which social differences are both invented and performed' (1995: 353). Hence a second theme of this chapter relates to 'performances of citizenship'. I venture into the realms of war recollections, state ceremonies and beauty contests, and scrutinize two things: first, the ways in which Britain is included within the Italian émigré terrain of belongings, and second, the kind of citizens that are produced in these performances. Moving away from the amorphous émigré emerging from the 'Italians abroad' discourse, I scrutinize practices that produce – and commend– particular kinds of Italian citizens: 'Italian citizens abroad', I suggest, are defined in terms of 'labour', 'honour' and 'duty', that are tightly bound to class and gender differences.

The vote for Italians abroad: universal rights for citizens with a difference

Italian people's relationship to national identity is complicated by a history of emigration. There are approximately 4.5 million Italian emigrants living outside Italy (LV 940, October 1995: 1–2) and an estimated 26 million emigrated between 1876 and 1976. When descendants of emigrants are included in the surveys, estimates reach up to 65 million people of 'Italian origins' living around the world (LV 938, September 1995: 1). Emigration is a household word in Italy, where a large number of people have friends, acquaintances or relatives who have settled abroad.

Though defined as a country of emigration, Italy is widely criticized by emigrant leaders for 'abandoning' (sic) its citizens living abroad and leaving them to their own devices in their struggles against discrimination or assimilation. After the downfall of Mussolini in 1943, relations between the Italian state and Italian emigrants loosened. Local *fasci* (social clubs established by the Mussolini government)[4] were closed down, and the local institutional structure was re-organized, usually under the initiative of newly arrived Italian emigrants. Locally based organizations flourished – there are currently more than 100 clubs, *circoli*, welfare organizations, professional associations, sports clubs, and so forth, in the Greater London area alone[5] – while state organizations were reducing their presence for migrants in favour of promoting Italian culture and consolidating good diplomatic relations with other European and American countries.[6] In this context, Mussolini's past interventionism is viewed today as a form of social redemption; for a number of London Italians, the *fasci* are remembered as testimonies of the Italian state's presence in, and concern for, emigrant communities and for reviving in them a 'sense of dignity', a sense of national pride (Marin 1975: 80).

In Italy, however, a number of boards and commissions have been set up to deal with emigrant issues both at the federal and regional levels. At the regional level, Italian emigrants may contact ERMI, *Ente regionale per i problemi dei migrante*, for any query that might fall under regional authority jurisdiction. At the federal level, the CGIE, *Consiglio Generale Italiani all'estero*, chaired by a high ranking officer of the Foreign Affairs Department, is a consultative body with strictly advisory powers. It is constituted by elected representatives of councils located in the countries of emigration. These local councils are called COMITES, *Comitato degli Italiani all'estero*.

None of these bodies, however, have legislative powers, and they are perceived, by some London based leaders, as 'empty shells'. Hence it was with great relief that those concerned with redeeming themselves from the forever-foreigner condition greeted Britain's integration in the EC in 1973, because they considered that it would clear a space for a renewed political role in Italy.

> [I] wish to repeat once again the reason I applaud the integration of Great Britain within the EC. We Italians from Great Britain expect many things, above all the following: that this favours the elimination from our continent of the plague of forced emigration, which remains the sole alternative to misery in some Italian regions, and that it will lead to redeem our emigrants from the ranks of *negroes (negri)* of Europe, that is of second class citizens uprooted from their own land and culture, deprived of all political power, anxious about the uncertain future of their children, recognised merely as instruments of production . . . The brand of foreigner will disappear only when the *political redemption* of émigrés will operate, when . . . fundamental political rights will be conceded to them (Marin 1975: 152, 154).

In addition, the prospect of European citizenship provides a new vocabulary for Italian intellectuals concerned with recovering an Italian presence in Britain; the representations of Italians *qua* Europeans offers a new language of differentiation for Italians in Britain.

> In this era of closer European integration the Italians in Britain are probably the most European section of British society – a position which is giving them increasing prominence . . . The British Italian Community is well-placed to think positively about Europe and about retaining its own identity within that structure, to look to 1992 and beyond and to help Europeanise Britain. (Colpi 1991a: 22, 258)

The representation of Italians as Europeans is a new signifier from which they can reformulate their contribution to Britain, namely by fostering a 'European conscience [within English society] whose temptation is always to shut itself off, to close itself upon itself', according to Graziano Tassello (LV 831, October 1990: 15). The European Union offers a new language of identity and difference, with the language of citizenship providing the vocabulary in which ideas of national allegiance will be embattled. What is more, the idea of a European citizenship crystallizes the congruence of culture, geography and origins. The rootings of European culture into a single line of descent also forecloses it into a racialized entity that silences and undermines the presence of black European populations (Miles 1992; Back and Nayak 1993; Solomos and Back 1994). Umberto Marin's use of the 'negro' metaphor is deeply woven with images of exclusion, oppression, exploitation, exile and loss.[7] This is a feature of what David Goldberg has labelled 'racial knowledge', which not only speaks of the Other, but which fabricates the Other (Goldberg 1993: 172). The 'negro' as metaphor of social pathology and 'underclass' constructs the 'negro' as Other. In asserting that the New Europe will liberate Italians from their status as second class citizens by virtue of their Europeanness, Italian leaders (in London and Rome) assert their whiteness and distance themselves from the oppressed blacks. Emancipation from foreignness, here, is tantamount to being accepted as white.

Informed by the rhetoric of European Community and citizenship, London Italians attempt to rescue themselves from oblivion. This stands in contrast with the Italian government's commitment to the dissemination and revival of Italian culture and language around the world. In 1993, Italian president Oscar Luigi Scalfaro stated to the European Parliament that 'Italy as an enormous cultural patrimony and has the right and duty to bring it abroad', while he simultaneously reasserted the depth of common European cultural roots 'which must, however, protect the specificity and the variety of its dense culture' (LV 900, December 1993: 2). London Italian representatives, for their part, are more immediately concerned with securing links with Italy while erasing their forever-foreigner condition in Britain. New voting rights for Italians abroad are one way of achieving this, and the European Community offers the conditions of its possibility.[8]

> The Italian immigrants had been waiting for these [European] elections because they saw in them something more than a simple administrative reality. It appeared to them that as a European fact, they were pointing to a possible area of social interaction where they could have been 'citizens' with full rights, equal to all the others (that is British and Italian people in their own country). In particular it appeared to them that the simple fact of being registered on the Italian polls for the [European] elections organised for them from Italy would defeat the reality of their everyday experience and show that in the home country they were being considered, and that they themselves were still able to have decisive ties with their own fatherland. (Bottignolo 1985: 50–51)

It is in this context that, in the early 1990s, leaders of a number of organizations in London rallied in support of a new election Bill that would allow all Italian citizens living abroad (regardless of the time spent away from Italy), as well as their children and grand-children (provided that they hold an Italian passport), to vote in Italian elections. To obtain the electoral certificate, it is not necessary to be born in Italy or to be on the list of contributors (LV 896, October 1993: 1).[9] A striking assumption underlying this provision is that Italian emigrants and their offspring, after years of living abroad, will even wish to have a say in the political life of Italy. In one of the rare expressions of dissent found in *La Voce*, a reader questioned the legitimacy of Italian emigrants' electoral participation: 'Is it fair that native Italians who have spent all or most of their lives in the country of adoption, not mentioning the millions who can claim as Italian only their name handed down by their grandfather or great-grandfather, have the right to decide which government will run Italy?' (LV 899, November 1993: 4).

The most contentious aspect of the bill, however, related to the election of representatives of Italians abroad to both houses of the Italian Parliament.[10] Rather than voting for a college within their *comune* of origin in Italy (or that of their parents/grandparents), Italians abroad would elect representatives for their own constituency abroad, which would be one of four: Europe, North-America, South-America, and Asia-Africa-Australia. The proposed legislation provided for the election of 30 émigré representatives: 20 MPs (out of 630) and 10 senators (out of 322). 15 MPs and eight senators would be elected according to majority vote, and the remaining five MPs and two senators would be elected by proportional representation. The details of the debates in Italy are not part of my immediate concerns. Suffice it to say that this particular clause was instrumental in the rejection of the Bill by the Italian senate in November 1993 (see Appendix 5).

According to *La Voce,* the main argument against the Bill was that those who pay no (or less) taxes[11] and who have tied their destiny to another nation should not have any influence on Italian political life. From *La Voce's* perspective, the Italian government is discriminating against Italians abroad on two counts: class and residency. These, it is argued, constitute the basis for the hierarchical order of citizenship, according to which citizens who pay more taxes and who not only reside but who anchor their destiny within the geographical boundaries of Italy have more of a voice than others. Supporters of the proposed amendment to the electoral legislation were quick to take issue with this and to denounce it as an infringement of the universal principle of equality (LV 938, September 1995: 1, 4).

The stakes involved in the claim for new voting rights were twofold: survival and national unity. Yet the relationship between both was conceived differently depending on whether the arguments came from Italian politicians or from representatives of Italians living abroad.

In Italy, Senator Giacovazzo of the Foreign Affairs Department argued that Italian emigrants' allegiance to Italy would be exemplary of 'unified Italy' that goes beyond regionalisms, a project that is still a point of contention within Italy itself. This was eloquently expressed in his reaction to the rejection of the voting bill in November 1993:

> [i]n these days of crisis for some important parts of Italian life, I have come to consider that our communities abroad still maintain alive, in a welcome delay, a sense of fatherland (*patria*) and of nation that we have not cultivated [in Italy]. They cultivate, instead, ideological belongings *(appartenenze)*, spreading this great patrimony, which is scarcely alive in our country. We maintain that the presence in Parliament of elected members from this population beyond our walls would have been useful to the sense of unity of our country, which is so vilified and lacerated. But this will not be. I am hurt because, in the words of a well-known saying, you can take a man out of a country, but you can't take the country out of the man. (LV 899, November 1993: 4)

For Senator Giacovazzo, if emigrants are exemplary in their patriotism, their survival is not even at stake, since they are eternal carriers of the sense of identification to Italy. As Italian president Oscar Luigi Scalfaro was reported to have said, their will for electoral participation is 'a sign of their attachment to the fatherland' (LV 899, November 1993: 1). The fears that Giacovazzo expresses are for Italian nationhood rather than for Italian emigrant identity itself. The vote is conceived, here, in instrumental terms, but in relation to an idea of 'identity' that is dissociated from 'belonging' in the sense of identification. For the Italian senator, 'the vote is something that *revives* in [Italian emigrants] an identity, more than [the expression of] a proper and true belonging' (LV 898, November 1993: 1; my emphasis). In such a view, identity is eternal and will be activated given the right political structures. This mimics neo-racist discourses in Britain, according to which national allegiance is something intrinsic, deeply entrenched in individuals so that it becomes 'second nature'. Nationhood, in this discourse, 'is the true state of man' (Casey 1982: 28); it is essentialized, naturalized and masculinized. I will say more on this in the following sections. My point at this stage is that the attribution of equal voting rights to Italian emigrants is conceived, in Italy, as an issue of national integrity and solidarity that will transcend regional differences. Italian politicians speak of emigration in terms that consistently seek to assert Italian national integrity over claims of both local (for example London or British Italian) and international relationships, without compromising the European community spirit. In 1993, President Oscar Luigi Scalfaro addressed the European Parliament in support of the political integration of the European Community. Scalfaro's idea of a politically unified Europe rests on 'commitment, will-power, political clarity and the deepening of common cultural roots' (LV 900, December 1993: 2). Likewise, Italian government representatives make sure not to offend English national claims by emphasizing that tighter links with Italy should not hinder the loyalty of emigrants toward the country of adoption.[12] During the campaign promoting new voting rights for Italians abroad, this guarantee was rhetorically presented by making the voting issue a cultural matter rather than a political one.

From the London Italian leadership's point of view, however, the issue took a different twist. Though defeated, community leaders still consider that the vote for representatives of Italians abroad would be a political lifeline for the émigré population. 'The vote represents today the ultimate area for the renewal of profitable contacts with émigré communities, who will otherwise disappear for good' (LV 897, October 1993: 1). London Italian leaders are fighting for the recognition of emigration as the basis from which a distinctive identity may emerge. In a meeting on the voting Bill, where Senator Giacovazzo met with London émigré spokesmen, Lorenzo Losi spoke of emigration in the following terms:

> I reaffirm that this emigration distinguishes itself by the way it integrated itself even if maintaining . . . its proper *italianità* and in fact imposing it to the host country. Silent labour, surpassing difficulties without making a fuss, acceptance of the typical and specific contradictions for those living away of their country of birth, are regular occurrences in many cases. On the other hand, the friends operating in the social, particularly the missionaries and heads of *patronati* . . . could tell us about so many other life stories, could tell us about the solitude and the difficulties encountered daily in cities as well as in the periphery . . . And it is for this reason that we disagree with those who claim that this community has no problems. Instead, we say that this community lives and often solves its problem without making a din. (LV 898, November 1993: 1)

It was on these grounds that Losi continued to suggest that emigrants need proper representation within the Italian state. It was on these grounds that he argued that Italians abroad must be 'craftsmen of their own future'.

Grafted to this central concern is the recognition of the unique vantage point from which émigrés might serve Italy: the 'Italian patrimony beyond the confines [of Italy]' represents an 'incalculable resource' for Italy. In the words of Graziano Tassello, with the vote for Italians abroad '[w]e will see the introduction, within the Italian fabric, of a precious concern for universality and a desire to surpass borders, which are typical emigration values' (LV 897, October 1993: 1). This version of the myth of return sees the emigrant maintain contact with the homeland not through a physical return, but rather in the repeated 're-turning' (Tölölyan 1996: 14) to the concept and reality of the 'fatherland' through political representation. Here, emigrants leaders want to re-turn and contribute to the political life of the 'country of origin' enriched with the very experience of migration. Therefore, the rejection of the Bill was read, by the London leadership, as denying the recognition of *emigration* as a legitimate point of convergence and basis for the formation of a political constituency.

In short, London Italian discourses of political community turn the Italian government politics of emigration on its head. While Italian political leaders speak of the representation of Italy abroad, the emigrant leadership emphasizes the representation of 'abroad' within Italy. As a result, these local politicians are not only proposing to expand the jurisdiction of the Italian state beyond the borders of the Italian peninsula. They are also speaking of 'new geographies of identity' (Lavie and Swedenburg 1996a: 170).

This was symbolically represented in the course of the vote debate, when *La Voce* introduced the *Simbolo degli Italiani all'Estero* (SIE). Designed by Giorgio Brignola, the Genoa-based emigration correspondent for *La Voce*,[13] the *Simbolo* is the logo for a non-aligned debating platform open to all Italians interested in the voting issue, and eventually in other political questions. According to Gaetano Parolin (former editor of *La Voce*), the SIE is the first stage in a longer term project of Brignola's, which would consist of a more united movement of Italians living in Europe. The logo represents a globe that is crossed lengthways by a pole, planted in the American continent, bearing the Italian flag, the three panels of which are parted, revealing parts of the globe between them. Insofar as the flag symbolizes the nation state, this images suggests both unity and parting as a result of the dispersal of Italians around the world. Thus the SIE represents a kind of global Italian citizenship, but one that remains deeply connected to Italy. The SIE is the symbolic representation of what is also coined the 'other Italy' (l'*Altra Italia)*, 'who lives far away' (LV 896, October 1993: 3). Both these labels suggest the preservation of the original fatherland, Italy, as a fixed geopolitical entity: its borders are preserved by locating the Italian diaspora *all'estero* or within *another* Italy.

The notion of 'Italians abroad' stems from a vexed position between the impossibility of return to Italy, and the quest for new solidarities based upon new forms of existence. The *Italiani all'Estero* identity is produced from this complex combination of cultural nationalism (locating an original fatherland and culture within the confines of the Italian state territory) and of diasporic awareness (rehabilitating the emigrant, multi-local mode of existence). It maps out a 'diaspora space inhabited not only by those who have migrated and their descendants, but equally by those who are constructed and represented as indigenous' (Brah 1996: 209). In this case, the indigenous are those who stayed in Italy. The space of Italians abroad, interlaced with genealogies of dispersion and genealogies of staying put (Brah 1996: 209), rises as a kind of third space, beyond the confines of territorial boundaries 'here' and 'there', strikingly conjured up in a section of *La Voce* titled 'planet emigration' *(Pianeta Emigrazione)*. This is perhaps a collective version of what Trinh T. Minh-ha labels '(un)location' that describes the necessary 'shifting and contextual interval between arrested boundaries' (Trinh 1991: 4).[14] Yet precisely because the boundaries remain intact, *l'Altra Italia* is a 'reassuring elsewhere' (Glissant 1981: 177) by virtue of enforcing the very familiar boundaries it attempts to breach. These boundaries are drawn around Italy, the first place of origin, but punctured by the creation of four political constituencies in four different parts of the world. In this respect, the *Simbolo* simultaneously defies and reproduces Italian *regionalismo.* It transcends the existing organizational structure in London, devised along regionalized origins – Piacentini, Parmigiani, Veneti, Siciliani – while its definition as a distinct political and cultural constituency produces yet another region within the Italian state apparatus.

In short, the relationship between Italians abroad and Italy is formalized by discourses of civil rights and duties. Issues of representation are embattled, however, in debates over the rehabilitation of an émigré identity within the Italian national project. Tensions arise between a diasporic awareness and a nationalist discourse, both of which ground the creation of an *Italians abroad* identity. Invested in this new geography of identity is not only the issue of representation, but also one of self-management on the basis of local particularism. Italian spokesmen for emigrants aspire to more power over rulings affecting Italians living abroad. As emigrants they consider themselves in the best position to represent Italians abroad by virtue of the shared experience of emigration. Emigration is construed as a distinctive feature of Italians abroad and as such, is constitutive of a community that is not all that Italian. In London, *comunità* is not reducible to, though it is woven with, *italianità*. In this respect, discussions around Italian language and culture classes for children of Italian immigrants are a case in point, for they reveal the tension between universalist ideals of national culture and claims for local particularism.

Language tuition and the affirmation of local particularity

The first Italian state schools for Italian children in London were set up in 1933 by the Mussolini government.[15] Up to seven schools were run by the *Direzione Didattica* of the London *fascio*. After the dismantling of the *fascio* during the war years, it was not until 1966 that new classes were set up thanks to the initiative of Italian emigrants and parents who financed, organized and taught the classes themselves.

Since 1971, the classes have been taken over by the Italian Consulate, under the supervision of two *Direzione Didattiche*.[16] The Consulate supplies funds and teachers, while the administration of the classes is the responsibility of COASIT *(Comitato di Assistenza Scuole Italiane),* registered as a charity organization in England. Also involved in the Italian language tuition are approximately 45 parent committees *(Comitati Genitori)* headed by FASFA (*Federazione delle Associazioni e Comitati Scuola Famiglia),* chaired jointly by Remo Finaldi and Giuseppe Giacon (at the time of the research). Giacon is a prominent and respected leader of the London Italian 'community'. He was responsible for reviving the languages classes in 1966, and plays a leading role in the promotion of 'community interests'. Apart from the positions mentioned above, he was, at the time of this research, chairman of the *Circolo Veneto* (Venetian Club), a member of COASIT, and a Consulate middle-man who attends to queries by Italians who cannot go to the Consulate offices because of its limited opening hours (it opens to the public only on weekday mornings). Giacon is Member of the Order of the Italian Republic, and has been honoured by the Mount Carmel School for Girls, in Islington, who created the *Coppa Bepi Giacon.* The plaque on the cup reads 'for triumph over adversities'. The cup is awarded to pupils who have shown their capacity to overcome life's adversities, and is sponsored by Giacon himself (LV 894, September 1993: 6).[17]

A recurring theme in my interviews with persons concerned about Italian language teaching to Italian children is the choice of teachers. The core issue is the claim for increased autonomy in the definition of local particularity, which interrupts the dissemination of a unified national identity. Teachers in London classes are sent from Italy for a period of two to four years,[18] having been trained in Italy following the Italian Ministry of Education curriculum (Baldwin, Carsaniga, Lymbery Carter, et al. 1980: 25, 27). The point of contention is that these teachers do not have an 'emigrant mentality' as Giuseppe Giacon puts it. A similar argument was also put forward by the former Association of Teachers of Italian (ATI): teachers sent from Italy 'project around the phenomenon of emigration an atmosphere of regret and nostalgia' which hinders the intellectual development of the emigrant children (Baldwin et al. 1980: 27).

According to local leaders, parents send their children to these classes so they can be in an 'Italian atmosphere', so they can 'feel' Italian. It follows that the Italian teachers should be replaced by Italian *emigrant* teachers, that is, individuals who are aware of the community life and familiar with the emigrant/settler experience, construed as *the* point of convergence for Italians in England. For the same reasons, the employment of English teachers (with no Italian ancestors) is also dismissed. These individuals, it is argued, would lack the 'Italian spirit' necessary to convey a more adequate image of Italian culture. Hence the basis of the arguments about who is most competent to teach young Italians is twofold: first, Italian emigrants have a particular experience that shapes their identity in a way that distinguishes it from Italian adults coming from Italy; their relationship with Italy and with Italian culture is distorted and transformed from years of living abroad and of settlement. Secondly, the relationship with the local English culture is also complicated by the experience of migration, as well as by the legacy of an inherent spirit, or mentality, that only Italians and their descendants can possess.

From the outset, this view suggests an essentialist definition of culture as something that pre-dates individuals, and that one does or does not have. Giacon's comment expresses a form of objectification and essentialization of Italian culture (or part thereof) as a thing to be transmitted from generation to generation: the Italian 'heritage'. In this view, language classes are conceived as instruments for the transmission and *preservation* of a cultural heritage, rather than of its *production*. But Giacon's argument cannot be reduced to this single comment; his politics are more sophisticated than that. If he suggests the need to perform and recreate a particular 'spirit', he also perceives the classes as instances for making the community. 'We, as parents, we see the Italian classes not only as a means to teach Italian but as a social [occasion], as a place for creating the Italian community. We create the Italian community.' Thus, contrary to common speculation about ethnic community leaders, they can be well aware that they are creating a community, that the community does not precede its institutions. It is not born out of spontaneous generation. It needs places and spaces where the Italian 'spirit' and 'feeling' are performed and inscribed.

Indeed, there is more to language and culture classes than creating a sense of solidarity and improving proficiency in oral expression. Classes provide reading and writing skills; families do not. If children or grand-children of Italian immigrants are seen as possessing an 'Italian spirit', they must nevertheless learn about the culture that is said to be its expression. In this respect, supplementary schooling constitutes 'inscribing practices' that Paul Connerton views as necessary to the maintenance of collective identity – along with 'incorporating' practices, that is the sedimentation of collective memory in bodily postures. In this particular case, the language classes fix cultural memory through the passage from its oral transmission to a literate one.

> The transmission from an oral culture to a literate culture is a transition from incorporating practices to inscribing practices. The impact of writing depends upon the fact that any account which is transmitted by means of inscription is unalterably fixed, the process of its composition being definitely closed . . . When memories of a culture begin to be transmitted mainly by the reproduction of their inscription rather than by 'live' tellings, improvisation becomes increasingly difficult and innovation institutionalised. (1992: 75)

The language taught in the classrooms is standard Italian (in contrast to regional dialects), in keeping with a standardized vision of national culture. 'Bringing the country into the classroom' is a dominant feature of foreign language pedagogy (Jackson 1990: 6). The point here is that the relationship to Italy is not only created, it is formalized and inscribed. In other words, supplementary classes not only inscribe a link with Italy, even if only symbolic, but they also create a unified version of Italian culture that, according to some critiques, obscures regional differences (ATI 1982).

However, Connerton perhaps overemphasizes the static consequence of the shift to print language. What is inscribed is not only a unified cultural emblem. As Benedict Anderson argues, print languages also allow for the creation of 'imagined communities' that break open the seams of national boundaries. '[T]he concrete formation of contemporary nation-states is by no means isomorphic with the determinate reach of particular print-languages' (1983: 46). The identity of 'Italians abroad' relies precisely on its association with belonging to the imagined community of 'Italophones', a term used by President Francesco Cossiga in his message to Italians abroad in 1990 (LV 831, October 1990: 9). But there is even more to it than that. As Sneja Gunew writes, the concept of the mother-tongue is part and parcel of the myth of origins that, within diaspora cultures, carries with it the obsession with their recovery, which in many cases 'focuses on language rather than on originating territory or geography' (1993: 10). The deep concerns that language transmission raise in migrant communities are deeply connected to the shift away from territory as a primary ground of identification. Moreover, the kinship trope from which the notion of mother-tongue stems further suggests the idea of gendered and generational differences that bear the hallmarks of ethnic difference (see below).

The Italian language is thus a vehicle of transmission of an original culture. Indeed, language, in popular and official conceptions of multicultural education, is commonly perceived as the best conveyor of a unique and singular culture (Tosi 1991: 207).[19] For London Italian representatives, the re-production of a cultural heritage, on the one hand, and the production of a local community of émigrés on the other, are competing in demands for increased autonomy in language tuition. Put differently, invested in the teaching of Italian culture and language is the negotiation between national homogeneity and integrity, and local particularity.[20] What is at stake, here, is the relationship amongst 'ethnic consciousness', identity and social integration. 'Italian language and culture are fundamental elements in the formation of second and third generations and an indispensable factor for a successful integration within the host society' (LV 831, October 1990: 19). '[The preservation of the cultural heritage is] an important factor in the building up of the children's personal identity, hence as a prerequisite for their participation in the life of the society of which they have become part of through their parents' immigration' (Mengon in Baldwin et al. 1980: 26).

There is an obsession, in multicultural education, for mother-tongues as originary sources of identity that, if lost, signal the loss of some originary self. The assumption is that descendants of Italians will acquire a stronger positive sense of selfhood by learning their cultural background via the language. A reinforced sense of positive self-identity would then favour a greater openness toward 'other' cultures, thus leading to greater social harmony. Personal autonomy is viewed as a cornerstone of collective well being.[21]

In the case examined here, the relationship between Italian children and the wider collectivity (the émigré community or the nation) is mediated by the family. For one thing, the classes are presented as having an important symbolic function for the parents themselves. As Bruno Bottignolo suggests, the classes play a symbolic role by offering a substitute to the fading dream of returning. '[Parents] think they are in some way reproducing themselves and passing their culture and world to their children. On the other [hand], all Italians have the impression that their distant homeland cares for them in some way and is near' (1985: 125). In October 1990, *La Voce* expressed its appreciation of the classes in similar terms: 'Thanks to the language and culture classes, the worker abroad becomes, through his [sic] children, the most useful conveyor of Italian language and culture beyond the confines of the Republic' (LV 831, October 1990: 19).

As I argued elsewhere, language is a link with the past, through which younger generations can get in touch with the lives and experiences of their forebears. Rather than an indubitable expression of identity, learning Italian is a gesture of remembrance that traces lines of continuity between generations (Fortier 1992). Likewise, for London Italian defenders of Italian language and culture classes, the Italian language is a bridge between 'old' and 'new' locations of dwelling, as well as between 'old' and 'younger' generations. And from this bridge a distinct local émigré culture and community can emerge.

The ongoing struggle to maintain the language classes is inseparable from intergenerational relationships. A noteworthy feature of this argument is that children's knowledge of Italian language and culture is re-imported not into the community, but into the family, thus re-asserting its centrality in the growth of the community. Ethnicity is rehearsed in the family setting, although it may not be entirely *re*produced there; indeed, the family is not solely responsible for the preservation of the 'cultural heritage'. On the contrary, the acquisition of Italian cultural values and language is removed from the exclusive province of the immigrant family: '[s]econd generation Italians will not appropriate Italian cultural values without proper structural support' (LV 912, June 1994: 5). The family is *a* space for producing difference, but not the only space. The formation of difference and the inception of a particularized form of collective identification spills over the family circle into civic organizations.

In conclusion, consulate-run Italian language and culture classes are necessary supplements for inscribing cultural values and linguistic competence, but images of *continuity* are re-located within the family – not the community – which is in turn mobilized by a system of generational differentiation. Put differently, the services of the family are called upon through a system of generational relations that place family, ethnicity and community on the same continuum. As for the language question, its centrality as the singular necessary basis for cultural continuity is disturbed by a more complex view of cultural change configured around the 'problem of generations'.

Through the 'culture line':[22] the multi-generational community

Whether in debates over the vote from abroad, or about the control of language tuition, the Italians abroad politics of identity wrap Italian emigrants into the homogenizing fold of shared experiences of migration and common language. Still, when debates turn to questions of continuity and change, the envelope splits along the seams of generational differences.

The recurring image of generations in the pages of *La Voce* alerts us to its significance beyond the family realm. Generations are typically used in immigration and ethnic studies to periodize the settlement and adaptation of a population within the 'country of adoption'. 'Ethnic groups' are consequently divided along generational lines. Yet as Werner Sollors suggests, generations are also used as a metaphor that works 'as a community-building device' (Sollors 1986: 223). While the generational atomization of the Italian emigrant population gives these units a semblance of coherence, generations also provide a particular way of speaking of changes within the collectivity as a whole, and to reify them as issues of common concern. Put differently, generational differences serve to create and unify the 'general' Italian émigré culture. This raises the question of the kind of narratives and strategies that are used to construct the 'generation question' as an issue of collective concern. What do 'generations' speak of?

In 1992, Italian president Oscar Luigi Scalfaro sent a message to Italians abroad in which he spoke of cultural continuity. Pointing out that he was the president of 'all Italians, in Italy as well as abroad', Scalfaro stressed his desire for deeper relations between Italy and Italian emigrants and concluded with an appeal about the revival of Italian identification.

> Yet another task of human, political and cultural significance imposes itself: that of re-establishing the ties with many generations of Italians and Italian descendants who have lost contact with Italy. I hope that this phase, which I shall call the detachment from the roots, is passed. For I know that in various modes, in various continents, a comforting rediscovery of Italy is already in progress among descendants of our emigrants.
>
> We will do our best to ensure that this rediscovery is confirmed and extended, for it is the best way toward the spread of our language and of our very rich culture. Hence the image of our Italy will become ever more alive in the world, through all of you Italians living outside the borders of the fatherland. (*Backhill,* July 1992: 30)

Setting aside the expansionist pursuits supporting this discourse, I want to focus on the language of generations used by Scalfaro. In a rhetoric typical of discourses on emigration/immigration, changes in the cultural life of Italian communities abroad are expressed in terms of generations. Indeed, the process of estrangement from Italy is portrayed by the succession of generations of emigrants and their descendants. Generations, in this discourse, punctuate the gradual *de*generation of an imagined 'original' culture. Likewise, it is in the name of the preservation of this culture that emigrant leaders seek to formalize cultural links between 'younger generations' and Italy by calling for new cultural policies 'which [sustain] the process of human, professional and social growth and which [ensure] continuity in the knowledge of Italian reality in all its developments, thus contributing to the conservation and transmission of the original identity' (*Il Messaggero*, incomplete reference).[23]

It was along these lines that an issue of *La Voce* reported a meeting held in Udine, in the northern Italian region of Friuli-Venezia Giulia, where 'new generations' were invited to discuss emigration-related issues: *L'incontro internazionale delle nuove generazioni in emigrazione* (International meeting of new generations in migration) (LV 894, September 1993: 5). The 120 delegates, representing Europe, North America, South America and Australia, 'all graduates and holders of diplomas, with a good knowledge of Italian' met to discuss what the region of Friuli-Venezia had done for the younger Italian generations abroad, to examine and indicate reasons for change, as well as to make propositions for future action.

> The comparison is now without any alternative: either we are in a position to solder the new generations to a new discourse between land of origin and land of adoption, or we will, within the brief consuming of the biological sunset, have to definitely close the great book of diaspora [sic] in a hundred countries around the world, the last page registering the eventual and irreversible assimilation of our people within an anonymous fold with no roots. (LV 894 September 1993: 5)

This lyrical statement emerging from the conference proceedings, brings together roots *and* routes, essentialism and pluralism, within a quest to keep some Italian memory and identification alive against the threat of assimilation. The image of the 'biological sunset' metaphorically speaks of the link between time, decay, and loss. If the sun sets, the land of origin will fall into darkness and it will disappear into oblivion, dragging the Italian roots and identity in its tow. What this discourse solders is an organic link between land and culture, emphasizing the distinction between 'land of adoption' and 'land of origin'. This distinction suggests two types of identification: one that is volitional, and one that is intrinsic; an 'identity-as-conjuncture' and an 'identity-as-essence' (Lavie and Swedenburg 1996a: 165). Such a split is concealed in expressions such as 'my blood and my heart are Italian, my brains are English'.[24] An aura of eternity surrounds the 'land of origin' and its organic Italian identity – 'Italians never die, they just *pasta* way'[25] – which stands in contrast to the contextual and historical undertones of the idea of 'adoption'. Cultural identity is brought into contact with geographically and genealogically coded 'origins', thus transforming it into a pseudo-biological property of human life.

By contrast, the land of adoption is conceived as the place of residence where new cultural forms menace the survival of age-old and faraway roots. Indeed, if adoption is volitional, it also connotes a commitment whereby immigrants tie their destiny to a chosen place. In the noticeable manner in which people presumably born in another country are still said to 'adopt' a place of residence and its culture, there runs the distinction between blood lines and historically situated lines; congenital culture and acquired culture. In this context, descendants of emigrants are asked to uphold their original identity 'with the will not to submit to the devastating process of homogenization which aspires to a total and global assimilation for all, with no roots nor memory for anyone' (LV 894, September 1993: 5).

But this threat is not always construed as inevitable. It may be reversed if the process of migration is itself reversed, that is if younger generations return to the homeland in order to rekindle with their origins, yet without necessarily confining their identity to the homeland. They are invited to act as mediators to link past and present in the construction of the future. In other words, the land of origin constitutes a 'detour through the past' enabling the future generations to 'produce themselves anew and differently' (Hall 1993: 362). It is 'a resource of history . . . in the process of becoming [more] than being: not "who we are" or "where we come from", so much as what we might become, how we have been represented and how that bears on how we might represent ourselves' (Hall 1996b: 4).

This was explicitly formulated at the 'Third Regional Conference on Venetian Emigration' of November 1992, held in Trevisto-Monastier, Veneto (north-eastern Italy). Resulting from the conference was a statement on the creative potential of regional mobilization around issues of emigration. Here is the core of the reprinted text:

> The formation of a hinge between the two Veneti[26] is explicit in the creation of a regional body for emigration with the ensuing management of the phenomenon, in a more creative and less political manner. In such a management, culture becomes the nodal point of the Venetian diaspora's [sic] strategies, the ideal bond between successive generations and between associations, who more than ever should engage in the path of a real connection . . . without denying the folklore and local aspects pursued by the provinces.
>
> The presence, however reduced, of second generations at the Conference . . . has contributed to table a noteworthy proposition. The will to establish contacts between groups of different nations, to continue research in the field, to attempt deeper connections with Venetians living *in patria*, indicating that the new generations see themselves as bearers of a more open culture, which shows solidarity and universality, and which decants in the region of origin. *It is the end of the culture of roots and the beginning of the culture of relations*, a true recovery of an essential Venetian trait. (LV 879, January 1993: 5; my emphasis in last sentence)

This text clearly engages with an open-ended conception of culture and the creation of a diasporic space of cultural relations: a transnational network for the deployment of a culture of relations between multiple locations. What is suggested, here, is a shift *from* a culture of roots *to* a culture of routes, but in a way that still engages with ideas of original identities.

This is what Edouard Glissant would name 'Relation', which is the founding principle of identity formations that rest on relations, mobility and multiplicity, yet which rely on some form of rootings that are on the ground's surface – the rhizomatic node as opposed to deep underground tree roots – and creative of new spaces of identification (Glissant 1981). Belonging, even 'on the surface' (Probyn 1996), entails the process of enclosing and suturing, however temporary and contingent. Hence the new culture of routes proclaimed in the Veneto Conference comes full circle back to the roots of the 'region of origin'. Indeed, the culture of relations is deemed an 'essential Venetian trait'. The aim of the passage to a culture of relations remains the recovery of origins, but these origins are then relocated within a relational system where they transit and cross with other cultural formations. In other words, 'origins' are put into circulation in a transnational network of relations. Moving beyond the problematic of generations caught between two cultures, these proclamations emphasize the creative potential of 'culture's in between' (Bhabha 1993), that contact zone where two cultures meet, each of which, however, is conceived, in the above account, as an enclosed and inalterable entity.

The key agents of this culture of relations are the 'young generations'. Called upon as soldiers of redemption, 'young Italians' are painted as carriers of an original culture and responsible for its revival around the world. Their task is to bridge Italy with the rest of the world in a reciprocal co-operation from each side. As such, it is their duty to proudly carry their heritage and to bring it into their 'land of adoption' (sic). The youths are presented as constituted by an 'original' identity and an 'adopted' one, which both decant into each other. To some extent, this is about the creation of a new ethnicity: one that features hybridization and 'diasporization', yet which proceeds from a return to the fatherland. Hence the detour through the past is not merely a stepping stone: it is rather a necessary touchstone in the construction of the new identity. Though origins circulate within a language of migration and change, they are construed as the necessary condition for the invention of a new Italian ethnicity that may bear some claim to authenticity.

The generation metaphor serves to consolidate solidarity around issues of cultural de-generation, loss and change. While Italian emigrant leaders clearly recognize the specificity of their descendants' experiences, their return to the nation brings them back into a constraining rhetoric of land, culture and origins that produces pseudo-biological underpinnings to their project for a new cultural politics. In this complex generational rhetoric, generations are both the problem and the solution. Generations are bound to an inalterable cultural origin that endows them with an inherent identity (the 'Italian spirit') and imputes to them a responsibility towards the community. Consequently, generations are agents of change, yet a change that is policed by the ultimate project of recovery and preservation. Biological undertones are concealed in a complex discourse where time is the active principle of cultural degeneracy, while multi-locality and dispersal are the vectors of a kind of hybridization that relates back to the fatherland where it introduces cultural changes.

To sum up what has been said so far, the politics of identity of Italians abroad are expressed in languages of citizenship that involve political, cultural and generational concerns. These three fields of concerns are stitched together by a foundational idea of culture based on common origins rooted in the fatherland and put into transnational networks of cultural exchange. Resistance to assimilation has led Italian emigrant leaders back to the nation, yet with the recognition of the unique émigré vantage point. It is a return with a difference that engages simultaneously with pluralist and essentialist conceptions of identity formations.

Images of nationals: soldiers, hard workers and beauty queens

Running through the discourse of 'Italians abroad' are allusions to amorphous men and women whose only defining character is to *be* 'Italians abroad', sharing the typical emigration experience of silent suffering and coping. Italian emigration is represented as an active thing animated by its own inherent characteristics: suffering, loneliness, estrangement, alienation, discreteness, but also displacement, settlement, and the negotiation of roots and routes. Emigration is something that is 'under*gone*, not under*taken'* (Jacobson 1995: 24): it appears as something that *happens* to people and puts them through the inescapable obstacles of its journey. But what kind of people are the émigrés? In what follows, I pull out the threads that reveal the specific ways in which gender, class and nation are re-articulated in Italian émigré culture, thus exposing more and less orthodox representations of the characters said to epitomize nationhood and nation: the soldier-hero, the emigrant worker, the beauty queen.

I want to begin with a vignette. It is the story of Nicola Nastri. This story was reported in *Backhill*, the monthly magazine of St Peter's Italian church. Nicola's story was told by Olive Besagni, who writes a regular chronicle on the life in London's former 'Little Italy' at the turn of the century.[27]

The story of Nicola Nastri is that of 'a war hero', as Besagni herself puts it (*Backhill,* March 1993: 30), and of a dedicated son. Indeed, Nicola, already serving in the British army when Mussolini declared war on the allies, volunteered to serve with the Special Service Unit in order to save his father from internment.[28] Nicola's story is told extensively – it takes up two of Besagni's features (*Backhill,* April 1993: 12–13, and May 1993: 12–13) – and carries all the ingredients for the making of a hero: a top secret and dangerous mission in Italy, his sacrifice for his father, his alliance with British soldiers, his imprisonment in Italy, hiding his Italian identity from his Italian captors, his Italian aunt denying she knows him when interrogated by his captors, and his post-war decorations. Nicola's story is a striking rerun of the war years, where the Italian state is unquestionably the enemy, but where some Italian citizens (here and in Italy) are allies.

The relationship between family and nation is brought together in Nicola's story. Nicola's allegiance to Italy passed through his father, whom he protected from internment by the 'enemy'. This is one version of nationalism's 'family romance'. Praised for being both loyal to Britain (a good soldier) and to his father (a good son), Nicola's drama is about dedication to the patriarch, respect of family values and national allegiance. But the latter has a double edge: protecting his father may also be read as protecting Italy, the fatherland, from the German threat. Nicola epitomizes honour: he is at once an honourable British citizen, an honourable Italian descendant, who showed his loyalty to both the 'hostland' and 'fatherland', and an honourable son, dedicated to his father. *Onore, Patria, Famiglia*: the Italian national motto writes the sub-text of this story which, in turn, emphasizes its masculinist configuration. The central subject of the Italian national family romance enacted in these war remembrances is not only a male soldier, he is also a son. The story of the nation at war is also the story of a nation of families.

The ultimate image of national allegiance is the men's willingness to fight and die for their country (Gellner 1983). Each year, the Italian consulate and embassy, jointly with the National Association of War Veterans *(Associazione nazionale combattenti e reduci),* organize a memorial service in honour of Italian soldiers buried at the military cemetery in Brookwood (Surrey). The service is officiated by the priest of St Peter's Italian church, accompanied by the Scalabrini choir. During the 1993 ceremony, the Italian Ambassador to London concluded the service with the following words: 'in these difficult times for our fatherland, liberty and unity are values which have been delivered by the sacrifice of our dead who therefore demand them to be maintained as guarantees of all civil life' (LV 900, December 1993: 3).

As he was speaking, I watched a woman gently laying flowers by some apparently selected gravestones. A son? A husband? A brother? The war mother, widow, sister, or perhaps cousin or fiancée, moved discreetly behind the scene while soldiers and veterans were praised for their patriotic sacrifice: two veterans were presented with medals by the ambassador during that ceremony. Similarly, the narratives of the war years in histories about Italian immigrants in Britain speak of 'wives and mothers . . . left at home to carry on as best they could' (Colpi 1991a: 126). As in narratives of migration, war remembrances relocate women's sacrifices, and identity, within the family setting. Women's contribution to the 'war effort' exists by proxy, through brave and patriotic husbands and sons.

Moving beyond this family romance, there exists a set of recollections of the war years that represent national allegiance as well as the relations between the warring factions in a very different light. Memories of the *Arandora Star*, and to a lesser extent of the internment of Italian immigrants, emphasize the suffering and alienation that distinguish British Italians from other Italians worldwide. In these stories, resentment towards Britain is strikingly absent. Alberto Cavalli, for example, does not blame the Britons for sending him to an internment camp: he considers that he was the victim of the circumstances and that Britain acted as any nation would. Likewise, public ceremonies honour the alliance rather than the enmity between Italy and Britain. In the Brookwood remembrance ceremony of November 1993, an Englishman was honoured for his contribution to the Italian resistance. His heroic story was told in detail and he was congratulated and thanked by the Ambassador in the name of all Italians.

Other displays of alliance appear sporadically in local publications, most often referring to POW camps. The most striking aspect of these accounts is their depiction of the soldiers and their legacy to the British cultural heritage. These memories depict pictures of 'cordial and kind' British prison guards, of Italian soldier-artists, craftsmen, bricklayers or carpenters who built lovely chapels. In an interesting twist of the highly masculinized image of patriotism, these soldiers are remembered for their architectural and artistic accomplishments, not for risking their lives for the nation. They are remembered for the cultural heritage they bequeathed to different parts of Britain, including the famous Churchill Barriers of Kirkwall, Orkney, and the 'Italian chapel' built on this location (LV 869, July 1992: 7). Another chapel, at the opposite end of the British Isles in Henlan, Wales, has likewise been recovered as an Italian cultural legacy to the Welsh country (LV September 1993, 894: 6 and 895: 7).

Anniversary celebrations that took place on these sites cancel out past enmities by highlighting past and present friendship and conviviality between English and Italians: honouring an English veteran, or praising the legacy of Italian POWs, represented as artists or labourers rather than enemy soldiers.

> Then, they were prisoners, enemies, condemned to forced labour. They have returned as guests of honour, welcomed and respected like important people. They have met again with the affection and esteem of the Orkney residents; the same affection and esteem that they have earned in the concentration camps [sic] and that have survived their departure. These are capable people, enterprising protagonists of a labour that no one had succeeded in completing – the barriers that connect the islands – and the creators of other artistic works that are the pride of the islanders, and the destination of pilgrims and tourists. (LV 869, July 1992: 7)

The barriers are a concrete example of the hyphen metaphor introduced in Chapter 1. Paths of connections, passage and exchange between the Orkney islands, they are also routes of reconciliation between past enemies. Routes of intercultural exchange that celebrate the legacy of a 'foreign' culture on Scottish soil. What is more, the connection is fulfilled through the gift: Domenico Chiocchetti, the architect and painter of the chapel, recalls a letter he wrote to the Orkney islanders in 1960: 'Dear islanders, the chapel is yours to love and protect' (LV 869, July 1992: 7).[29] This is a gift of reconciliation which creates a space of legitimacy in support of the recovery of the Italian presence in Scottish (and British) culture.

The performed sites – the chapels, the barriers – become 'trembling spaces' (Stewart 1996: 95), vehicles of connections and of conflicting memories (imprisonment and entrepreneurship, forced labour and creative work, enmity and alliance) that are at odds with masculinist representations of soldier heroes, patriotism and nationhood: pride for the nation passes through gifts of art and architecture, rather than the sacrifice of life. Undoubtedly, they are material traces of the 'hybridization' of the British social and cultural landscape that results from histories of forced labour and internment. As Lisa Lowe rightly argues, '[h]ybridization is not the "free" oscillation between or among chosen identities' (1996: 82). In this particular case, hybridization resulted from the uneven process through which Italians encountered the violences of the British state, captured in Winston Churchill's infamous words, 'Collar the lot!' (Gillman and Gillman 1980).

Yet war memories speak of the struggle between estrangement and alliance, where the latter wins in the end. Britain, here, is the 'host country', where even former hostages were well treated and respected. Nationalistic claims are not *embattled* in the remembrances: rather, we witness an instantiation of European alliance. In other words, these remembrances are not reruns of the war;[30] they are rather reruns of the armistice between Italy and England and the ensuing (re)integration of Italians in British society.[31]

All told, these events, and the images they foster, ride on the glorified position the soldier occupies within nation-based narratives of collective selfhood. Other national subjects, however, are also commended as models of citizenship. The London Italian calendar of events includes a ceremony of conferment of honours bestowed by the Italian government upon Italians (and a few non-Italians) living in Britain. This event is one of the rare moments where Italian state officials and Italian emigrants meet. In contrast to other meeting places (the Consulate, or promotional fairs for Italian products), these occasions publicly congratulate men and women for promoting the Italian national values inscribed in the Italian national motto *Onore, Patria, Famiglia*. Again, this shibboleth of patriarchal values operates from, and emphasizes, gendered differentiations through which the limits of citizenship are defined.

Each year, on the occasion of the *Festa della Repubblica,* the Italian embassy holds a ceremony of conferment of honorary medals to Italians or non-Italians in Britain. The awards, bestowed by the Italian ambassador, are numerous. The most prestigious is that of *Cavaliere* (the equivalent of knighthood) which goes to recipients of the Order of the Republic *(Ordine al Merito della Repubblica).* Many British Italians – and some non-Italians – have acquired this title in recognition of their significant contribution to Italian national development through their work in the British Italian community. As mentioned earlier, Terri Colpi was honoured in June 1995, for her work in support of the Italian community (LV 934, June 1995: 6). The same year, Ada Pizzuto and Sebastiano Petrillo were made *Cavalieri*: the former for her volunteer work in prisons, the latter for his key contributions to a variety of Italian associations (including the Association of War Veterans that organizes the annual remembrance ceremony in Brookwood; LV 934, June 1995: 6). In 1994, Lazzaro Servini, a former war internee, was honoured for his engagement in promoting Italian language and culture in Wales, and Dr. Elisa Provini-Walker for her similar commitment within British academia (LV 912, June 1994: 6). Other *Cavalieri* include Giuseppe Giacon, the business magnate Charles Forte, and the president of the Italian Women's Club (*Club Donne Italiane*), Roberta Mutti.

Another honorific medal is the *Stella al Merito del Lavoro*, the recipients of which merit the title of *Maestro*. This medal is granted to an Italian individual whose hard work contributes to producing a respectable image of Italian labour abroad *(lavoro italiano all'estero)*. One Maestro, Nicesio Fantini, was honoured for his activities in miners' unions as a spokesman for Italian miners, thus 'acquiring esteem and respect for Italian labour abroad' (LV 912, June 1994: 6). Another Maestro was honoured for marketing Italian ethnicity – Giuseppe Belloni, Master Chef, received the Stella in June 1995. He is esteemed, the text reads, for his dedication and hard work in the hotel industry, 'ultimately promoting, in this way, the image of the Italian worker abroad' (LV 934, June 1995: 6).

Echoes of Mussolini's doctrine resonate in the praises of the emigrants' labour as a reflection not of the poverty of the country, but of the force and energy of Italian-style labour (Mack Smith 1959: 242). Likewise, Italian emigrants are also honoured for their actions as ambassadors of Italian culture. Tributes speak of hard-working labourers; of generous donors of artwork; of significant contributions to the Italian 'community'. The honoured are usually Italian 'co-nationals' who have suffered out of their duty to the country or to their trade. In Italian immigrant historicity, labour is tightly bound to suffering and sacrifice. But in these state functions, labour is valued as productive of a respectable image of Italy. What is featured in the state ceremonies is the profit and prosperity of Italian nationhood by virtue of individual efforts. The award of these Medals by the Italian state honours the 'active citizen' who 'engages in "doing good" but purely in private capacity' (Hall and Held 1989: 174). And doing good, here, means promoting and disseminating Italian culture. Hence those 'workers' who do not 'trade' in Italian ethnicity are unlikely candidates for the Italian national honours. Unless, of course, they achieve remarkable success, such as Charles Forte. On the other hand, how likely is a man like Toni to be made *Maestro?* Class operates in these ceremonies in ways that are deeply embedded in injunctions of national belonging. Class divisions are also obscured under the guise of national pride and identification; the economic and social achievements of *Maestri* and *Cavalieri* are congratulated on the basis that these are represented as *expressions* of Italian identity and identification. Moreover, they are presented as expressions of the inherent qualities of Italian culture, that is, of Italian *ways*.

Moreover, the fact that eighteen men, and no women, have received the *Stella* between 1993 and 1996 indicates that the values promoted work in a gendered way. To put it simply, the title of honourable hard worker is available predominantly to men because it is granted for their actions within the labour market, where men hold the economic power and occupy most decision-making positions. Without arguing for the reification of 'female' values and the need for the recognition of women *qua* women, there is something to be said about the circulation of national values and the class and gender orders that are produced through them (Walby

1994). Differences of class and gender are obscured and produced through contentions that 'honour, fatherland, family' are universal values. Italian citizenship – like the universalized, abstract modern definition of citizenship – is invested with class and gendered systems of differentiation and has developed in relation to them (Walby 1994).[32]

This is not to say that women are not recognized as citizens. In the Italian nationalist discourse, the centrality of the family suggests the political inclusion of women as mothers and wives, whose duties, however, are relegated to the 'private' sphere of social life. 'A woman's political relation to the nation [is] thus submerged as a social relation to a man through marriage. For women, citizenship in the nation [is] mediated by the marriage relation within the family.' (McClintock 1995: 358) Denied any national agency – nationhood and patriotism are masculinized in the figures of the soldier-hero – women are conscripted as emblems of the nation.

In Italian London, this was exemplified for a time in the *Miss Italia nel Mondo* beauty contest. From 1991 to 1994, the London-based Radio Spectrum – a multiethnic radio station directed by Wolfgango Bucci – organized a contest for *Miss Italy in the World*. The contest involved the selection of a Miss Italy for Great Britain (sic), who would then go to Italy to compete against peers for the title of *Miss Italy in the World*. This contest was the offshoot of what used to be *Miss Emigrante*, and involved descendants of immigrants: usually second, occasionally third generation Italian women. The change of title signified, for Terri Colpi, 'the change in attitude towards emigration and the general strengthening of links between Italy and the expatriate Communities' (1991b: 171).

Truly, both *Miss Emigrante* and *Miss Italy in the World* speak of how communal identities are inscribed on women's bodies. The beauty queen is a particular version of the widespread portrayal of nations as women (Mosse 1985; Parker, Russo, Sommer, and Yaeger 1992). By contrast to the fallen soldier, honoured as an active, brave, patriotic citizen, or to the Cavalieri/Maestri, congratulated for their individual efforts for the national good, beauty queens are chosen to embody the nation (or a collective referent of identification such as 'emigration'). Beauty queens are living embodiments of how a nation projects itself to the world. Often said to act as ambassadors of their country, beauty queens commonly define their role as promoters of peace, care and good will. Beauty queens represent the 'soft side' of nationalism.

The *Miss Italy in the World* competition was also another instance where the connections between the Italian diaspora and Italy were deployed. Wrapped around the women's bodies was a banner identifying the Beauty Queens *as* the nation: Miss Italy in the world, or Miss Italy for Great Britain, and so on. During its short-lived existence,[33] *Miss Italy in the World* was a specific instance where gender, ethnicity and nation came together in the construction of a gendered nationhood.

As national allegiance is masculinized ('you can take a man out of a country, but you can't take the country out of the man'), the nation is feminized.

Here, 'women are subsumed symbolically into the national body politic as its boundary and metaphoric limit' (McClintock 1995: 354). These women's bodies become the 'flesh' (Grosz 1994) through which local particularity and nation are inscribed, *in and against each other*. The idea of *Miss Italia nel Mondo* was that young women publicly compete against each other, thus staging a number of rivalries at once: between nations, between 'Italian communities', and between women. The boundaries are multiple, and their limits blurred: the thresholds of Britain, Italy and émigré culture converge on the women's bodies as they circulate on the stage in this dated performance of nations in conflict. The national trope fashions this feminized version of cultural ambassadorship, where women portray an array of collective identities at once.

Finally, *Miss Italy in the World* is a sadly familiar instance where women's bodies are conscripted and displayed as exemplars of 'beauty'. Ethnicized as Italian (or British-Italian, German-Italian, and so on), they are also assessed according to Eurocentric norms of elegance (the evening gown competition), physical beauty (the swim suit competition), character (personality competition), and skill (the talent competition). Injunctions of young, white, Italian-European womanhood were spelled out in this moment where the 'great book of diaspora' adopted a distinctly feminized narrative. *Miss Italy in the World* is to the nation what emigrant women are to the émigré culture: the living embodiment of collective experience (see Chaper 5).

Final remarks

The ambivalence about physical return and attachment to the 'fatherland' is one vector of the London Italian 'drama of emigration' (see next chapter) that London emigrant leaders seek to resolve by a return to the nation expressed in languages of citizenship and origins. These politics of identity combine notions of a fixed and inalterable original culture with notions of migration, change and transformation. By positing emigration as a central collective signifier, while calling for cultural preservation, community leaders simultaneously challenge and conform to nationalist conceptions of identity that rely on narratives of an original core culture.

Origins appear as the nodal point linking political, cultural and generational concerns and stitching 'here' and 'there' together. The language of origins emphasizes descent and roots and substantiates ideas of an authentic, pure, a-historical, core culture confined within the borders of the 'fatherland'. The necessary return to the land of origin – enacted either in the actual return to Italy, or in the transmission the Italian language – acts as a touchstone in the construction of a new identity, which also proceeds from a diasporic mode of existence.

Italian politics of identity emerge from what Rosi Braidotti has labelled a 'migrant consciousness', 'caught in an in-between state whereby the narrative of the origin has the effect of destabilizing the present' (1994: 24). The politics of identity of London Italians seem to be juggling with the Italian national myth that relies on narratives of origin, on the one hand, and present living conditions that are increasingly estranged from any notion of 'origin' as a single, primary ground of identity, on the other. Emigrant leaders move between the two structures of local and national authorities. They re-turn to the land of origin for national identification but work hard to integrate the local experience into émigré identity formation. Performances of citizenship that take place outside the immediate purview of Italian officialdom produce this kind of cultural citizenship that is grounded in multilocality. These performances are not only 'trembling spaces'. They are also what May Joseph calls 'nervous enactments' of citizenship, which are recast within a transnationally inflected public arena (1999: 5). They are nervous insofar as they stem from the awareness that public narratives about the Italian political and cultural subject do not cohere with lived experiences of migration, while the language of citizenship provides the definitional frames through which Italian express their will to be recognized as public actors.

The possibility of transculture seems to appear in regional locations. The meeting in Veneto on the future of generations in migration, or the festivities in Scotland and Wales, speak of a culture of relations that results from the combination of transnational and regional links, thus overstepping nationally bound belongings. These events perform a form of transnational citizenship where the 'Italian abroad' is at once a legal and cultural subject. The London organizational structure, defined in terms of regionalized origins, also suggests that 'origins' are not strictly nation based. Such localisms, as it were, emerge within an arena shaped through trans-cultural relations and multi-local belongings.

London Italian practices of nation are tightly bound to what Anne McClintock refers to as nationalism's family iconography (1995: 357). Italy is referred to as the 'fatherland' *(patria)*, immigrants and their descendants are said to 'adopt' other countries and their cultures, ideas of 'mother-tongue' support the concern about the preservation of Italian culture, 'younger generations' are emblems of the paradoxes of diaspora, and soldier-heroes are also sons and husbands of wives and mothers waiting at home. In sum, the political struggle over the definition of the Italian emigrants' destiny is deeply woven into kinship narratives that spell out ideas of generational responsibility embedded within gendered systems of differentiation. By fusing nation and family together, discourses of national allegiance naturalize the different positions men and women occupy within national and ethnic communities: men defend and protect, women reproduce and embody. On the other hand, the family acquires a special significance, in migration, as it becomes a key stage of ethnicity – as testifed in the rehearsal of the Italian language in the family before it circulates within the 'community'. Though the national discourse frames definitions of origins, collective belonging and political subjects, the family is the privileged site and frame of memory within Italian émigré culture.

To be sure, this localized culture is more than a political and social category. Institutional practices of identity offer an array of forms of self-representation that both mimic and disrupt historical and political meta-narratives of identity. The second part of this book is devoted to the daily life of the Centro Scalabrini and St Peter's church, two organizations that play a significant role in shaping an Italian émigré culture, in London as well as in Britain.

Notes

1. The sophisticated debates among some political theorists over 'the rights of minority cultures' tend to start from this premise and to overlook the kind of culture that is spoken of and created by the cultural claims of minorities. My concern is for identity formation itself, rather than the moral and political implications of minority rights. See Taylor 1994; Kymlicka 1992, 1995a, 1995b; Kukathas 1992.
2. I remind the reader that quotes drawn from *La Voce degli Italiani* are my translations from Italian, unless otherwise indicated.
3. For instance, leaders of *La Voce* were involved in the foundation of two federations of press organizations that are distinct from Italian-based ones; organizations that practice a journalism *by* Italians abroad as opposed to *for* Italians abroad. FEDEUROPA, i.e. the Federation of Italian Newspapers in Europe (*Federazione dei giornali italiani in Europa)* (1965) and FMSI, the World Federation of Italian press abroad (*Federazione mondiale della stampa italiana all'estero*) (1971).
4. The first *fascio* outside Italy was established in London in 1921 (Cliff 1995; Marin 1975: 80), followed in 1922 by the Glasgow *fascio,* also known as *Casa d'Italia* (Colpi 1991a: 92). It bears repetition that members of the *fascio* were not necessarily fascist sympathizers. See endnote 18, Chapter 2.
5. Many of the London organizations are members of a federation established in 1975, the *Federazione Associazioni Italiane England* (FAIE). According to the 1993 Italian Directory published by *La Voce,* the FAIE includes 38 member organizations, most of which (at least 30) are based in London.
6. Italian organizations based in London include: the Embassy, the Consulate, the Military Attaché, the British-Italian Society (which is under the patronage

of the Italian ambassador) and the Italian Cultural Institute (ICI). The latter is a good exemplar of Italian state intervention to promote Italian culture. Created in 1951 under the Anglo Italian Cultural Agreement, the ICI has the mandate to promote and encourage cultural exchanges between Britain and Italy. Among other roles, the ICI acts as the 'official advisory agency to the Italian Authorities on the equivalence of certificates and courses of studies' (ICI brochure). Apart from providing Italian language classes at relatively high cost, the ICI holds a variety of cultural and intellectual events that gather Italian and British aficionados of Italian 'high' culture.

The Italian Consulate, for its part, has educational departments that organize, fund and supply teachers for Italian language and culture classes for children and grandchildren of Italian immigrants (see third section in this chapter).

7. The use of the 'negro' as metaphor for underclass had wide currency in nineteenth century America (Roediger 1991, 1994) and was used in various political discourses. More recently, it was used during the 1970s 'ethnic revivalism', and seems to be making a come-back in the 1990s. In Québec, for instance, a leading nationalist pamphlet of the 1970s nationalist movement was titled *Nègres Blancs d'Amérique* (Vallières 1979). A revised second edition was published in 1994, the same year that a book on Irish nationalism appeared bearing the title *Ulster's white negroes* (O'Dochartaigh 1994). This is not to say that the metaphor is used in equivalent ways in all settings: closer scrutiny would indeed reveal the locally and historically specific ways in which race and class articulate in representations of social marginalization.
8. Voting rights for Italian *émigrés* was first raised in 1908 at a Conference of Italians abroad held in Rome and has been the subject of an ongoing debate over the last 40 years. It has been recently revived in the context of constitutional changes occurring in Italy in 1992 and 1993.
9. Italian citizenship follows the principles of the right of blood.
10. In Italy, the government is elected by a combination of proportional representation and majority vote (since 1994). Voters elect members of the Chamber of Deputies (lower house) and the Senate (upper house).
11. Including, for example, taxes on properties in Italy.
12. President Cossiga in LV 831, October 1990: 9, and Senator Giacovazzo in LV 898, November 1993: 1.
13. At the time of this research, Giorgio Brignola was also correspondent for other Italian emigrant newspapers in Europe, and he had a regular slot in the weekly BBC radio programme in Italian: *BBC Mondo Italiano.*
14. I am grateful to Magdalene Ang-Lygate for drawing this point to my attention.
15. Other schools did exist prior to these. The first Italian school was founded in 1817, subsidized by the *Regno di Piemonte.* This *scuola popolare* was first based in Lincoln's Inn, under the Sardinian Chapel *(Cappella Sarda).* It became

St Peter's school in 1837 and it eventually moved to Clerkenwell and was run by the Pallottini Fathers of St Peter's church. In 1841, Giuseppe Mazzini founded a school for poor Italians, offering Italian language classes to children and illiterate adults. The clearly patriotic aims to transmit a sense of *Italianità* to children of Italian immigrants (Palmer 1977/1991), and the 'anti-religious' views of the school did not appeal to St Peter's and hostility grew rapidly between the two schools. Mazzini's school closed in 1848, shortly after its founder returned to Italy. St Peter's then became the only school for most of the second half of the nineteenth century. It ran until the 1939–45 war broke out.

16. The Italian Law 153/1971 is aimed at providing courses for Italian workers' relatives, in order to facilitate their insertion in the host country's schools and in view of keeping alive *'l'origine linguistico-culturale'*.
17. The fact than an emigrant is selected as sponsor for a cup honouring determination and guts is probably no accident. Emigration and its teleology of suffering is emblematic of adversity, and emigrants such as Giacon are often deified as symbols of resilience and success.
18. Although some do decide to stay, and manage to continue with their teaching.
19. Such a conception also underlies the EEC directive no 486/1977, which provides compulsory bilingual and bicultural education to the children of emigrants who must integrate in the language and culture of the host country, 'but without ceasing to identify to the language and culture of their country of origin' (Lazzari 1990: 416; also Stubbs 1985: 384, for a copy of the Directive). Such views have been criticized on a variety of grounds, all of which question the metonymic relationship between language, culture and identity (Fortier 1992; Rodriguez 1983; Edwards 1985; Hewitt 1991; Khan 1980; Giles, Bourhis, Taylor 1977; Oriol 1985).
20. Moreover, at a time when Italian authorities are reducing their funding, some leaders are considering asking more intervention from the British government. Their concern, however, remains one of self-management and the preservation of their heritage.
21. Some critics of the present system add another element to the debate: the position of Italian language and culture within the British national education curriculum. For Arturo Tosi (1991) and for Bruno Cervi (1991), full integration of Italians in Britain would be achieved by including Italian as a 'community language' within the British education curriculum, rather than maintaining it on the margins of the national curriculum, thus keeping Italian culture in a peripheral, foreign status. Giuseppe Giacon, for his part, is ambivalent about the issue. What Tosi and Cervi are suggesting is that 'integration' is not accomplished by self-esteem alone. A sense of belonging to the British national culture is best fostered through multicultural education, an issue that has fuelled

a longstanding debate in Britain as in other parts of the Western world. For a totally opposite viewpoint, expressed in the American context with regards to bilingual schools (English and Spanish), see Rodriguez (1983) who contends that bilingual education merely keeps minorities on the margins of the 'crowd', as it were. Full individuality is achieved, he argues, 'by those who are able to consider themselves member of the crowd' (Rodriguez 1983: 27). And this is possible only when given the same opportunities, such as the same education, as the rest of the population. Although his argument is compelling, its limitation is that it rests on the premise of a clear-cut division between the 'private' and the 'public'. Cultural difference, in his view, is and should be produced within the confines of the family.

22. This phrase is borrowed from Paul Gilroy's forthcoming book on multiculturalism.
23. I am thankful to Father Giuseppe Blanda, former director St Patrick's International Centre in London, for bringing this article to my attention. The cited passage is my translation from Italian. *Il Messaggero* is a Catholic publication for Italians worldwide.
24. I first heard this expression in February 1993, from Francesco Giacon, editor of St Peter's magazine, *Backhill*, and son of Giuseppe Giacon. I subsequently heard it from his sister, Joanna Giacon, who identifies as Italian *and* English (no hyphen). At the time of the study, Joanna worked at St Peter's parish office.
25. This was printed on a t-shirt sold at the annual pilgrimage to the monastery of Our Lady of Mount Carmel in Aylesford, in June 1993.
26. Veneto is a north-eastern region of Italy. The reference to the two Veneti, here, is meant to include Veneto *within* and *without* Italy, that is, the symbolic reproduction of Veneto through the Venetian emigration outside of Italy.
27. Also known as 'The Hill' or *Il quartiere italiano*, Little Italy consisted of a small area located in what is now Clerkenwell, central London. In Chapter 5, I explore the ways in which The Hill is constructed as a second place of origin within Italian émigré historicity. Besagni's texts are written in English.
28. The fate of Alberto Cavalli – whose story is referred to in Chapter 2 – was different. During his trial after his arrest as an 'enemy alien', Cavalli was asked if he was ready to serve with the British army. He replied that he would on the condition that his father was released. This did not satisfy the tribunal, and both he and his father were sent to an internment camp.
29. The chapel has been under the care of a local preservation committee since 1960, and in 1993, the Orkney Island Council has taken the responsibility of its protection. .
30. War reruns appear rather in the football field, and the question about whether you are willing to die for your country is transposed into the pitch. During

the World Cup of 1994, London was riddled with nationalistic displays of allegiance and division. Italians of all creeds flew their flag and rooted for their country. The football field has become the place where nationalistic claims and allegiances are embattled, and sometimes the source of tension for people who foster multiple senses of belonging. Indeed, the question can potentially be problematic, as Alberto Cavalli explained: 'If the Parma football club was to meet Arsenal, that will be something! What will the Italians do? If it was any other team than Arsenal, they would certainly go for Parma's team. But Arsenal, a London team. They wouldn't know who to cheer for!'

31. In 1943 an estimated 75 000 Italian prisoners of war were liberated, thousands of which stayed in Britain, recruited as manual labourers. Lucio Sponza considers that there were 150,000 Italian POWs in Britain at the end of the war (Sponza 1995).
32. The development of democratic rights in Italy, as elsewhere, interweaves with class and gender-based social differentiations. In Italy, universal male suffrage was introduced in 1918, and women first voted in 1946.
33. The contest no longer takes place for lack of response from young Italian women; Mr Bucci blames it on apathy. A similar contest apparently existed in Toronto, and ended for the same reasons (Harney 1998).

Part II
Spaces, Memories, and Displays of Identity

–4–

Space, Place, and Icons: Creating 'Habitual Spaces'

Mamma dami cento lire/che in America voglio andar

Italian folk song[1]

June 20 1993, lunch time, Centro Scalabrini in Brixton. Dressed in a white blouse and black skirt, I am reporting for duty. In order to access the Father's Day lunch organized by the *Club Donne Italiane* (CDI; Italian women's club), I volunteered to wait on tables. This was my first observation of a 'community function'.

That Father's Day was my first of a 'social whirl of dos' that was to last a year. June, pilgrimage and picnic. July, the Procession. August, summer holidays, clubs are 'dark'. September, grandparents' day lunch. October, Charity bingo. November, Armistice ceremony. December, Christmas party. January, *briscola* competition. February, Valentine's lunch. March, Easter lunch. April, CDI Quiz Night. May, *La Voce* Solidarity Banquet. To this day, I watch the months go by and recall which event might be bringing together Monica, Luisa, Silvia, Domenico, Roberto, Angelo,[2] Father Russo and Father Giandomenico (with his camera). The calendar of events frames the 'community' life. It punctuates it into a predictable, rhythmic continuity. Each year is much the same as the other. May, the banquet . . . June, the pilgrimage and the picnic . . . July, the procession . . . Each month, *Backhill* and *La Voce* record the events, with details of the themes, speeches, distinguished guests and, occasionally, the menu, all with the obligatory photographs.[3] This calendar of events, by virtue of its predictable and repetitive character, structures what may be labelled London Italian time. This is a textured time, layered with other events organized by regional or other kinds of organizations: February is the *Circolo Veneto*'s annual lunch;[4] March is the gala of the *Trinacria* Association (Sicilians in England); December, the *Trentini* Association.[5] Hence, the calendar also encloses a geographical reconstruction of Italian diversity, which all comes together in October, at the annual FAIE[6] dinner dance. Moreover, events may occur simultaneously in different parts of England: in Scotland, Wales or Nottinghamshire. London Italian time, then, is the product of the combination of temporal and geographical structures that are inscribed in a 'calendrical rhetoric of re-enactment' (Connerton 1992: 65): the structuring of the events, their calendrical organization into an incessant flow patterned into a predictable yearly timetable. The regular recording of these occasions in the local papers conveys a sense of connected dispersal of the Italian population living 'here' and 'there'. A series of interconnected movements and moments, some occasional others habitual, are framed by a calendrical logic that, year after year, provides a sense of continuity and stability.

Returning home from the Father's Day lunch, with aching feet and back, exhausted and hungry, I could not but admire all those volunteers who invest so much in 'community events'. The time and effort spent in keeping the 'community' alive is tremendous. Communality is not a natural outcome of an assumed shared identity. Women of the *Club Donne Italiane*, and men from the churches and numerous associations spend days organizing lunches, games, sporting events, daily excursions, travels abroad, and other gatherings that bring together, and indeed produce, the 'community'. These women, most of whom are volunteers, and men, some of whom are 'professional' community organizers, or 'cultural brokers' (such as the Scalabrinian priests), actively *create* the community, to repeat Giuseppe Giacon's phrase.

What initially struck me, however, is the closure of such activities. For a while after the Father's Day lunch, each of my visits to the Centro Scalabrini left me with a sense that the events were utterly fixed into stasis. Behind the closed doors, there seemed to be a life on the margins: on the margins of London, of England, of Italy, as well as on the margins of the daily working life of the patrons. In July 1993, I wrote the following entry in my field diary:

> It's as if, [in the realm] of the 'community' the past is encapsulated and re-lived through small packages, delimited in time and space. Enclaves of Italy, repeated, sporadically, like the beat to a tune, which keeps the rhythm. The beat, incessant, reliable, without which 'we are lost', without which the tune cannot be, without which 'our future' is compromised.

Life at the Centro takes place exclusively inside, invisible to the neighbouring Brixton residents, available only to a handful of people connected to each other through a close 'community' network. At first, this produced for me a sense that the place, the building was wrapped in an 'invisible pulsing membrane' (Myerhoff 1979: 5) that separates it from the immediate surroundings.

But this is indeed a 'pulsing' place. A place that vibrates, lives and is lived in ways that are continually redefined. Precisely because one crosses the building threshold to 'commune' with others, and to do so *as* Italians, the Centro is stasis *and* process at once; it is both fixed location and 'trembling space', to use once again Kathleen Stewart's telling metaphor (1996: 95). There is a constitutive tension between appropriating the Centro as a cultural object that is to be added to the elements cobbled together in the name of an identity project, and the incessant flows that constantly displace its symbolic boundaries and meanings. De Certeau's distinction between place as location and space as relational, is useful here. Space is the 'practised place', its acting out. It is 'composed of intersections of mobile elements. It is in a sense articulated by the ensemble of movements deployed within it' (de Certeau 1980/1990: 117). Linda McDowell makes a similar distinction, taking her cue from Raymond William's notion of 'structure of feeling': a *sense of place* centred on a specific territory. McDowell emphasizes 'that spaces and places are not only sets of material social relations but also cultural objects. Thus we must investigate not only patterns of flows but also the meaning of place, of place as absolute location, and of place as stasis, albeit with varying boundaries' (1996: 32).

In the pages that follow, I move between these two polarities – stasis and flow – that are part and parcel of the dual project of identity of place and identity of 'community'. The first two sections are devoted to the meaning of place: I examine the ways in which the Centro leaders (re)define the role of their organization in the face of the ebb and flow of London Italian life. I scrutinize their discourses as well as the manner in which the building itself has been shaped to express local particularity. What interests me here, are the forms of self-representation that circulate in the Centro Scalabrini and that construct its identity as a collective belonging. In short, I propose to unpack the ways in which the Centro and its church are defined as cultural objects; not only as spaces of belonging, but as places that belong to Italians.

In the third section, I turn to an examination of the *Club Donne Italiane* (CDI; Italian Women's Club), by way of questioning the identity claims made in the Centro. This is an analysis of forms of sociality that inhabit the space itself, and that complicate its boundaries, yet which operate through fixed definitions of modes of being.

From ethnic church to émigré church

The Centro Scalabrini of London is part of the Scalabrini congregation, an Italian missionary order founded in 1887 to minister mainly to Italian emigrants and their descendants around the world.[7] The Scalabrini order may be defined as diasporic: Scalabrinian fathers and sisters travel toward migrant 'communities' in order to provide them with pastoral and social care. Routes and roots intermingle as they seek to recreate a familiar environment in order to facilitate the smooth transition of migrants into a new social environment. These men and women are émigrés with a mission. What is more, the institution of the Church itself is figured as migrant. This is clearly illustrated in the Scalabrini vademecum: 'This is the mission that the Church has entrusted itself through the Founder, the bishop of Piacenza

Giovanni Battista Scalabrini: to make itself migrant with the migrants' (Missionari di San Carlo Scalabrini 1987).

Since its foundation in 1968, the Centro Scalabrini of Brixton has played a leading role in London Italian institutional life. Most of the present Italian organizations and associations of London were founded in the years following the 1939–45 war and many have emerged from the Centro. Apart from being a meeting place for a number of regional or other clubs and associations, the premises are often used for meetings or conferences about the life and destiny of the Italian 'community', gathering representatives from a number of different organizations. For these reasons, the Centro is commonly associated with what some still view as the 'new community' (Colpi 1991a), that is the immigrants who arrived after 1945.

Apart from the administration offices, the building houses the Italian Women's Club, a club for retirees, a youth club, and the Church of the Redeemer (*Chiesa del Redentore*). The organization also runs two hostels for students (one for men, one for women), a nursery, and a retirement home. The grounds of the retirement home, in Shenley, is the location for one of the biggest annual picnics of the London Italian 'community'.[8]

Four priests reside at the Centro in Brixton and share different religious and social responsibilities, including officiating masses not only in their own *Chiesa del Redentore*, but also in the parishes of Sutton, Lewisham, Croydon, Epsom and Walton on Thames. At the time of my closer involvement in the Centro, one of its leading priests was Gaetano Parolin. Father Gaetano lived in London for 20 years, from 1974 to 1994, most of which were spent in Brixton. In 1979, he took over the directorship of *La Voce degli Italiani*, succeeding Umberto Marin, and ran it until his return to Rome in 1994. As a result, Gaetano Parolin played a crucial role in shaping the life at the Centro and in defining its aims and directions.

Parolin spent his first years in England as an MA student in theology, at the University of Canterbury, where he completed a dissertation on the religious practices of Emilian emigrants in London (Parolin 1979).[9] This text provides interesting insights into the principles supporting the foundation of the Centro Scalabrini. According to Parolin's view – reasserted in my conversations with him in 1993–4 – the role of the 'ethnic community' is essential for the 'safe process of integration of immigrants into the host society', a process proceeding from a position of strength rather than the state of weakness and premature disruption resulting from migration (Parolin 1979: 131). It is, he argues, the role of 'ethnic associations' in general, and of the 'ethnic church' in particular, to provide the cultural resources and surroundings necessary to support immigrants in their adaptation to the alien environment. This position purports that the proper integration of immigrants requires resources available beyond the family realm. This point of view is shared by other Scalabrinians, such as Graziano Tassello, who emphasized the role of newspapers and missions in the creation of new identity for Italian 'invisible immigrants'. Tassello also co-authored a study on second generations Italians in Britain, in which he drew similar conclusions (Tassello and Favero 1976).

Key to this argument is that 'community' cannot be created from families alone. True to languages of civil society, Parolin seeks to consolidate the role of the church as a key institution in promoting, defending and fostering claims of peoplehood and self-determination. Given the centrality of family values in the Catholic ethos, however, what strikes me in Parolin's argument is his ambivalence toward the family, which appears as both a hindrance and a linchpin in the establishment of closer links between individual and communal senses of belonging.

The main finding of Parolin's MA study is that Emilians (like most Italian emigrants) practice a form of 'familistic religion'. That is, their religious practice is mainly connected to family related ceremonies of rites of passage (from christenings through weddings to funerals). As such, Parolin concludes that this form of religious practice 'will be fundamentally anchored to "memory" and become functional to family life' (Parolin 1979: 6). He opposes it to religious practices in rural areas of Italy, where the compactness of the village community provided a social support no longer present in emigration. Thus, '[r]eligious practices which had individualistic and social functions in the village now take on solely familistic roles leaving aside the social functions of religion' (Parolin 1979: 6). In other words, village churches were stages for nurturing a form of community awareness that seems to be withering away in the context of migration.

For Parolin, familistic religious practice signals a form of private devotion that isolates individuals from the 'community'. And for Italian children brought up in this way, this disconnection will intensify.

> Another trait typical of the religious personality of the Anglo-Italian youth is the scant community awareness and socio-political concern. Religion is confined to a private sphere and has not anything [sic] to do with other people's needs and social commitment . . . [T]he religious practice of the Italian young people almost entirely depends on the primary family acculturation and on personal choice once they have come of age. As they were born in England, they did not live the unifying experience between religious participation and social life which their parents lived at the village. (Parolin 1979: 80)

A feeling of uneasiness for private practice irradiates from Parolin's thesis. His discomfort with the privatization of religious practices by Italian emigrants is associated with his concern for the future of religious faith, on the one hand, and for the future of community awareness, on the other. Parolin distinguishes between the individualistic nature of 'traditional' forms of worship, and familistic forms of new practices of worship that emerge in the context of migration. The passage from rural Italy to metropolitan England, old to new, past to present, indeed of 'tradition' to modernity, is signalled by familyism, not individualism; but a familyism, here, which is viewed as acting against 'tradition' and which menaces communalization.

Parolin's disquiet may be partly understood as an expression of Catholicism's scepticism toward private religious practice. Before the demise of high ceremonies ratified by the Second Vatican Council in the 1960s, each person stood before God as an individual and was simultaneously joined to the others *in the institution,* through the priest. Catholics were institutional worshippers, not individualistic ones (Rodriguez 1983: 110). But a crisis of faith in Europe and North America motivated the Vatican to introduce changes in forms of worship that would 'popularize' religion and breakdown its stiff, hierarchical and authoritarian character. The use of vernacular languages (replacing Latin), pop music, 'rites of peace' where communicants exchange wishes of peace with a gentle handshake, were introduced to unite Catholics living in an increasingly non-Catholic world. As Richard Rodriguez points out, the display of collective worship not only left little space for private prayer, but concealed an increasing suspicion for it.

> To such Catholics – increasingly alone in their faith – the Church says: You are part of a community of believers. You are not single in your faith. Not solitary. We are together, Catholics. *We* believe. We believe. We believe. This assurance is necessary because, in a sense, it no longer is true. (1983: 106; emphasis original)

In migration, we might think that saying 'we believe' in 'our' language would add an additional power of communalization to collective prayer. But Padre Parolin's findings speak of a real tendency within the Italian population of London to attend an 'Italian' church only for special, family events. When it comes to religious affiliation, a large number of Italian immigrants feel part of a wider, transcultural 'community' of Catholics. No matter in which language they utter the 'Hail Mary', they are happy to attend their local church; the important thing is to have a place to pray as Catholics in Britain. This was a common view among those I met throughout my study.

In this context, what becomes of the role of the 'ethnic church'? For Parolin, and many of his colleagues, its role is to create a community, and to sustain it (Tassello and Favero 1976). Ethnic church-cum-centres are spaces for (re)constructing communities by aggregating members of the same 'ethnic group'. They are 'institutions where the old environment is somehow recreated' (Parolin 1979: 73), where Italian emigrants will find an 'Italian atmosphere' (Parolin 1979: 132). This, in their view, is what distinguishes 'ethnic' churches from local Irish Catholic or Anglican churches. Parolin argues that 'ethnic churches' place less emphasis on religious beliefs and more on the possibility of expressing beliefs in a way familiar and habitual to immigrants. Ethnic churches 'shelter' the ethnic group from assimilation, while securing a smooth transition into the 'host' society. In an interesting combination of attachment and movement, the 'ethnic church' is presented as a bridge, enabling newcomers to 'remain ethnic' in the integration process. Luigi Favero, former Superior General, reiterates this position in a booklet of the London Centro Scalabrini published in 1993. He asserts that the Centro is 'a space open to all Italians living, working, studying in London . . . a space for Italians to meet with their own roots and traditions, with other *compaesani*, to find again the identity and the warmth with which to confront the great cold of the anonymous city' (Centro Scalabrini di Londra 1993: 23).[10]

The perception is that it is the role of these institutions to enhance and reproduce ethnic religious practices, thus to reinforce the sense of belonging to, and inheritance of, a particular ethnic background. Parolin joins his voice to those of most of the men and women I interviewed in London, especially clergymen, who view their role in terms of social responsibility and *re*production rather than in terms of producing new forms of identity. Yet in the face of great indeterminacy about the definition of the London Italian 'community' in general, and the future of the Scalabrini Centre in particular, the priests are seeking to re-define their purpose. Giandomenico Ziliotto, Parolin's successor as editor of *La Voce*, speaks of this period as one of the 'crisis of civil society', where organizations are increasingly out of touch with the people. Conflicting views compete in attempts to reconfigure the Centro's and the missionaries' purpose in the face of social changes. Throughout this debate, the key issue remains to solve the indeterminacy and fragmentation of the Italian collectivity, and by extension, to ensure a future for the Centro, which Ziliotto declares possible by deploying the centre's 'creative capacity to create a community'.[11] The object is to create a community that would constitute a pole of aggregation for the disparate Italian population. But it is also about creating a collective identity, a narrative of coherence that stitches together the different segments of the 'community'. As testified in Graziano Tassello's speech on the invisible immigrants (see Chapter 1), identity is a feasible project for these men who are intent on using their position and their missions as 'instruments for a new identity' (LV 831, October 1990: 15).

My purpose, here, is to examine how the manufacturing of this identity entails the shaping of physical spaces into mirrors of who 'we' are, on the one hand, and the creation of subjects, on the other. In light of the ongoing redefinition of the centre's purpose, I shall revisit what Parolin sees as the *re*production of a culture, and explore the ways in which this particular place embodies the project of identity. What interests me here is the way in which the materialization of culture takes on multiple forms: from turning physical buildings and spaces into cultural objects, to images of human bodies as symbols of collective identity. In line with a growing catalogue of work on how bodies, artefacts and places are used as instances of collective memory and symbols of continuity (Rowlands 1996/97 for short overview; also Gillis 1994a; Boyarin 1992; Young 1993; Savage 1994; Radley 1990), I want to raise here the ways in which the materialization of places as/of belonging results from a combination of competing definitions of history and presence, as well as from the circulation of different lives and experiences of identity. For instance, how can a place, a physical building where individual bodies circulate, come to embody collective memory in the same way as a monument can? In a recent article, Gaetano Parolin used the phrase 'habitual space' to qualify the Centro/Chiesa (LV 967, February 1997: 5). This phrase captures the play of memory, body and materialization in defining, indeed fixing, an identity of a place. By this I mean that definitions of the identity of a place, in migration, are largely grounded on the interplay of remembrances and materializations. This is what I look for when I scrutinize what the Centro, as a cultural *object*, is made of.

In order for a place to be recognized as a 'habitual space', some kind of 'architecture of reassurance'[12] is required. That is that the material organization of space is such that it will interpellate its users and call upon them to 'feel at home' in the setting. This, at least, was the objective of the Scalabrinian priests when they had their church renovated. In the words of its conceiver, Aldino Albertelli, the church's interiors were restored in the Italian classical style 'to bind a Church loved by many of our community, to our history, to our cultural tradition' (Centro Scalabrini di Londra 1993: 9). For the church leaders, this represents 'the best of our culture, that the community, and particularly the younger generations, *could proudly identify with* in front of the English. It is an accomplishment worthy of the fantasy, enterprise and generosity of the Italians who live in South London' (Centro Scalabrini di Londra 1993: 9; my emphasis). The church is a space where these leaders express and hope to transmit the purpose and pleasure of their selves as Italians in London. It is objectified as a distinct marker and *expression* of the Italian presence in South London, standing at the junction of identity/difference, at once locating and projecting Italians in relation to English culture and in relation to themselves. England emerges as the 'significant other' which is located outside, yet which surrounds, thus includes, the church and Centro. Consistently represented as a hostile environment – 'the great cold of the anonymous city' – where Catholics are but a 'small minority' who must proudly display their cultural heritage 'in front of the English', Britain is also coveted as the necessary, indeed unavoidable site of integration. There is a narrow clearing for the establishment of a 'habitual space', or comfort zone, where the projected identity can be at once different *and* integrated. For the Scalabrinians, the challenge is to provide such a space that draws individuals outside of the privacy of family life and fosters a communal sense of belonging in Britain. The inauguration of the new church, in December 1993, provided the opportunity to lay down the new grounds of Italian émigré belonging in present-day Britain: an idealized form of belonging born out of, and liberated from, migration.

The church's inauguration coincided with the Centro's 25th anniversary, which was marked by a series of events spread out over a seven-day period. During this momentous week, the Centro re-assessed its role and, more importantly, asserted its ecumenical character. This, in my view, signalled a shift away from the idea of 'ethnic church' toward the 'émigré church', in an attempt to solve the religious anxieties about the future of the Italian Catholic faith in London. More importantly, the inauguration of the new church coincided with an attempt to re-orient the meaning of this location in order to adapt it to new social parameters that the 'fathers of emigrants' now have to deal with. A striking feature of this shift is the combination of continuity and change, indeed of permanence and evanescence, in the meanings projected onto the church. The church stands namely as a symbol of defiance against the detractors and objectors to the initial project of its construction, who contended that emigration is provisional and the emigrants need assistance only in the early years of their arrival. For the Scalabrinian fathers, who maintain that emigration is continuous but changing, the issue is not whether to have a church or not, but to reassess its pastoral structure and methods (Centro Scalabrini di Londra 1993: 6).

The essence of the Scalabrinian project remains the same as that expressed by Marin in his monograph of 1975: to emancipate emigrants from the forever-foreigner condition. Thus the very foundation of the Centre is explained in these terms:

> Residing in a nation where Catholics are a small minority, and with ecumenical sensibility, we thought to dedicate [the church] to the Redeemer under whom all, at least all Christians, may and must find themselves, thus cancelling the notion of *foreigner.* On the façade, alas rather modest, is a mosaic of Jesus-Christ *Pantokrator* who holds the globe in one hand, symbolising Christian universalism which is a fundamental instance of the migrant people. (Centro Scalabrini di Londra 1993: 6; italics original)

In line with their political discourse, the Scalabrinians ground the identity of the church and the 'community' in the drama of emigration. Emigration is the recurring theme running through the images displayed in the church. It is located as a point of departure in a project of continuity, change and liberation. 'People do not know where they are going, if they ignore where they are from', writes Umberto Marin (Centro Scalabrini di Londra 1993: 7). The drama of emigration, however, is not a site for indulging in nostalgic recollections or for dreaming of mythical returns; there is no going home. Emigration is rather retrieved in images that shape a new kind of belonging and entrust individuals with the 'courage of the future' (Centro Scalabrini di Londra 1993: 7). Emigration is re-articulated in the constitution of a new, localized, yet deterritorialized identity. Hence the very grounds on which the church is built are made of different versions of remembrances. The earlier ethnic church rose from the necessity to provide a space of comfort, a stage for Italian kinds of sociality re-enacted by recently arrived immigrants. Today, the émigré church has become a habitual space, where people are enjoined not so much to remember, but rather to 'unforget' the drama of emigration. That is to say that emigration is not merely recovered in a master narrative that aligns a series of anecdotal moments in the story of collective growth. Unforgetting, as Kathleen Stewart views it, is an inversion of the 'hierarchy of concept over event', idea over example (1996: 80). Emigration, here, is retrieved as a mode of being and a mode of knowing in itself.

This is where Scalabrinians diverge from their own political discourses of identity. Emigration here acquires a special significance as a result of its association with religious languages and beliefs. This entails a move away from nationalist forms of territorialization and localization, toward the universalist idealism of Christianity. The émigré, here, is emphatically abstracted from any material context, indeed from any material body. Emigration is deployed in a discourse of liberation that re-inscribes the 'empowering paradox of diaspora' (Clifford 1994: 322) within a project of transcendence. Yet the project is given substance in material representations that are not so disruptive of master narratives of history, or of modern forms of knowledge. In response to Kathleen Stewart, I want to excavate the social grounds of unforgetting. What I suggest is that the deep discomfort associated with the émigrés' 'foreignness' expresses itself through the project of transcendence, which is idealized in masculinist terms. I want to develop this point further by way of returning to the pictorial narrative of migration that is displayed in the church's premises.

Travel metaphors and the iconography of transcendence

Picture it. You are walking through the double doors of the Chiesa del Redentore. Its classical interiors are sober, simple. Corinthian pillars align each side of the vaulted nave. In the lateral walls, four stained-glass windows filter the sunlight in colourful strands that dot the pews and floor with speckles of red, blue and yellow. Small round windows are inserted in the nave vault. The stations of the cross are niched along the alley walls. The marble alter stands at the front of the church. All seems reduced to a small scale and free from the burden of the ornate decorations of so many Catholic churches.

But on a first visit, the discreteness and details of the church interiors may easily go unnoticed, eclipsed by the large fresco that dominates the altar in lieu of the usual crucifix (Plates 1 and 3). A male figure, young, white, muscular, arms stretched out in a cross, hovers against a sky-blue backdrop, the colour of God. His head is hanging sideways, eyes closed. His face expresses both pain and rest. He is naked except for a piece of cloth wrapped around his hips, covering his genitals. His feet are crossed and marked with blood stains. Above him, an opening echoing those of the vaulted ceiling, is painted in trompe-l'oeil; light floods through it, seemingly drawing the floating body upwards.

The most striking feature of this painting is the truncated body: arms, legs, torso and head are sliced so that we see the blue backdrop in the spaces left by the missing parts. But despite its fragmented state, the body occupies the space as a whole, unified body.

Few have not been taken by this awesome representation of the crucifixion. Indeed, it was the subject of many whispers, frowns and smiles among the parishioners, for some time after its unveiling. My friend Monica[13] disapproved because Jesus is 'too muscular'. Luisa,[14] for her part, likes it simply because it is different and certainly powerful. To her, it is 'very symbolic' and captures both the vulnerability and strength of Jesus. In any case, she appreciates how 'it definitely doesn't leave you indifferent.'

This figure is remarkable for many reasons. Firstly, it emphasizes the human, physical, bodily nature of Jesus. Though such 'manly' representations of Christ are not new (Morgan 1996), this depiction nevertheless contrasts starkly with the suffering, slim, weak crucified body most often seen in Western Catholic churches. Secondly, the fresco breaks away from the traditional crucifix by leaving out the cross, a gesture that enhances both the suffering and spiritual strength of Jesus. Hence the fresco further troubles traditional Catholic representations of the crucifixion by suggesting the strength of hope and redemption, rather than overemphasizing the suffering and pain of an earthly life of sacrifice.

The fresco constitutes a highly resonant background motif for an émigré religious organization that is juggling with the project of creating unity in dispersal. Deemed postmodern by Gaetano Parolin, this fresco symbolically captures 'the present day search for unity in the face of increased fragmentation' (Centro Scalabrini di Londra 1993: 9). It also seizes all that the Scalabrinian fathers are striving for: unity with multiplicity, without forgetting suffering, aspiration and hope. Finally, in the present period of transition, the choice to replace the former wooden crucifix with the fresco signals a turning point in the mandate that the London Scalabrinians are defining for themselves.

More importantly, the fresco constitutes a striking version of bodily representations of collective identity. On the night of the Centro's 25th anniversary choir concert, Padre Giandomenico Ziliotto deemed the Calvary as '[t]he most dramatic story of migration'. For Umberto Marin, the crucifixion is 'the image that best represents that which animates the emigration event: sufferance and hope' (Centro Scalabrini di Londra 1993: 6). The body of Jesus, in this respect, epitomizes the émigré condition.

Migration, travel, movement, permeate the Scalabrinian discourse and make migration the inaugural moment in the formation of a future community. These travel metaphors operate in emphatically masculinist and patriarchal terms, replete as they are with male figures of migration: Padre Scalabrini and his spiritual heirs, the 'fathers' of emigrants; the Calvary; or the colour print hanging in the social club representing a man walking away, head down, shoulders slightly hunched to convey a sense of sadness. The caption is a passage from the Bible: 'I was a foreigner and you welcomed me'.

Redemption from foreignness is likewise represented in male and patrilineal terms. The Pentecostal 'fraternity' (sic), for instance, the subject of another stained glass window in the church, stands as the paradigmatic figure of inter-cultural encounters that result from emigration.

> The experience of human migrations is a stimulus and a recall to the Pentecostal fraternity, where differences are harmonised by the Spirit and charity lives through welcoming the 'other'.
>
> We are called, as Church amongst migrants, to contribute to the emergence of a new world, open to the experience of the gift God made in the person of his Son, denouncing the inhuman world of forced migrations as expressions of relations of interest and exploitation, and announcing and testifying to the absolute gratuitousness of God. From migrations themselves come the call for a concrete and symbolic mobility, which breaks all structures of rigidity and of absolutism: Exile always precedes the Ascension, which prepares for the Pentecost. (Scalabrini Order vade-mecum in Centro Scalabrini di Londra 1993: 13)

It bears repetition that central to the Centro's aims is to go beyond the drama of emigration. Viewed as a 'one of the most complex and dramatic events of history' (Pope John-Paul II in Centro Scalabrini di Londra 1993: 12), or a 'social calamity' which has reached 'breathtaking proportions' (Umberto Marin in Centro Scalabrini di Londra 1993: 6), emigration is not fossilized into a 'tradition' to be re-enacted ad nauseam as the ultimate symbol of collective belonging. The purpose of the church, rather, is to overcome this drama, to transcend it. 'In emigration', states Umberto Marin, 'the Holy Mass . . . represents the major force of aggregation and liberation' (Centro Scalabrini di Londra 1993: 5).

The image of Christ, in this respect, speaks volumes of the ideal of transcendence that operates through a tense relationship with the body. 'The body of Christ, crucified, real man, in tension because it signals sufferance . . . is invaded by God's blue which alleviates it, transforms it, exalts it, enlivens it . . . Crucified Christ is real man, constituted by God, in the mystery of death and resurrection, real Son of God' (Centro Scalabrini di Londra 1993: 9). This visual depiction of emigration-as-Calvary speaks of the hope of transcending the suffering body. In the fresco, the power of God manifests itself not within nor through the body, but in its absence. In line with Western philosophical thought, transcendence is the attainment of a higher sphere of knowledge that is liberated from the immediate materiality of the body, and it is associated with men (Lloyd 1984; Massey 1996). It is opposed to immanence, which Massey refers to as 'static living-in-the-present' (1996: 113). Equally, the opposition between transcendence and immanence, in Catholicism, operates through the figures of Jesus and Mary. In the following chapter, I explore the link between the worship of Mary and collective displays of presence. But in the Centro Scalabrini, in contrast to St Peter's, the project is one of liberation, of moving into a higher, metaphysical realm of being, where the burden of the suffering body – Christ the 'real man' – is 'exalted' by the touch of God.

The Italian émigré identity is perhaps deterritorialized and disembodied insofar as it is projected in a realm beyond the reaches of daily experiences, desires and struggles, but it is also undeniably embodied as it is deployed, firstly in a place which is reified as the material expression of cultural specificity and local particularity, and secondly within a discourse of migration-as-transcendence that is materialized in representations of male bodies. In Chapter 2, I showed how a teleology of sacrifice places patriarchal authority at the centre of a system of generational responsibility. Similarly, the theological discourse of migration casts the conditions of possibility of redemption along masculine lines of descent. Lines of continuity and belonging originate in the life of Jesus, the son of God made 'real man'. His life, here, is retold in terms of migration: from the Flight to Egypt,[15] deemed the 'first drama of emigration' (Centro Scalabrini di Londra 1993: 13), to the crucifixion.

Religious language provides a legitimacy that significantly appears to be above politics and beyond the present. It has the power to sanctify and to universalize cultural behaviours and social injunctions, rendering them somewhat timeless and spaceless. A new migrant Christianity now appears as a 'new ethnicity' (Hall 1988) ideally uniting people from different national, cultural or class backgrounds. In this project, the church, the physical building, becomes a place to call home, a space of familiarity that joins people in the metaphysical realm of 'fraternal' kinship as children of God. It is, in other words, shaped to 'reflect' and display Italianness as well as to project the drama of emigration into an other-worldly realm of belonging. This 'church among migrants' is a site of 'global localism' (McDowell 1996: 31), that is that it stands at the crossroads of different ranges of belonging located on different spatial scales. The very shift from 'ethnic church' to 'émigré church' creates a terrain of belonging that both maintains and exceeds the boundaries of immediate locality. This is a belonging that is at once local – being Italian and Catholic in a non-Italian, non-Catholic world – and global – being part of the world 'community' of Catholic/Christian migrants.

In addition, the project of visibility is pronounced through the modality of invisibility. First, representations of collective belonging are confined within the walls of a building, to be seen primarily by the migrants themselves, hence 'invisible' to 'others'. Second, they are deployed within a pseudo-universalist rhetoric of 'invisible' masculinity that needs not to be qualified for it stands for humanity. The pseudo-universality and impartiality of Christian fraternity constitutes a logic of identity that denies and represses the social relations of power that construct categories of identity/difference. Though I do not propose a research or analytical practice that reconstructs absolute difference, I want to question, here, the very assumptions of universality inscribed within this religious discourse. Moving away from iconographic narratives, I now explore how the Centro is a *lived* space, occupied and contested differently by differently positioned subjects.

Club Donne Italiane and the definition of 'italian woman'

The projected 'community' is in fact many and divided along a variety of lines that criss-cross in the centre's basement, known as 'the club'. The weekly flow of people and groups that use the place on a regular basis is structured along generational and gendered lines: Tuesdays, women's club;[16] Wednesdays, lunch for retirees; Fridays, youth club. These vectors, in turn, are inhabited by individuals with different memories of 'being' Italian in England. Many of those who lived in London during the war years remember the hatred and humiliation they suffered as Italians, which younger men and women have no experience of whatsoever. Post-1973 immigrants have a different experience of circulating freely between countries and jobs from those who arrived under bulk recruitment schemes in the 1950s. People from different regional and class backgrounds mix and mingle during the number of events that take place in the club. Hence different kinds of sociality prevail in the Centro Scalabrini, resulting from different experiences of, and identifications with, the 'drama of emigration'. By way of exploring different forms of 'being' Italian, I focus on the *Club Donne Italiane* (CDI) – also known as the 'Ladies club' – where I encountered a definition of 'Italian woman' that both collides with and fits in the Centro's grand narrative about the universal émigré subject.[17]

As I explain in the opening chapter, it was through my links with the Women's Club that I accessed the London Italian 'community' life. To many of my first interlocutors, during the preliminary stages of my study, it seemed only 'natural' that I join the women's club, as opposed to, say, St Peter's Social Club which is very much a men's club. Yet I did not slip painlessly into the CDI. My gender, in other words, did not dissolve the distance between myself and these women: 'being a woman and being with women is not necessarily the same thing' (Probyn 1993: 32). As I wove my way, and my 'self', through the 'field-world' (Harstrup 1992) that resulted from my relations with these women, I grew increasingly aware of the negotiable character of gender. Likewise, it soon became clear the 'Italian woman' is multiple and varied. Differences of class, status, migration experience, ethnic identification, criss-cross the CDI's social fabric. Members of wealthy business families, workers in catering services, professionals, academics, or housewives, will meet for choir practice, the mad-hatters' Easter party or an Italian beer tasting evening. Some women barely speak English, others are fluent in English, Italian, and perhaps an Italian dialect, or even another language. Women born in England, others born in Italy, others born elsewhere (Spain, Greece, Canada), will relate to Italian culture and the 'homeland' in different ways. Some are of Italian parentage, others of mixed ancestry: Italian-English, Italian-Scot, French-Scot, and so on. The women identify differently as Italians, British-Italian, or as the British, English, Scottish, Greek, or Spanish wife of an Italian man. Some women have children, some do not; some have grandchildren. Some travel to Italy several times a year, some only once, some not at all. In short, under the veil of 'Italian woman', are multiple lives and negotiations that complicate the meaning of 'Italian womanhood'.

Nonetheless, the *Club Donne Italiane* seeks to promote 'the identity and role of the woman [sic] within the family and the Italian community and other charity organisations' (CDI statute; my translation). In line with the general object of this study – which, it bears repetition, focuses on institutional representations, not individual experiences – what interests me here is the kind of 'Italian woman' that is 'promoted' and produced in the CDI, and how it connects with the broader project of Italian specificity.

During my first evening at the CDI, Antonia asked me why I chose to study Italians, to which I replied that I wanted 'to study a European minority in Britain'. 'Minority?' Antonia exclaimed. 'We're not a minority. We're well integrated, we speak English, our children studied here, we've got good jobs. We're not a minority.' Antonia's remark alerted me to the ways in which being an Italian in London may be lived differently by different people, and how institutional forms of representation may be contested.

Antonia had other opportunities to voice her disagreement, namely on the two evenings when I presented some of the findings of my study to the CDI.[18] Both times, when I broached the Scalabrinian discourses of emigration as a founding principle of shared belonging, reactions quickly surfaced and rose in an animated debate about the accuracy of this label that was foisted upon them. '*I* don't consider myself an immigrant. I live here, I'm English.' 'How can I define myself? My children are British. I'm Spanish. My husband is Italian.' 'I'm just an Italian who lives in London, I feel at home here and in Italy. I'm not an immigrant, and I'm not an emigrant'. 'We *are* emigrants, whether we like it or not.' 'And why do they spend so much time fighting for our voting rights in Italy *anyway*? I'd like them to fight for our rights here, in Britain. I've been here 20 years and I still can't vote.' At this point they all agreed.[19]

As I listened and engaged with the women, it seemed to me that in the midst of the animation surfaced an anxiety to belong. The energetic rebuttal of 'emigration' as a defining trait of collective identity goes hand-in-hand with a fear of being marginalized. In a country and continent where 'immigrant' means black and foreigner, some of these women refuse to be pushed to the margins of belonging in Britain – just like the 'young' migrants discussed in Chapter 2. As Europeans who move freely between two countries, who cross borders without hassle, who are organically integrated in the British social and economic fabric, these women's experience of migration is not that which is associated with 'immigrants' or 'emigrants'. At once foreigners – culturally and politically – and no-longer-immigrants, they are searching for a vocabulary that would adequately define their modes of living, their senses of identity, and, more importantly, that would not emphasize their marginality in British society.

For some women, the anxiety may be little more than semantic. But other women's experience of immigration has produced a lived anxiety that results from a deep sense of isolation. Consider Micaela, who had an air of sadness and loneliness in her eyes that barely dissipated when she smiled. Married to an Englishman for over 20 years, she confided in me that she enjoyed the CDI evenings because they were 'like home', a place where she did not have to explain herself or who/what she is, in contrast with her own household in the working class English suburbs of South London, where her loneliness was compounded, she felt, by her life with her husband and two sons. That night, she disappeared a few minutes after our conversation, after explaining apologetically that she did not want to keep her husband waiting that extra minute that would make him angry. Each subsequent meeting, she would greet me with a powerful hug, and we would sit down and 'have a natter'.

One of the motivations supporting the foundation of the women's club in 1988 was precisely to offer some momentary comfort to women like Micaela. The story of the club begins in 1973, when Umberto Marin approached Luisa to join the school committee in order to fill the need for a woman's voice. She joined and found at first that she was a 'pleasant ornament'. 'Oh, I was good to serve coffee and all that, but my opinions were no more than cute.' She nonetheless fought to get her ideas through, until they were heard as valid opinions in their own right. From then on, she says, she was included as 'one of them'.

In 1984, Luisa joined the fund-raising committee for the Villa Scalabrini retiring home. As the campaign was going rather slowly, she suggested to create a sub-committee with women only. She gathered nine women from her circle of friends and acquaintances, and the 'Villa Scalabrini Ladies Committee' was founded. They raised close to £30,000, thanks to a variety of activities and events that were anything *but* dinner-dances, the institutionalized 'social do' which 'may be good for high brow mundanities, but not so efficient for fund raising', as Silviana, a regular at many such events, once said to me.

In 1988, the CDI was set up to develop, promote and advance its goals: to reach out to the women who were house-bound and isolated, and to educate women into associative life – 'to give them the ability and confidence to speak up in community politics' in the words of Luisa – and to promote 'the potential role of the Italian Woman [sic] in our community.' To be sure, the CDI plays an important role in London Italian associative life. Thanks to its fund-raising activities – a biennial sponsored walk, and annual *briscola* competition (see further on in this chapter), quiz-night and gala-charity bingo – the CDI has donated funds to St Peter's church, and to the Centro/Chiesa. The CDI also holds Sunday lunches for Mother's day, Father's day, Grandparents' day, Valentine's day. These seemingly mundane events play a significant role in 'making' the community and sustaining the very *raison d'être* of the Centro Scalabrini. Finally, the CDI is perhaps the most 'visible' Italian organization outside of the Italian 'community'. As a registered charity, the focus of which is the welfare of babies and young children, the 'ladies', as they call themselves, are in regular contact with non-Italian institutions (hospitals or other charities), to whom they represent themselves as distinctly Italian.

In 1997, the women's club had over 300 members, only a small number of which attended the CDI's meetings on a regular basis. At the time of my regular involvement with the CDI (1993–95), weekly meetings were divided in two parts. The first hour was devoted to a form of collective exercise: yoga, keep fit, or the like, during which time those who did not participate could sit around and talk in the bar area. The second hour, after tea break, was devoted to talks, presentations, demonstrations, videos, and so on. During my two years of regular attendance, the topics ranged from Italian cooking to Italian classic architecture, art classes, and 'an evening with a difference' in the company of none other than Jeremy Beadle.[20] Other themes revolved around the care of the self: Avon products; hair removal ('Sugaring: take the "ouch" out of hair removal'); women's health; and fashion shows. And it is here, I argue, that ideals of femininity were repeatedly performed and its fields of constraints delineated.

One such event encapsulates the complex social dynamics inherent in what may be best referred to as the 'work of femininity' (Winship in Lury 1997: 134) within the CDI. The event was a presentation on 'making your wardrobe work for you', by Laurel Herman, who sells second-hand designer clothes – which she buys from 'friends' – and offers consultations on 'making good use of your wardrobe.' The presentation was set up like a stage play, with a basic plot that served the purpose of illustrating how one can creatively put a few clothes items to appropriate use for different occasions. Herman introduced the story as a 'fairy tale': it was about a business woman travelling to New York for three days. On the plane, she meets a man whom she then sees while in New York. Consequently, aside from her tightly scheduled business meetings and lunches, she is invited to a wedding, a 'high-class dinner', and a concert. Throughout the performance, the female character moves swiftly between social events, transforming her appearance with the help of a few accessories, with the soundtrack from *New York, New York* in the background. Slight alterations to the make-up, and a light teasing of the hair completed each transformation. Predictably, the story concluded with the marriage proposal.

Herman's performance was steeped in the view that now dominates the representation of women in relation to consumption: women are invited to consider 'their own lives as their *own* creation' (Lury 1997: 134; emphasis original). This is linked to the growing importance of the 'work of femininity'. That is to say that women are increasingly interpellated as agents who, in order to measure up, in order to be loved, must work on their bodies and appearance to achieve the goal of respectable femininity (Skeggs 1997). This work of femininity, moreover, operates in relation to the institution of heterosexuality: though he is physically absent, the male onlooker is central to Herman's entire plot, and he is presumed to be white and economically 'well-off'. The whole purpose of creatively 'working' your wardrobe is defined in relation to the white, 'successful', male onlooker. And the 'success' of the performance is asserted by the marriage proposal.

But while femininity is performed for the ideal male spectator, it is also performed for a female audience. As we watched Herman's show, clapping to each new outfit, we were not only taught some basic fashion 'skills', but we were also invited to look at the 'feminine' woman, and to look at her being looked at by the omnipresent male. We were taught to look as well as to be looked at (Lury 1997: 146). In this respect, this was a resolutely postmodern fairy tale, where women are at once objectified by the male gaze, and active participants in this objectification (Lury 1997: 143).

This tale may be read as a metaphor for the way that the CDI operates in relation to the omnipresent male gaze, insofar as the CDI 'is' what its administration committee makes it. Keeping 'our' men happy was an integral component of the CDI's life. Once a year, the committee members prepare an elaborate meal for their husbands to 'thank them for letting us out once a week', as Anna explained (without irony). In addition, the women have recently accepted to include men in some of their short weekend trips, because some husbands had complained that they felt 'left out'. While some women perceived this as 'giving in', others accepted it as a necessary accommodation in order to maintain harmonious relationships within both community and family. Whether the women legitimate the power of masculinity, or whether they trivialize it and 'keep it in its place' by keeping the men happy, is hard to say. The point is, however, that the club operates under the surveillance of the male gaze: men feel licensed to comment on what the women are up to, and women are called upon to respond.

Moving back to Laurel Herman's show, a key feature of her performance is that it reveals the imitative character of femininity: the repeated acts of femininity effectively reveal that femininity is not a 'natural', 'instinctual' given, but rather a carefully constructed appearance that can be displayed. The imitative structure of gender leads Judith Butler to suggest that 'all gender is like drag, or is drag, [that is] that "imitation" is at the heart of the *heterosexual* project and its gender binarisms, that drag is not a secondary imitation that presupposes a prior and original gender, but that hegemonic heterosexuality is itself a constant and repeated effort to imitate its own idealization' (1993: 125; emphasis original). To be sure, the 'work of femininity' is effective when it covers the conventions, and indeed the effort and repeated rehearsals, to create the appearance of a natural, fixed identity. But the class and race inflections of respectability reveal that if *all* gender is like drag, not all gendered subjects have equal access to the necessary resources to effectively pass.

Laurel Herman's display was deeply entrenched in class conditions that positioned her, and her clientele, as distinctly 'well-off': from her friends who sold her the second-hand designer clothes, to offering consultations about how to use your 'wardrobe' (one needs to *have* a 'wardrobe' to begin with), her location in Hampstead, and the fairy tale about a jet-setting business woman, all came together to create clear definitions about 'tasteful' and respectable femininity. As the show came to an end, Laurel Herman concluded by stating: 'If you wear quality clothes, no one will ever imagine that the accessories are from the high street.' The distinction between high-street and designer labels relays class distinctions that shape definitions of femininity. As Beverley Skeggs argues, 'femininity requires the display of class dispositions' (1997: 100), suggesting that bodies bear the imprint of social class and produce a class informed version of femininity. And the necessary cultural and financial capital for the effective performance of respectable femininity is not equally available to all. This was clearly recognized by some women in the audience whose comments, during the performance, caught my attention: 'So far, she hasn't shown us anything under 100 quid!'; 'I could never afford that!'

Which is not to say that middle-class femininity is aspired to by *all* women of *all* classes, nor is it necessarily easier to perform by women from a middle-class background. 'I know nothing about labels and I don't give a damn!' 'I couldn't possibly look smart with a scarf wrapped around my chest!' Some woman choose to 'distinguish' themselves from the middle-class conventions, whether they have the economic resources or not. Hence while the category 'woman' is decidedly 'occupied, resisted, experienced and produced through processes of differentiation' (Skeggs 1997: 98), these processes are not necessarily based on class inequalities. They are also a matter of cultural distinctions that are not solely the prerogative of middle-class women.

But the point is that the CDI represents itself as ostensibly middle class. The CDI committee is dominated by middle-class women, including professionals, wives of Italian businessmen (some very successful), and 'honorary' members such as the wife of the Italian Consul General, and the Italian ambassador's wife, who is the club's patron. Also known as the 'Ladies Club', the CDI still fashions itself on ideas of respectability invested in this eighteenth-century term 'lady', which emerged alongside the formation of the ideal of femininity that was modelled on 'the habitus of upper classes, of ease, restraint, calm and luxurious decoration' (Skeggs 1997: 99). Today, the term remains inflected with ideas of refinement, elegance and superiority. As the OED puts it, a lady is 'a woman regarded as being of superior social status or as having the refined manners associated with this.' Hence the accepted label of 'ladies' further instantiates the idea that the CDI represents, and recruits, respectable women. This ideal dominates the overall way of 'being' in the Club, and establishes lines of distinction, and exclusion, that members need to negotiate. However performative it may be, what one does, and how one does it, may be the source of one's exclusion, which is often self-attributed.

Such was the case of a woman I saw only once, at a CDI weekly meeting. Standing on her own, in a corner, I noticed her observing us as we mingled and talked before the evening's main event. I went to her to introduce myself. She explained that she had come to the evening only because a friend had invited her (the friend had not yet arrived). But, she added, she is not a member of the CDI, nor did she want to be. When I asked her why, she simply explained that she did not get along with the 'posh' ladies, and preferred to join the group from the *Chiesa* for their activities. Her perception of the 'ladies' as 'posh' overrode the differences that existed among the membership itself, and led her to exclude herself from the CDI.

Class-inflected distinctions shape the overall character of the CDI. This is perhaps best exemplified by the Club's 'travel culture': each year, the committee organizes a trip to places like Thailand, Pakistan, China, Moscow or, as in March 1997, a long weekend in New York. For a number of the CDI members, especially committee members, these trips are the highlight of the club's calendar. While the trips constitute significant moments in consolidating ties between the women travellers themselves, they also produce exclusions between those who cannot afford the expense, and those who can; or between those who cannot take the time off from work, and those who have more freedom in the choice of their holiday time; or simply between those who are not interested, and those who get much enjoyment out of such travels in foreign countries. At the same time, the trips stand in contrast with other important CDI events, such as the charity Bingo or the sponsored walk. But though somewhat marginal, they occupy a significant space in consolidating a 'core culture' that is perceived as representing the CDI.

The CDI's travel culture brings the production of this 'community' of women outside of the Centro Scalabrini. More importantly, this is one of the key activities where the women represent themselves as Italian. The photographic recording of each trip always includes one group photo, foregrounded by the CDI pink banner bearing *Club Donne Italiane* in black lettering. It is interesting to see how these trips abroad constitute an opportunity to reinstate the women's ethnic specificity. Away from 'home', as it were, Italianness and femininity are brought together, and subsequently brought back 'home' when printed in the pages of *La Voce*, inviting its readership to witness the display of Italian womanhood abroad.

Performances of femininity such as the ones described above are by no means specifically Italian, nor do the women from the CDI claim that they are. And the activities that are Italian – demonstrations of Italian cooking, Italian beer tasting, a talk on Italian classic architecture – are not about femininity. Hence some activities are about acquiring Italian cultural capital, and others are about the work of femininity. On the one hand, gender and race are articulated under the discursive conditions of class; on the other, gender and cultural ethnicity rarely meet. It bears repetition, however, that the central goal of the *Club Donne Italiane* is to promote the role of the 'Italian woman' in the community. Hence it may be argued that overall, the activities organized for the Club members serve to support an assertive femininity and act as resources for 'specifically feminine cultural competences' (Lury 1997: 150) that subsequently serve to revisit established definitions of 'Italian woman'.

In London Italian cultural life, gender differences operate through gendered uses of space, such as the Centro's social club, where men move rarely into the kitchen, and women do not sit at card tables. Unless, that is, they are participating in the CDI's annual *briscola* competition. *Briscola* is a card game from northern Italy. For southerners like Toni and his brother, the preferred game is *scopa* (literally meaning broom, 'for when we clear the table', as Toni explained). In a parody of the Italian north–south conflict, northerners and southerners continually tease each other, boasting the highly sophisticated skills required for 'their' respective game, and mocking the rules of the other as simplistic and childish.

According to the CDI's president, the aim of the competition is to encourage women to compete in this traditionally male activity, as a way of challenging the gender order of Italian cultural life. By inviting women to participate in this card game – and to prepare the *polenta*, which is what draws many male players to the CDI competition in the first place – the CDI is not only questioning the exclusion of women from the card game, but they are also performing another version of Italian womanhood: the woman card player, who can also cook *polenta*.

As an integral part of London Italian social life, card games are important cultural signifiers in the establishment of a specific gendered ethnicity. At every community affair I attended a number of men would inevitably gather at some point during the day and pull out the deck of cards for a few games. Occasionally, people would stand by, observing and commenting on the strategies of the players.

Like that day Robert, Silvia and I stood there, killing time while we waited for the rest of our group to arrive for Valentine's Day lunch. Robert, an Englishman, knows the rules of *scopa* inside out, yet he admitted that he wouldn't play because he's too slow to react. 'They've been at this game since they were children. They remember each card that comes out and know which are left. So they know in advance what you'll play.' Silvia added that Robert could not join these men in their card games because he would destabilize them by not playing the right cards. His ignorance of their 'ways', their manner of playing, their implicit codes, as it were, would disrupt the pace of the game. Using a language of 'acquired instinct', Robert effectively excludes himself from the game, respecting one of its key unsaid rules: outsiders (women and non-Italians) are not invited to play.

Card games, in Italian émigré social life, are cultural practices where a number of boundaries are played out at once – between north and south, Italianness and otherness, men and women. Card games become microcosms where multiple differences are performed and parodistically embattled. By challenging the male prerogative over this activity, the women of the CDI are thus questioning a complex web of social relations of power through which gendered ethnicities are established. This is not only about gender; it is also about *Italian* gender differences.

As I lingered there admiring the tarot-like cards, Toni approached me and set out to explain the difference between *scopa* and *briscola*.

> You see, normally, you have the jack, the queen and the king: 11, 12 and 13. But in our game [i.e. *scopa*], the Jack is worth more than the queen, because women in the South are worth less. We keep the women as they should be [he looked at me, smiling teasingly]. In the North, the queen is worth more than the jack, or the mother is worth more than the son. But in the south, any man is worth more than a woman [he laughed as I looked at him feigning anger].

What struck me in Toni's explanation was that the privileged metaphor to render cultural differences visible and comprehensible is gender. 'If you marry an Italian man, don't expect a modern man', I was warned by Monica one day, as the Villa Scalabrini picnic was coming to a close and we were waiting for 'the men' to finish their game of *scopa*. 'It's like that with Italian men. We wait for them, they say when it's time to go', she added as she was absently looking at the swift shifting of cards from hand to table to hand. And so Monica expressed her idea of cultural specificity through the neat entwinement of gender and ethnicity captured in the marriage trope. Monica conflated ethnicity and gender to separate 'modern' cultures from 'traditional' ones, clearly locating Italian culture in the latter. Monica's striking phrase – like Toni's metaphor – speaks volumes of the ways in which gender is the modality in which cultural specificity is represented, and, moreover, how it is the principle through which cultures are hierarchized within the modern world order. In addition, it mimics the *famiglia* teleology discussed in the introduction and Chapter 2, whereby gender and ethnicity are locked into each other through the marriage trope. A common narrative emphasizes the centrality of family ties in Italian people's lives: hence to be born in an Italian family is to be brought up within a 'domus-centred' culture (Orsi 1995; Goddard 1996), and to eventually reproduce it in your own family life. Family as teleological: the point of departure and the end point, fatalistically inscribing, and inscribed within, the Italian *modus vivendi*. This is a common feature of wider definitions of ethnic cultures: the folk knowledge that ethnic communities are inherently family based and, by extension, deeply homophobic (Takagi 1996).

'If you marry an Italian man, don't expect a modern man.' With these words, Monica was also expressing her conviction that I would, one day, marry. My marital status was indeed a point of curiosity, if not concern, for many of the women I was in regular contact with, especially during the first months of my research. In the women's club, I circulated as a young, white, middle-class, single, heterosexual woman and was perceived somewhat as an oddity because of my unmarried and 'unspoken for' status at the advanced age of thirty something. I was expected, however, to aspire to marriage and to look for a husband. I was never asked if I want to marry, let alone if I wanted to share my life with a man. In any case, whether I wanted to or not was not the point. It was, rather, that I was assumed to be a heterosexually desiring subject.

Assumptions such as this one signal the extent to which women's subjectivity is profoundly constructed through sexual categorization. While the women in the CDI were differentiated by class, they were normalized by heterosexuality. This was clearly spelled out in a talk given by Gaetano Parolin, in June 1993, at one of the CDI evenings. Entitled 'The morals of our time', the presentation (his second in a series of two) was about the Vatican's new position on sexuality. The priest explained that since the Second Vatican Council (1962–5), sexuality is no longer exclusively linked to procreation. It is rather considered an act of communion between two 'persons' (sic). A communion which is first and foremost essential to the foundations of a solid family unit. This communion is to be aspired to and consolidated before having children. From this, he drew the conclusion that sexuality is more important that procreation, and that the stigma attached to it as a sensual need no longer stands.

Running through this talk, and through the ensuing discussion, was the notion that heterosexuality is the only recognizable, acceptable, mentionable sexuality, indeed the 'only known way of speaking sexuality' (Skeggs 1997: 120). Furthermore, it is a sexuality that remains linked to procreation, as it is the founding basis for a stable family unit. As an act of intimacy through which the partners learn more about each other, sexuality constitutes an essential step in the building of a solid and stable family. If sensual desires and pleasures are now recognized, thus marking a slight shift away from traditional Catholic taboos related to 'desires of the flesh', sexuality remains linked to procreation, and sexual practices are policed and normalized according to this equation.

Parolin's talk constituted an instance where sexuality is framed in education. Assuming that the women are in need of basic advice to 'get it right', he regulated sexuality by maintaining heterosexuality through the process of exclusion, thus deploying sexuality along domains of constraint that set limits to what is unimaginable, unthinkable, unspeakable. In his rendition of the Church's position, Parolin re-instated that marriage and heterosexuality are inevitable, that marriage is the only acceptable future positioning, and that the deep and meaningful relationships involved in marriage and family life are so special that they cannot be experienced elsewhere (Skeggs 1997: 126).

It is this discursive context that surrounded the negotiations of my own sexual position in the CDI. As I describe in more detail elsewhere (Fortier 1996, 1998a), my gender ambiguity was *fixed* (both stabilized and mended) through projecting me as a heterosexual subject. I was repeatedly invited to perform heterosexual desire through the double act of looking and being looked at: nudging and winking as soon as a single man was spotted in one of the social events, or being asked to respond to 'the young man whose been eyeing you'. As Judith Butler says, 'there's a specific notion of gender involved in compulsory heterosexuality: a certain view of gender coherence whereby what a person feels, how a person acts, and how a person expresses herself sexually is the articulation and consummation of a gender' (1994: 36–7). For Butler, 'the injunction to *be* a given gender . . . takes place through discursive routes: to be a good mother, to be a heterosexually desirable object, to be a fit worker, in sum, to signify a multiplicity of guarantees in response to a variety of different demands all at once' (1990: 145). What I observed in the CDI, however, was that these injunctions were organized in a linear narrative. Though I was a 'young woman', I was yet to journey on the routes of accomplished womanhood: to be a heterosexually desirable object, a wife, a lover, a good mother. In sum, I negotiated a number of injunctions of womanhood that are not only multiple, but which are organized in sequence. Or, as Mary Melfi puts it in her own fictional account of being a 'proper' Italian woman: they are organized in ascending order, with motherhood placed as the ultimate achievement (1991: 117). This bears important implication on understanding identity as performative. If performative acts repeatedly produce what is seen to be natural, they are also lived as an organized sequence in individual lives. In other words, gender is lived, by these women, both as a narrative, with a beginning and an ending, and as performative, that is, produced in 'performative moments all along a process: repetitious, recursive, disordered, incessant, above all, unpredictable and necessarily incomplete' (Prosser 1998: 29–30). Ontological grounds of identity are thus deeply reliant on teleological narratives that secure and connect different and pre-determined states into a continuous line of 'becoming': 'the sexed body (female) as recognizable beginning and gender identity (woman) as clear-cut ending' (Prosser 1998: 29), which is ultimately *completed* in child-birth and motherhood.

Final remarks

The fictitious banner of 'Italian woman' draws limitations as to how women could 'be'. Although class-inflected definitions of femininity may have been contested, resisted or accommodated differently by different women in the CDI, the category of 'Italian woman' was normalized through middle-class consumer culture, whiteness and heterosexuality. The various sessions about the care of the self produced a class-informed version of respectable femininity that was captured in the self-ascribed label of 'ladies'. Whiteness, for its part, was accepted as a given, and reinstated as the unmarked, normative position from which to look at the world. And heterosexuality was explicitly lived as an organized sequence of 'becoming woman' that follows the predetermined teleological path that leads to the final accomplishment of gender: motherhood.

The life of the CDI slightly distorts the narrative of self-representation deployed by the Scalabrini fathers about the Centro Scalabrini and its church. The Centro/Chiesa is an enclosed space shaped by the retrieval of the past within a project of liberation and emancipation. It is a space where 'we' unforget where we come from (the drama of emigration) in order to entrust ourselves with the courage of who we are (Italian Christian emigrants), and where we are (part of a world religious community in south London). Here, memories rather than territory constitute the place of origin, the place where the redemptive project begins but does not end. Not only are origins not the homeland, but 'where we're from' is not teleological. As stated earlier, there is no going home. In sum, the very grounds of the Scalabrinian project of identity are shaped from remembrance and unforgetting, and are consequently deterritorialized. This, in my view, is the empowering potency of diaspora: its liberation from the necessary rootedness of origins in a single territory, or a single place. Here, origins are emphatically evanescent, even metaphysical.

However, the manner in which emigration is retrieved and circulated by the Scalabrinians also reveals the social grounds of difference that feed into the identity project. Both the identity of the émigré church and the project of 'community' are ossified within an iconography of migration-as-transcendence, which reprocesses emigration in a theology of liberation that operates in emphatically masculinist and patriarchal terms. These terms interpellate Italian women to conform to an ideal of Italian womanhood deeply entwined in definitions of femininity inscribed through discourses of heterosexuality.

In contrast to the Centro's neat entwinement of ethnicity (émigré culture) and gender (masculinist narratives of migration), however, connections between gender and ethnicity are much more tenuous in the CDI. Likewise, narratives of heterosexuality reinstate ontological securities about gender differences, without necessarily rendering them Italian specific. In the next chapter, I further explore the relationship between gender, sexuality and ethnicity, and reveal how bodies and spaces may be simultaneously gendered and ethnicized.

Notes

1. 'Mamma give me one hundred lire/for I want to go to America.' This song was included in the programme of the choir concert for the Centro's 25th anniversary, discussed further on in this chapter.
2. All names are pseudonyms.
3. Such details are usually found in *La Voce* rather than in *Backhill.* The latter usually provides a photograph with a short paragraph informing the readers of the nature of the event.
4. Veneto is a region in north-east Italy, bordering the Adriatic sea.
5. Trentino-Alto Adige is also a region in north-east Italy, bordering Austria and Switzerland.
6. Federation of Italian Associations in England (*Federazione Associazioni Italiane England*).
7. Though some 'missions' also cater to other Catholic migrants, such as Poles in Boston (Tomasi 1986) or Mexicans in Florida. In addition, apart from establishing 'ethnic churches' world wide, the order has a very active research culture. Scalabrinian-run research centres are found in Rome (*Centro studi emigrazione* – CRE), New York (Center for Migration Studies – CMS), and Buenos Aires (*Centro de Estudios Migratorios Latinoamericanos* – CEMLA). The journal *Studi Emigrazione/Études migrations* comes from the CRE, while the *International Migration Review* is issued by the CMS.
8. It competes in popularity with the picnic of the prestigious, though moribund, Mazzini-Garibaldi club for men. This club was founded in 1864, at the time of Garibaldi's visit to London, and succeeded a society of Italian workers which had existed since 1840, the Union of Italian Workers (*Unione degli Operai Italiani*) founded by Giuseppe Mazzini.
9. Emilians are from Emilia-Romagna, north-east Italy. The dissertation was written in English.
10. All excerpts from this booklet are my translations from Italian to English.
11. Padre Giandomenico Ziliotto made this statement on the evening of the Centro's 25th anniversary choir recital, 4 December 1993.

12. This was the title of an exhibition on Disney Land held at the Canadian Centre of Architecture in Montreal, 17 June–28 September 1997. The phrase referred to the re-creation of familiarity in a world of fantasy.
13. A pseudonym.
14. A pseudonym.
15. The Flight to Egypt is the subject of one of the four stained-glass windows of the Chiesa.
16. The women's club met weekly up until 1997. It now meets every fortnight.
17. Note that all women's names used hereafter are pseudonyms.
18. In November 1994 and April 1996.
19. Since then, Scalabrinians have slightly shifted their tack to consider more closely the position of Italians in Britain, and their political contribution. See the concluding chapter in this book.
20. Jeremy Beadle was a popular British television figure at the time, host of a weekly stunts show called *You've Been Framed*, a British version of the American *Candid Camera*.

–5–

Re-membering Places and the Performance of Belonging(s)

Gender is a project which has cultural survival as its end.

Judith Butler

Pattern is the soil of significance; and it is surely one of the hazards of emigration, and exile, and extreme mobility, that one is uprooted from that soil.

Eva Hoffman

When I first entered St Peter's Italian church, I was overwhelmed by the sense of *déjà vu* conveyed by the surroundings: the aromas, the light, the statues and icons, the holy water, the pews, the priests' robes . . . I easily performed the proper bodily movements, drilled by the cues of rising, sitting, kneeling, crossing, heart pounding with a closed fist while whispering *mea culpa* . . . Despite the fact that I renounced Catholicism years before, the familiarity of these weekly masses alleviated the sense of estrangement one might feel when engaging in a new research world. This place constituted a strange terrain of familiarity and comfort in a country where I had recently arrived from Montreal. Even though the ceremonies were not performed in the French vernacular I was brought up with, my first visit to St Peter's struck me because it was a 'habitual space'. A space where I need not try to make sense of what was going on: all was familiar, intelligible, in an unpleasant and troubling way.

My engagement with Judith Butler was crucial in these initial stages of my study. As I state in the opening chapter, her insistence on repetition helped me come to terms with understanding cultural identity as more that a mere social construct. As I sat there in the pews, it seemed as if I was watching a re-run of part of my identity *in the making:* the 'stylized repetition of acts' (Butler 1990: 140) reached into some deep seated sense of selfhood that had sedimented into my body. The rituals cultivated a sense of belonging. This short episode made mc realize the extent to which cultural identity is embodied, and memories are incorporated (Connerton 1992), both as a result of iterated actions. And how these, in turn, are *lived* as *expressions* of a deeply felt sense of identity and belonging. This small experience gave me some insight into what it may mean, for some Italians, to return to St Peter's. Going to the Italian church momentarily solves the ontological problem about belonging to the Italian culture in a non-Italian, non-Catholic world.

Moving on from the spatial materialization of identity examined in the previous chapter, I now take a slightly different look at the connection between gender, ethnicity and the construction of place. Like Angela K. Martin (1997), I propose a 'corporeal approach' to group identity. I am informed by recent developments in feminist theory that explore how bodies constitute the raw material through which place is both experienced and inscribed, and how bodies, in turn, are inscribed by and become the signifiers of particular notions of place (Martin 1997; Grosz 1994; Colomina 1992; Valentine 1993). Identity, here, 'is formed and continually reinforced via individual practice within culturally defined spaces, which are themselves in turn continually constituted out of these same practices' (Martin 1997: 92). But it seems to me that the focus on the sexing of bodies neglects the processes through which bodies (and spaces) are also ethnicized. In other words, embodiment is reduced to sexualization and thus becomes the matter and symbol through which group identities are sexualized within already culturally defined spaces. This is also implied in the work of symbolic anthropologists, namely Victor Turner, whose thick description of the 'ritual process' (1969) examines the circulation and transformation of bodies as they circulate within pre-defined cultural and physical spaces that circumscribe the different stages individual bodies go through in the ritual process. In contrast, my version of a corporeal approach to group identity takes account of the simultaneous genderization and ethnicization of bodies *and* space. In a manner akin to Angela McRobbie's appraisal of Catholic Glasgow (1995), I shall pursue an investigation of how bodies and space produce each other in both ethnically and gender specific ways.

My analysis is grounded in the life of St Peter's Italian church, which differs from the Centro/Chiesa on two key aspects. First, the public 'displays of presence' stand in stark contrast with the Centro's enclosed practices of identity. Life at St Peter's spills beyond the building's walls, and its identity is inseparable from the local neighbourhood, the past of which is re-membered in a set of practices – written recollections, commemorations, rituals – that serve to display the enduring presence of Italians in London. Second, St Peter's is the preferred Italian church for the practice of 'familistic religion',[1] which, as I argue below, is a site where the fragmentation and discontinuity of Italian London are challenged head on. In sum, St Peter's occupies a special position within the London Italian (indeed British-Italian) historical environment.

Like the Centro, St Peter's is a main focal point of the Italians' associative life. Founded in 1863, it stands at the heart of what used to be 'Little Italy', in Clerkenwell, central London (Holborn). It was established by two Pallottini fathers, Raffaele Melia and Giuseppe Faà, who were sent to London for fear that Italians might be converted to Protestantism if they were not provided with a place of worship of their own. The site of the church was obtained in 1852. The architect, Sir John Miller Bryson,[2] drew the plans for the church interiors, modelled on the Basilica San Crisogono in Rome (see Plate 2).

The crypt was open on Christmas Day 1862. The solemn opening of the church followed on 16 April 1863, 'under the most auspicious circumstances, there being present . . . twelve Prelates of the Church and a very large number of the Clergy Regular and Secular' (*The Tablet*, 18 April 1863). Initially, the church was to be named St Peter's Roman Catholic Church of all Nations (*The Builder*, 14 May 14 1853: 312), but when it opened it was simply called St Peter's church. At that time, it ministered to the religious needs of the large number of Catholics residing in, or constantly hurrying through, London: Irish, Poles, French, Germans, and of course Italians. In October 1871, Irish republicans and 'home rulers' used the premises for their political meetings (Sponza 1988: 139, 202). Poles used the church's crypt as a place of worship for the National Polish Church. Gradually, as this multicultural presence moved on, or established separate churches – such as the Irish with St Etheldreda's Catholic chapel nearby in Ely Place, in 1879 – St Peter's catered predominantly to Italians and acquired its status as *the* Italian church.

Linked to St Peter's church are a social club, *Casa Pallotti*, a youth club, and a number of small religious groups such as the *consorelle*, women who meet for mass one Friday a month. There exists a male counterpart: the *confratelli*, who can be spotted seated in the nave during special religious ceremonies. Two parish priests are appointed to the church: Father Carmelo di Giovanni and Father Roberto Russo, each of whom has been living in London for over 20 years.

St Peter's publishes its own monthly magazine, *Backhill*. Subtitled 'magazine of the Italian community' *(Rivista della comunità italiana)*, *Backhill* was created in 1977 and prints articles in Italian or English. Vittorio Heissel, who runs *Casa Pallotti* and the youth club, approached Francesco Giacon, son of the prominent community leader Giuseppe Giacon, to ask him to start an 'extended parish bulletin'. Both men agreed that there was a need for a new type of Italian magazine, one that would not be as political as *La Voce* or as highbrow as *Londra Sera*.[3] As Francesco Giacon explained to me, they established 'a more family type magazine'. The pages of *Backhill* cover parish announcements (weddings, baptisms, special masses), general information for Italian émigrés, local activities and events, news from Italy, news from the Vatican and another 'religious page', news from the EEC, entertainment, leisure, sports, and a history of 'The Hill', the pet name for former Little Italy in Clerkenwell.

St Peter's occupies a mixed position within the local Catholic hierarchy. On the one hand, it has a national parish status, which means that its membership is based on ethnicity instead of place of residence. On the other, it answers to the diocese of Westminster. In the mass celebrating its 130th anniversary (9 May 1993),

Father Carmelo publicly assured Cardinal Basil Hume, then archbishop of Westminster who was invited for the occasion, that St Peter's considers itself part of the British Roman Catholic Church, dismissing its national parish status as 'not important'. Concomitantly, Father Carmelo simultaneously de-ethnicized and re-ethnicized St Peter's by stressing that it is part of the 'British Catholic family'. However, the church retains a role in the formation and assertion of a specifically Italian presence in Catholic London, as I shall show.

St Peter's is, for most Italians I have met, acknowledged as *the* Italian church. It stood at the centre of the 'original settlement' and is still seen as the heart of the present day 'community'. Indeed, its enduring life is read as the guarantor of survival of the Italian 'community', however dispersed and fragmented it may be. St Peter's is viewed, and lived by many, as *casa nostra* as Father Russo likes to call it, where Italians return for their weekly visit, to attend the annual procession della Madonna, or to celebrate the rites of passage that punctuate their life. In a manner similar to the Centro Scalabrini, the church is perceived, by its leadership, as a place where Italian culture is inscribed; a reliable enclave in the hostile, 'vast city'.

> The Church of course, IS THE COMMUNITY. It ably fulfils the needs of Italians in London on so many levels – religious, social, moral – dealing with the problems of drugs, bringing solace to the dying, and comfort to prisoners, visiting the sick and elderly, and also performing the joyous rites of the Church, such as weddings, Baptisms and Confirmations etc., again the list is endless. No one needs to be told the many different roles our Priests have to fulfil, meeting daily problems of the community with patience and good spirits. We NEED OUR CHURCH AND OUR PRIESTS very much, but especially for us, in this vast city where we are exposed to many bad influences. The Church is like a rock, keeping us steadfast in our faith. Without the physical presence of a Centre (the bricks and mortar), the Community would begin to flounder, and eventually cease altogether.[4]

The church, *casa nostra*, is wrapped in images of protection and 'body buffer zones' associated with the family and the household in the textual narratives examined in Chapter 2. It is asserted as the institution where ethnicity is tried and preserved. Without it, the community would flounder. As such, St Peter's is defined as the cradle of London Italian authenticity, and the repository of British-Italian history. For instance, up the stairway, in the portico, are two war monuments. One is dedicated to the memory of the Italians residing in London who died in the Great War of 1914–18. This monument lists 175 names and was erected under the auspices of the National Association of War Veterans in November 1927. Above this memorial, a bronze bas-relief represents a lifeboat, overloaded with men, arms stretched out, expressions of horror on their faces: it honours the 446 Italians who lost their lives in the sinking of the *Arandora Star*. The inscription reads: 'To the memory which lives on in the hearts of the relatives, the survivors and the Italian Community.' The location of these national memorials on the church's premises brings together nation and religion and testifies to the national status of St Peter's. But these memorials are also landmarks of past alliance (in the 1914–18 war) and enmity (in the 1939–45 war) with Britain. These memorials thus reinstate the ambivalent social and political position of Italians within the British historical landscape.

In contrast to the Centro, St Peter's sense of itself is very much set within its very presence. While the Scalabrinians seek to create a new identity and community, St Peter's positions itself as responding to the needs of an already constituted community. Its leaders view their role primarily as one of cultural reproduction and preservation. My objective, here, is to visit a number of events that take place at St Peter's and examine them not as moments of cultural *re*production, but, rather, as instances through which physical, symbolic and bodily (terrains of) belongings are created.

My argument is organized around three episodes drawn from the daily life at St Peter's, and which are to be read as a collage rather than an organized sequence that composes a plot. These episodes capture a number of layers embedded within the process of identity formation, and which tie up with broader theoretical questions about the reterritorialization of identity, the invention of tradition, and the embodiment of culture.

First episode: 'The Hill' as a second place of origin

It was on a hot and sunny Sunday of August 1992 that I first ventured into a section of Clerkenwell, where 'The Italian church' stands. Having read Lucio Sponza's history of Italians in nineteenth-century London, my first visit to Clerkenwell was daunting. Instead of finding a Dickensian[5] street life bustling with markets stalls, cries, music and aromas, I discovered what is now a quiet, desolate quarter of London. This is more pronounced on weekends, where shops are closed, the market stalls of Saffron Hill are shut down, leaving two local pubs and a hole-in-the-wall off-licence open to the odd customer. The stillness and deserted character of the area contrasts starkly with what once was the most densely populated area of London and a main settlement of Italian immigration.

As I wandered in the empty streets, I came across a discrete trace of the past. Above the door of a barber shop tucked away in a side street is a plaque, erected in 1922, in honour of the renowned leader of the *Risorgimento*, Giuseppe Mazzini. It is made of a large, rectangular stone, bearing a bas-relief of Mazzini's head. Under it, a string of laurel leaves and a text that reads: 'In this country, Giuseppe Mazzini the apostle of modern democracy, inspired young Italy with the ideal of the independence, unity and regeneration of his country.' This testimony is what

Jonathan Boyarin would see as a sign marking something that 'was and no longer is' (Boyarin 1992: 4). Mazzini played an important role in nineteenth-century Italian life in London, namely by establishing a school for poor children in former Little Italy, the area surrounding St Peter's church. Remembering his presence is also connected to remembering the past presence of an Italian community in the area. Indeed, this is a place where a face-to-face community of daily interactions *was and no longer is*. However, this is not a simple absence. What 'was' is remembered in a variety of ways that all revolve around St Peter's church.

St Peter's acquires a special significance within London Italian historicity as a result of its association with its immediate surroundings. Known as 'The Hill', this section of former Little Italy is repeatedly retraced, its history retold and its confines redefined through written recollections published in St Peter's monthly magazine, *Backhill*. Started in November 1992, 'The Hill', as the column's title goes, is written in English by a British-Italian woman, Olive Besagni. Its typical pieces are on families or portraits of individuals, all of which emerge from stories told to Besagni by former residents of *il quartiere italiano* (sic), or their descendants. These short biographies are set against the backdrop of the everyday life of Little Italy in the late nineteenth or early twentieth centuries.

To a large extent, this chronicle bears the hallmarks of the textual narratives examined in Chapter 2. The community, here, is symbolically reconstructed through the lens of the patriarchal family, with its systems of gendered and generational differentiation. In Besagni's series, the story of *il quartiere* is the story of families who share the experience of (e)migration, hardship, hard work and hope, all of which will be redeemed thanks to the successful integration of the 'second' generation.[6] Yet Besagni's column also carries a distinctive feature, which I want to discuss here: that is the way in which genealogy and geography are worked into the creation of new grounds of belonging.

In her accounts, readers are introduced to the characters of each story through their links – kinship, professional, or other – with other former residents, some of whose stories could have been told in previous issues. In other cases, the genealogy is more conventional and retraces the family tree of the characters. Such genealogical tracings usually provide a trans-generational backdrop to the main story, linking past to present, linking memories to 'real' people, linking former Little Italy residents to the present day, geographically dispersed, English Italian population. 'The Nastri sons . . . all married to English girls, all had good marriages and as you can imagine there are plenty of young Nastris growing up in England today. All as a result of that journey made by Trofimena and Alfonso way back in the year 1908' (*Backhill*, March 1993: 30).

Olive Besagni resorts to genealogy as a metaphor for continuity. It may be argued that languages of descent trace blood lines between generations, thus concealing racist notions of culture and belonging as genetically endowed

(Micheals 1992). Without denying that family trees re-emphasize the family as the natural foundation of 'community' founded on blood lines, Besagni, in my view, does not imply that the culture of the present day 'community' is *biologically* determined by its lineage. To paraphrase Daniel and Jonathan Boyarin (1993), there is a difference between saying that one is Italian because one has Italian ancestors, and saying that one *behaves* like an Italian because one has Italian ancestors. The signification of ancestry and generations is central here. In Besagni's texts, trans-generational links collapse the past into the present and give substance to London Italian historicity and continuity. As the chronicles extend into one another through the generational trope, the complex fabric of communality and continuity slowly surfaces and clears a space, in central London, for the creation of an Italian terrain of belonging predicated on remembrances of beginnings.

Besagni herself views her column – and her other writings such as the musicals she writes, and produces almost yearly for the Italian 'community' – as an act of nostalgia. As she puts it: 'I'm always into nostalgia.' Hers is a nostalgia that stands in between the 'useless act', on the one hand, and the politicized remembrance that would serve 'to illuminate and transform the present' (hooks 1990: 147), on the other. Hers is a nostalgia entangled with a desire to leave a trace, to bear witness.

Judging from the mail she receives, many of Besagni's readers are former residents of the area. By reading her column, they are thus bearing witness to their own story, which some warrant and others contest. To be sure, 'The Hill' is remembered in a variety of ways: as a rough, poor area where outsiders were less than welcome, or, in contrast, as a place of close-knit community life of solidarity and mutual support – which some remember as equally enclosed upon itself. For some, Little Italy is not worth remembering and Besagni's nostalgia is condemned as a useless wish of retrieval of an imaginary and romanticized past which, they argue, 'actually never existed'. She is derided for what is perceived as a naive longing for things to be as they once were – an accusation that she refutes: 'Of course I don't want to re-live the past! I simply want us to remember.' Other readers, however, bask in the written memories of past times which 'bring Little Italy to life again', and warmly recall the daily life on 'The Hill'. Others, still, simply appreciate it as a source of historical knowledge: 'it tells us about the history of the place, the history of the community', thus providing them with an historical environment that serves to legitimate the actions undertaken to claim the Italianness of St Peter's and 'The Hill'. Finally, 'The Hill' may also appear as an Italian enclave, separated from the rest of London/England, where conflicts and solidarity combine, and where the 'community' is tightly woven through stifling 'traditional' family values and injunctions of womanhood. This version is best exemplified in a fictional rendition of life in The Hill written by Besagni's niece, Lilie Ferrari (1993). The story of *Fortunata* extends between 1920 and 1990, and is about the life of an independent Italian woman committed to anti-fascist politics, who struggles against 'traditional' Italian family values that confine her to married life with a man she does not love. Written in the genre of popular romance, this text clearly has feminist intentions. Ferrari's account offers real attempts to disturb hegemonic discourses on Italian womanhood. Yet it remains deeply grounded in stereotypical images of what typifies Italian culture: *la famiglia* with its clearly divided gender roles where women are oppressed and victimized. Other central themes of the narrative concern political conflicts within the Italian population – namely between pro- and anti-fascists – or the alliances between Irish and Italians in anti-imperialist politics, portrayed in the passionate love affair between Fortunata and Joe O'Connel.

These contested views about the 'beginnings' are constitutive of the creation of Little Italy as an ancestral space for Italians of England or Britain. In one instance, Besagni reprints a letter she received, where a reader from Birmingham, tracing his 'family-tree' in order to find his 'roots' (sic), asks for information regarding the Alberici family that once lived in 'The Hill'. He then tells of his journey to Clerkenwell.

> [S]o I decided to visit Clerkenwell and discovered St Peter's Italian Church, as it seems to be the heart of the Community, and I felt so close to my ancestors and tried to picture their marriages taking place there. On entering the Church Arcade I noticed to the left a commemorative plaque in honour of Italians who died in the 1st World War, and to my surprise was listed an ancestor 'Giampietro Alberici'. I have twice returned to St Peter's to celebrate the Procession in Honour of Our Lady of Mount Carmel which is held in July. Both occasions have been enjoyable and I have really felt that I am re-tracing the surroundings and traditions that would have been familiar to my ancestors. (*Backhill*, June 1993: 10)

In Besagni's column, details of street names and addresses, shop and pub names, photographs and accounts of the street life, identify sites and places people can return to and re-member: they join together elements of a(n imagined) past which is projected onto the area. Her stories, in short, constitute a form of memory work that is particularly rich with images of duration. There is more to this series than mere juxtapositions; it is more than simply overlaying images from the past onto the present. It is part of a creative process that creates and locates an historical environment, adding substance to the immediate, lived experience of the present. Besagni's series conjures up lives of the past to create a habitable space for her contemporaries (de Certeau [1980] 1990: 162).

Another constitutive feature of this space is migration. While *e*migration is the inaugural moment leading to the formation of Little Italy, migration is a recurring event in the lives of those who are also known as the first 'settlers' of the present-day community (Sponza 1988: Colpi 1991a; Marin 1985). Flows of migration act upon the delineation of *il quartiere italiano* as an enclosed space, surrounded by an imagined boundary. We rarely go beyond its limits, in Besagni's stories, and when we do, it seems like a temporary migration. Even the daily journeys of workers to the West End convey this sense of moving between two different worlds. Similarly, in *Fortunata*, images of workers getting off the bus at the top of Clerkenwell Road, or on Farringdon Road, mark out the border between the outside, 'other', English world and the familiar, unified 'Italian Quarter'. In sum, *il quartiere italiano* emerges from Besagni's narrative as a space enclosed and distant from the rest of the world. She cites Victor: 'whenever we represented [St Peter's] school in competitive athletics or football, we always felt that we were competing for Italy, rather than the school' (*Backhill*, March 1993: 30).

This suggests that in the minds of some of the residents, Little Italy *was* Italy. However, overlaying the boundary between Little Italy and Elsewhere is another boundary that separates this Italian quarter from another Italian 'colony' (sic) nearby, in Soho. Historiographers (Sponza 1988; Colpi 1991a) as well as former residents of the areas, speak of the well-known rivalry between the two areas; the 'West End Italians', as the Soho Italians were known, were the 'posh lot'. Interestingly, in her column Besagni retraces a boundary line between them not by emphasizing their differences and rivalries, but simply by obliterating the presence of the 'other'. It is as if Italians from each sector had no contact; as if there were no cycling trips joining 'The Hill Italians' and 'West End Italians', like those Olive and her husband Bruno recalled in my conversations with them, where they contrasted the 'Hill Italians' with their battered, rusted, hand-me-down bicycles, and the 'Soho Italians' with their shining new vehicles. Memory and forgetting work together in the struggle over differing histories and geographies that construct the identity of a place.

What is more, London itself is remapped according to the (dis)locations of Italian 'settlements' (sic) and their relationship with the rest of the world. In British-Italian historicity, The Hill is construed as the original settlement, the second place of origin for Italian immigrants. 'The history of Italian immigration to Britain', writes Lucio Sponza, 'is to a great extent the history of the Italians in [Holborn] . . . This is true both in terms of sheer numbers and, more importantly, in the sense that the occupational structure and living conditions were reproduced in a scattered manner in almost all the Italian settlements around Britain.' (1988: 19) In written renditions of the Italian presence in Britain, The Hill is both an end point and a starting point; a point of arrival and a point of departure. It is an interval; a spatial and temporal 'moment' that marks off the passage from migrancy to settlement, which, as I showed in Chapter 2, is figured through gendered distinctions between migrant workers and settler wives.

The Hill, then, emerges as an 'envelope of space-time' (Massey 1995: 188) constituted out of particular claims about the history and geography of the original settlement. It is part of the communal project of recovery; of the 'rediscovery' of a past, of a place, a *grounding*, which, as Stuart Hall points out, is grasped through reconstruction (1991: 36). The Hill is remembered in a way that draws essentialist and exclusionist boundaries – indeed it obliterates the presence of Irish and other residents that lived in this area at the time, while it traces generational bloodlines of belonging and continuity. But although it is place *based*, this history is not univocally place *bound*. The Hill is arguably elevated as the emblem of Italian settlement in Britain but it is inserted within a network of many similar settlements scattered in Britain (and elsewhere). It follows that London's Little Italy becomes a surface of beginnings within the diasporic horizon of Italian emigration. The image of the rhizome comes to mind: diaspora as a rhizomatic network of nodes that foreground the possibility of new beginnings. Little Italy, here, is a space of belonging that proceeds from remembrances of beginnings (Probyn 1996: 113) and that roots them, as it were, within English territory.

Second episode: the annual procession

The most important affair of St Peter's is its annual procession in honour of Our Lady of Mount Carmel. It occurs on 16 July or the first Sunday thereafter, and attracts diverse segments of the Italian population. This is not unique to the procession: the pilgrimage to Aylesford (Kent) and the annual Scalabrini picnic are also multi-generational, multi-regional and multi-class events. As such, although it does not take place in the outskirts but rather in central London, the event may be viewed as a pilgrimage: a place where Italians return to, every year, in a collective remembrance of traditions (see below). What distinguishes the procession from other Italian gatherings is its association with a multiculturalist discourse. The procession is a 'public' event, held in selected streets of Clerkenwell, attracting a large crowd (Plate 4) which is perhaps predominantly Italian, though increasingly non-Italian. It symbolizes the multicultural fabric of London by displaying the presence of an enduring Italian culture. It is not as well known as the Notting Hill Carnival, but it has been listed as an 'Ethnic London' event in the *Time-Out London Guide* and draws many tourists and non-Italian Londoners. The procession, then, is marked out as an 'Italian event'.

It is easy to label such manifestations as 'ethnic' and to ossify them as traditions that testify to the continuity of some authentic, original culture. Yet the devotion to Mary is not specifically Italian, nor is the feast in honour of Our Lady of Mount Carmel. Likewise, the event is not only held in London's Italian community. On the contrary, this is what I call a diasporic moment:[8] that Sunday, Italians of London, Toronto, Montreal, New York, as well as in some parts of Italy, hold a procession in honour of Our Lady of Mount Carmel, and in some cases re-map areas known as Little Italies. As Olive Besagni puts it, on that day 'the streets of "Il Quartiere Italiano" come to life once more, just as they did in the old days "Down the Hill"' (*Backhill*, September 1996: 9). For these occasions, Italians from different parts of the world join families and friends, like Besagni's relatives from America who 'strive to get [to London] for that day.' (*Backhill*, September 1996: 9).

The first procession of London occurred in 1883 in the context of Catholic emancipation among Irish residents of Holborn and Islington, and was instigated by an Irish priest (Sponza 1988: 315, n.78). Hence the concurrence of the first procession with Irish Catholic emancipation questions the ethnic specificity of this practice. More to the point, it destroys assumptions about the transit of a pristine, original culture from Italy to London. Even when considered in the context of Italian popular religion itself, the procession appears as the result of the merging of two practices that have been widespread in Italy since the fifteenth century: the veneration of a local village saint, and the devotion to Mary (Carroll 1992). Clearly, this consists of a 'tradition' that is born out of cultural re-processing rather than the accidental re-enactment of a pristine culture. A number of participants I spoke with agree. As one of the organizers told me: 'Since we cannot have separate feasts for each patron saint, we hold this big event for all of them and we chose to honour Our Lady.'

Preparations for the big day begin several weeks in advance: sketches are drawn for the floats, costumes are mended, flowers are ordered, food is prepared, stalls are repaired, volunteers are recruited. On the eve of the event, seven floats are built by a number of volunteers: families and friends arrive early afternoon and set out in teams to work on each float. Many extended families, like the Besagnis or the Giacons, set this day aside as one of the rare annual occasions for a get together. Parents, grandparents, children, grandchildren, brothers, sisters, aunts and uncles pitch in to build 'family sponsored floats'. Inside the church, food and drinks are laid out. Father Russo walks around, beaming with his contagious smile, looking around him with pride, obviously enjoying the presence of his parishioners, gathered for this special event. Dressed in his black suit and white dog collar, he stands at the door or in the dining room, greeting and chatting with people, teasing the younger ones, joking with others. Father Carmelo, for his part, is casually dressed, sometimes stepping out from his office, but generally more discreet than Father Russo. He approaches people in a more intimate way, often holding one by the arm and chatting quietly. Meanwhile, men, women, children build the floats and by seven o'clock, all is practically finished: just in time for the Saturday evening mass, which some will attend before heading home.

On the day of the procession, crowds begin filling the streets from one o'clock, strolling among the stalls to try their luck at the tombola or eat an Italian sausage, apple fritter, or strawberries and champagne. They buy the programme, an Italian flag, and a Bart Simpson or tricolour heart-shaped balloon for the children.[9]

Around three o'clock, the Madonna emerges from the church, supported by four porters, framed by a flowered arch (Plate 5). She is the centrepiece of the day's event, and will be closing the procession behind a trail of seven floats, each representing a biblical scene. On each float, yesterday's builders and artists are turned into angels, saints, Jesus or the Virgin Mary. The procession also includes the *consorelle* and the *confratelli*; army veterans; the year's first communicants; altar servers; and statues of patron saints, which village or regional organizations parade each year, extracting them from the church where they are stored. The long file closes with praying and singing parishioners led by Father Carmelo and, occasionally, the Bishop of Westminster. Organizations from South London (Epsom, Croydon, Sutton), Gloucester, even Birmingham signal their presence with their banner. Finally, an Irish pipe band joins the procession and lingers after its conclusion, entertaining the public for a while before it disperses again among the stalls of the fair (*sagra*).

The procession travels through the winding streets around St Peter's church in a long and slow re-mapping of Little Italy's 'core', the heart of which is the church, where the procession begins and ends. The long file travels through what used to be the heart of Little Italy: Back Hill, Bakers Row, Farringdon Road (formerly Coppice Row and Turnmill Street), Cross Street, Leather Lane and back onto Clerkenwell Road, to the church's main entrance.[10] During the hour it takes to complete, the map of 'Il Quartiere Italiano' is re-drawn, the streets of the former 'Little Italy' are re-appropriated and invested with sounds, colours, odours and images of Italy.

The fair marks the distinction of London Italian Catholicism, where the sacred has a taste and a smell. As in all 'community' events, food and wine are part of this religious celebration. The *sagra*, however, is a relatively recent addition to the day's event. It was introduced in the 1970s in order to attract the dispersed Italian population, and to make their journey 'back' to The Hill 'worthwhile', as a volunteer explained. This yearly performance is a celebration of the Italian presence in London, where demonstrations of faith and culture are simultaneously displayed. In contrast to the weekly masses, this version of religious worship is much more secularized. Worshippers, organizers and participants celebrate Italian culture, or, rather, Italian religious culture, displaying their difference in a non-Catholic, English world. As Father Carmelo once proclaimed to the worshippers gathered in the church after the procession: 'This is a display of our faith. We show our faith to the world.'

In the early evening, the crowd slowly disperses. The noise dies out, the stalls are dismantled, and the cleaning agency comes in to clear up. Once again, Italians of London have expressed their faith with a difference. This annual event is, for some, an imperative moment of worship and religious devotion. For others, it is a feast, a time of reunion with friends or family, a brief immersion in 'Italian culture' for their children or grandchildren.[11]

At one level, the invention of tradition is tightly bound to the (re)creation of ethnicity that surfaces from reprocessing history and memory (Hobsbawm and

Ranger 1983). Ritualization and formalization lie at the basis of the invention of tradition, thus exalting into timelessness a culture that is said to be *re*presented by the different forms of remembering. Yet beyond the processes through which a tradition is invented, I want to emphasize how it becomes, when performed, a ground of remembrances and how, as such, it becomes an open site for multiple memories.

The annual feast features several kinds of events at once: it is an ethnic festival in a plural society, a collection of village feasts and thus a display of Italian diversity, a demonstration of enduring Roman Catholic devotion, an occasion for 'family unification', a 'community' gathering, and a reprocessing of popular religious practices – Italian and Irish – within a new environment. The procession itself is a trail of different temporalities, histories, boundaries and 'communities'. Italians from Birmingham and Gloucester come to London and project the 'community' beyond the metropolitan area. Village-based groupings gather around their patron saint, re-enacting their local festival. Elderly women pray in earnest, while young British-born teenagers and children pose as angels, or proudly represent St Peter's Youth Club, and young girls parade in traditional regional dress. The Irish pipers recall the Irish presence in the neighbourhood, and testify, according to St Peter's leaders, to the 'continuity of collaboration between the two communities' (St Peter's church 1996: 18).[12]

Whether it is a display of faith, culture, enduring presence, pluralism, or all of these at once, the procession states the undeniable presence of Italian Catholicism in London (and England). The very performance of the ceremony defines this 'truth'. In this respect, the procession consists of what Barbara Myerhoff has called 'definitional ceremonies': 'performances of identity that state the unquestionability of truths, made unquestionable by their performance' (1979: 32). The procession is lived as an irrefutable, and necessary, testimony to Italian identity and continuity. For many participants or bystanders, the procession is a moment of nostalgia. A return to the neighbourhood they grew up in: 'I lived just around the corner, here. I come here for nostalgia.' 'You know, in those days, the *festa* lasted four days. It was great!' 'I lived there, just down the street. I went to St Peter's school. Ooh we was a tough lot!' Memories flow into the air, weaving a net of nostalgic remembrances that wrap the procession and tie it down as a moment of 'attachment, a base, a closeness, a point of reference, *a point of refuge*; without them, you are a drifter. It's to preserve a particular way of life, a particular community. It's about bridging the gap between generations. You do what your forebears did. I do it out of some sense of duty; to keep [the traditions] up.' Francesco Giacon expresses, here, the extent to which the procession, however much invented, is lived as an ossified tradition, that which constitutes, he adds, the 'kind of ground work on which we base our lives.' It is a display of presence, where Italians – and increasingly non-Italians – are called upon to bear witness to the Italian past and present/ce.

Each year, hundreds of men, women and children parade through the winding streets, reclaiming the sector as the old Italian neighbourhood. As it unfolds the procession simultaneously traces the confines of a territory and reiterates the identity of 'The Hill' as an Italian place. In the words of Doreen Massey: 'The invention of tradition is . . . about the invention of the coherence of a place, about defining and naming it as a "place" at all' (1995: 188). Commemorations such as the procession allow for memories to be not only lived and re-processed in a ritualized pattern of continuity. They are also located within a specific territory in a collective claim of belonging. The ritual thus produces a distinct timespace in the very heart of London. Streets are blocked, taken over for a day when 'we show our faith to the world'. It is in part a gesture of affirmation that mobilizes volunteers and families, and gathers hundreds of people every year to either join in or simply stand by and watch the trail unfold. Once again, the notion of the changing same pointedly stresses how remembrance and commemoration, rather than a primordial culture, are the principal grounds of belonging in diaspora. The procession, in short, is another version of the 'living memory' (Gilroy 1993: 198) of Italian presence in London – the living memory of the church and 'The Hill' as the place of belonging for all Italians, past and present, in London and elsewhere in England.

But there is more to the procession than tracing London Italian culture onto a map. This is where most accounts of processions in other Italian diaspora communities come to a halt (Primeggia and Varacalli 1996; Migliore 1988; Trebay 1990; Swiderski 1986). In contrast, I want to suggest that the procession della Madonna is not exclusively about cultural (re)production or territorial claims. It also concerns the construction of an ideal of femininity that relates back to the creation of local particularity. In a manner akin to the 1970s and 1980s formation of the 'good' white ethnic communities in the US, Italian émigré culture in London rests heavily on the Madonna-like image of the unselfish, hardworking, 'head of the household' mother. An image which contrasts with those of the 'lazy', overbearing but 'incapable of controlling their children' black mothers (which circulated in the US and Britain alike),[13] or the cold, rigid and selfish WASP women (di Leonardo 1994: 177). But beyond the argument about the general imagery of the Madonna, I explore how the London procession connects back to 'community' formation – and in this respect I also move beyond the general reasoning that confines the Marian devotion in her relationship to family and family roles (Orsi 1985; Carroll 1992). Rather, I propose to examine how this devotion takes on a particular significance as a threshold figure of collective belonging.

In the booklet for the 1993 procession in honour of the Madonna, we find the following text:

> Today we honour a woman who, in human terms, should hang her head in shame. She gave birth to a child, not fathered by her husband. Her son had the audacity to claim to forgive sins. Her son was condemned to death as a blasphemer who dared declare to be the Son of God. But throughout her life she never questioned the motives of the Lord, never doubted His actions, never criticized His ways. Her Faith, her trust in the Lord, never faltered or wavered, however little she understood. Rather than condemning God she praised him. 'My soul proclaims the greatness of the Lord' (Luke 1:46). When we look at Our Lady's life, not through a rose coloured filter or sentimentality, but in the harsh reality of how it must have been, one can understand why she is revered above all other human souls.[14]

This text echoes the narratives discussed in Chapter 2, where the location of 'woman' is never a thing of her own. It is contingent on that of a father, a husband, and a son. This is what leads Amy-Jill Levine to remark that 'woman is, in effect, in perpetual diaspora' (1992: 110). In turn, it may be argued that the London Italian diaspora is figured as 'woman'. 'First-generation Italian women of the southern Italian communities', writes Terri Colpi, 'are the living embodiment of the difficulty and sadness of emigration' (1991a: 218). The isolation of these old women, confined in the home, not speaking English, becomes the epitome of the sacrificial and suffering immigrant condition of existence.

For Levine, the exaggeration of women's captivity and passivity in Judaism, asserts the freedom of male migrants and exiles, and simultaneously stabilizes the world of the exile (Levine 1992: 117). Yet when contemplating the feminization of the Italian diaspora through the body of the Madonna in the light of Catholic popular religious practice, the figure acquires both utopic and dystopic aspects.[15] This ties in with the historical paradox that has invested definitions of 'woman' in Western thought. A number of feminists have pointed out the mixture of attraction and repulsion (Julia Kristeva), or recognition and wonder (Luce Irigaray), that makes '"woman" . . . the eternal pole of opposition' (Braidotti 1994: 83). Mary, as 'woman', is indeed a paradoxical figure, one which is both loved and feared; giving and narcissistic – 'Italian Catholics . . . see Mary as a goddess who craves veneration' (Carroll 1992: 54) – unitary and splintered – in contrast to Protestants, Catholics have tended to splinter the figure of Mary into a range of images and personifications, including Our Lady of Mount Carmel, each of which has become the object of an extensive cult (Carroll 1992: 2). Mary, then, is at once human and supernatural. The 'unnatural' birth of God suggests that Mary was, in some ways, not quite human, not quite flesh, indeed not quite 'mother'. The birth of Jesus 'inscribes an antimaternal dimension at the very heart of the matter' (Braidotti 1994: 84). Though Mary 'is the premier female within the Catholic and Orthodox faith . . . she seems to transcend womanhood itself' (Dubisch 1995: 246). Finally, within Italian popular religion, the Marian devotion supersedes devotion for God and Jesus (Carroll 1992), while at the same time, she is the very product of a male-dominated church and a patriarchal theology (Warner 1976/1990; Dubisch 1995).

But within contemporary Catholic discourse, voiced by the London Italian clergy, Mary's ambiguity is levelled through the sanctification of motherhood. Likewise, the multiple representations of Mary are unified within the single body of motherhood. Mary's is a vulnerable body, a body that has been invaded, hurt and its desires utterly suppressed – the virgin. But it is also a fecund body – the mother – and celebrated as such. To be sure, this constitutes one version of Italian *mammismo*, that is the veneration of the mother figure as 'the symbol of what is most sacred within a family' (Bottignolo 1985: 59; Colpi 1991a: 216).[16] And *mammismo* is one dimension of a wider system of meaning that surrounds *la donna*, in Italian culture. Indeed, as Maureen Giovannini writes (1981), 'woman' is, historically, a dominant symbol that serves to delineate and protect family boundaries. But not all women are worthy of collective worship. This 'privilege' is reserved to the mother, the virgin and the Madonna.

Historically, in Italy, the singling out of women as a group and their location within the family has been variously systematized through the concerted efforts of Catholic teaching and Fascist policies (Caldwell 1986; de Grazia 1992; Passerini 1996; Pratt 1996).[17] It is difficult, in this regard, to speak of Italian *mammismo* outside of the Catholic discourse of motherhood deployed in the cult of the Virgin Mary. This ties in with the Church's position on the family as a sacred institution, as well as on sexuality, the primary function of which is reproduction. Within this discourse, the Catholic Church has displayed an obsessive interest for the mysteries, duties and obligations of motherhood. This became particularly explicit in recent discourses which appeal to women as descendants of Mary, as it were, and where ideals of love, devotion, and sacrifice are woven through the conflation of femininity and motherhood and the sublimation of female sexuality (Kristeva 1983; Warner 1976/1990). The Pope's letter to women published in 1995 goes one step further: womanhood, in his discourse, *is* the essence of a divine and pure humanity by virtue of the effects of the 'love work' of motherhood. It is through the care of their mothers that men learn about 'loving thy neighbour'. Mary, then, is no longer 'alone of all her sex' (Warner 1976/1990), for she joins all women in the accomplishment of her 'natural' gift of motherhood. Women's bodies, their wombs, become the sites of authentic human experience that clear the path to redemption and divinity (Pope John Paul II 1995). In this respect, the integrity of humanity is interchangeable with womanhood/motherhood. Yet the affirmation of the primacy of womanhood, of the maternal function, is defined within a gender position. In Catholicism, languages of authority are written on male bodies, while languages of purity are inscribed on female bodies, and they are arranged in a hierarchy.

Universalist Catholic discourses of womanhood, within the procession, essentialize and celebrate motherhood as the supreme experience of human life. In contrast to the Centro, St Peter's role is essentially defined in terms of displaying the presence of a 'community', but a 'community' that, rather than seeking transcendence from the 'drama of emigration', re-members a place of origins, a place of nostalgia, a place of being and of 'living-in-the-present, of simple reproduction, which has been termed immanence' (Massey 1996: 113). And immanence, in Western philosophical thought, is female (Massey 1996; Lloyd 1984). Woven through Mary's body, the procession becomes a narrative of presence-as-immanence; that which is contained within the very nature of being.

The signs of Italian Catholic presence, then, are not just engraved on the church's stones, its adjacent deli, or in the re-tracings of boundaries onto a map. They are also displayed on women's bodies that emphasize the primacy of womanhood: as the Madonna is carried out of the church gates, leads the motley file, and travels through the winding streets of former Little Italy, she marks out the boundary of Italian Catholic culture. The female body is once again a symbolic threshold in the process of inventing traditions and naming places. Here, the living memory of The Hill as (former) Little Italy is given substance through the circulation of female bodies. The following episode further explores this process.

Third episode: the sacraments of ethnicity

She is standing in front of the church, in her white dress, with her white gloves and her hair adorned with white flowers. She smiles shyly as her mother takes some photographs before the ceremony begins.

The interior of the church is decorated as for festive days. Flowers hang on the pews of the central aisle, flowers at the altar, all lights brightly shining. This is a big day.

After the photograph, she must get ready to enter the church. 'We don't want to keep the assembly waiting, do we?' She kisses her mother on the cheek and, nervously, lets go of her hand. The mother enters the church and finds her seat.

The church is packed. Families meet, laugh, hug, wave to each other or call out to those who still haven't found their seat. Men in dark suits, women in colourful dresses circulate in the aisles, wafts of perfume and after-shave trailing behind them. Children run around while teenagers look on indifferently, sticking together near the entrance, at a safe distance from their parents.

The ceremony finally begins and all falls silent. They enter the church, in a double file. Girls in white dress, boys in suit and tie. There are thirty-six who are receiving the first communion, la prima comunione.

The celebration of life cycle events that constitute Italian émigré 'familistic religion' is viewed by some as expressive of an Italian specificity: 'steeped in ritual and tradition . . . it is mainly in this area that differences between British and Italian Catholicism are highly visible' (Colpi 1991a: 235). That is to say that the particular manner in which rites of *passage* are celebrated is where Italian Catholic specificity is located. The ritualized *becomings* are displayed as emblems of ethnic difference. In other words, performances of generational difference are reified as emblems of Italian émigré identity and continuity. In contrast, I argue that the ritual also consists of a set of behaviours cast in a stylized and formalized pattern, which simultaneously produces a communal appreciation of continuity, acts upon the identity of St Peter's as *casa nostra*, and constructs particular kinds of subjects that cannot be dissociated from the collective project.

Within the array of practices that compose familistic religion, the first communion is invested with a special significance for it is viewed as an event that brings young Italian children in touch with Italian culture and institutions (Colpi 1991b: 126). It is singled out in a souvenir booklet on St Peter's church, as 'an important occasion in [a child's] life, and a delightful event in the church's calendar' (St Peter's Church 1996: 20). The first communion is a site where metaphysical and institutional practices of identity meet. At these moments, community and generations articulate together to inscribe a terrain of communality that is cast within the church's premises. St Peter's church, *the* Italian church, is a space where trans-generational discontinuity is challenged head on. Seeing itself as the cornerstone of the 'community', the church offers a space for the re-enactment of continuity to dispersed and fragmented families who gather regularly for the different rites of passage that punctuate their members' lives. 'My father took me here for my first communion and I want my children to have their first communion here.' Thus the church provides what transnational and dispersed families cannot: a stage for the performance of continuity. A refuge, as Francesco Giacon says, against the threat of loss, of losing ground.

As argued in Chapter 3, generations, in migration, are the living embodiment of continuity and change, mediating memories of the past with present living conditions, bringing the past into the present and charged with the responsibility of keeping some form of ethnic identity alive in the future. Called upon as bearers of an 'original' culture, and an 'adopted' one, they embody both continuity and change, culture-as-conjuncture and culture-as-essence that decant into each other and combine in the formation of a distinct émigré identity and culture. Their very presence in communal displays of presence seems to be a defiance to discontinuity and loss: girls dressed in regional apparel, first communicants parading in the procession (Plate 6), or introduced to the Archbishop of Westminster on the occasion of the 130th anniversary of St Peter's church. Their circulation in an array of cultural activities repeatedly enacts both generational differences and cultural continuity.

Images of generations work differently on male and female bodies. For the first communion, boys wear dark suits and ties, dressed up like little men. But when seen standing next to the girls, the 'little men' become grooms. The girls are all in white: white dresses, white gloves, white stockings, white shoes, and something white in the hair (veil, headband, or flowers). For one woman volunteer the 'true' meaning of the white dress is 'purity and joy'. Indeed, the bridal gown projects girls' bodies into a metaphysical realm, where their sexuality is sublimated into the more venerable virginity. The girls 'don the symbols of purity . . . for the first time and dramatically affirm the ideal of virginity which they are expected to maintain until they appear in church again dressed in white as brides' (Giovannini 1981: 412). This denial of female bodies is deeply enmeshed with Catholicism's distaste for 'things of flesh' that work through a particular connection with women (Plate 7). As Mary Douglas suggested (1966/ 1984), sexual taboos shape the contours of individual bodies. Female bodies, in particular, symbolize the threshold between purity and danger. Wrapped in images of purity, the bodies of young girls in white are utterly trapped in Catholicism's fear of 'desires of the flesh'.

According to Victoria Goddard, the ritual of the first communion 'expresses the recognition of liminality, from the time when a girl is no longer a child but is not yet a wife and mother.' Virginity, for Goddard, embodies liminality, or the liminal state, which is 'ideally not abandoned until the ritual or marriage ends liminality, and the girl becomes a woman as wife and an expectant mother' (1996: 193). For Goddard, the ritual is about producing a liminal subject, that is, an ambiguous subject who is 'neither here nor there; . . . betwixt and between' (Turner 1969: 95) the two clear-cut positions of girlhood and motherhood. The virgin hovers perilously between two states, being somewhat of an unintelligible entity. Hence virginity is conceived as a temporary stage of ambiguity that individuals go through, but which must be, and will be, resolved in the ritual process. In short, virginity, for Goddard, is not a sexual category – let alone a sexual identity or practice.[18] In contrast, what the narratives of becoming outlined in the previous chapter reveal is that virginity is part of the process of sexualizing female (and, in different ways, male) bodies. The first communion constructs unambiguously heterosexual subjects, re-emphasizing virginity as an utterly feminine feature. Virginity, here, constitutes one of the sexual categories through which women's subjectivities are constructed. Within the narrative of 'becoming woman' outlined in the previous chapter, the virgin is a distinct, even if momentary, identity position that is figured through a distinct sexual practice.

At first glance, all girls are alike (and boys as well). The uniform dress code erases individual distinctions, thus 'purifying' the bodies in order to re-inscribe them with the norms and conventions attributed to the next 'stage'. Yet when considered in the context of consumer capitalism, the ideal of 'innocence' is undermined by the extensive cost of the outfits (which may easily reach £100 or more). As some mothers told me in the days preceding the first communion of their daughters, 'we have no choice, do we? I don't want my daughter to feel left out, so I have to buy the whole thing: gloves, veil, socks, shoes . . . I think it's too much [of an expense], but what can I do?' Avoiding the shame of exclusion is a key motivation for going along with the expense, for these women. Like in the Italian Women's Club discussed in the previous chapter, class differences affect the ways in which families negotiate 'community' life, in this case, the celebration of the First Communion. Hence different ways of 'being' an Italian girl co-exist in the performance of Italian childhood: but class differences are erased in the display of universal purity and virginity – unless, that is, one child is not 'appropriately' dressed. Then s/he stands out as a disturbing reminder of difference.[19]

Likewise, gender differences also cross cut universalized definitions of generations. If boys will be men, girls will be brides. The volunteer agreed with me: 'Parents tell their daughters that they are the brides of this big event. But they tell their sons that they are little men. I've never heard boys referred to as grooms.' Yet as the children walk down the aisle, in pairs, the evocation of a wedding ceremony is unmistakable. The first communion is a wedding rehearsal.

Marriage vows, as Judith Butler argues, are performative acts that perform heterosexuality through the heterosexualization of the bond it names. '"I pronounce you . . ." puts into effect the relation that it names' (Butler 1993: 224). At the same time, the subjects themselves are brought into being as agents, in performativity: as willing, gendered human beings (Butler 1993: 220). The entire ritual, entrenched into stylized and formalized gestures and act, projects into timelessness the relationship between man and woman, and thus renders it natural and outside of history. But within Italian émigré culture, the wedding also acquires a special significance as a result of its association with sacrifice. The wedding serves as the ultimate reminder of the drama of emigration where sacrifice – displayed and re-enacted in the grand wedding feast – becomes the binding element of a system of inter-generational responsibility (Cavallaro 1981: 84). In a wedding reception, a guest expressed his congratulations and best wishes to the newlyweds, as well as to all 'young persons' present, 'so that they appreciate and follow the example and the sacrifices of their parents, who do all that is in their power to support their children throughout their lives and to accompany them to the altar on their wedding day' (LV 869, July 1992: 10). Sacrifice becomes the symbol that relates generations to community through the institution of the family. Both the first communion and the wedding, then, are stages for the enactment of inter-generational responsibility and as such, are elevated as emblems of collective continuity within the project of identity formation.

But sacrifice also operates differently with male and female subjects. As they are consecrated full Catholic subjects, the female first communicants are also 'preparing for womanhood, marriage and the sacrifice of their virginity' (Goddard 1996: 193). In addition, a feature of *mammismo* is the praise of women for devoting their lives to their families. Self-sacrifice is what distinguishes virtuous women (the mother, the virgin, the Madonna) from the unvirtuous (the whore, the lesbian, the adulteress, and so on).

In sum weddings and first communions are institutional sites of repetition steeped in ritualized patterns of behaviour that repeatedly perform heterosexualized generational and gender differences. It is by *passing* as/into particular *kinds* of boy/manhood, girl/womanhood, that generations enter the communal fold. As young girls and brides mirror each other, and boys mirror men (grooms), gender, sexuality, and generation blur into the display of an enduring Italian presence in London.

Final remarks

To be sure, other forms of life also take place at St Peter's. Twice a week, the parish offices are open to young men, who find food served by volunteer workers, and advice dispensed by Father Carmelo, while the Italian housekeeper meanders her way through, going about her daily tasks. Excluded from the 'community' (see Chapter 2) these youths nevertheless find a welcoming meeting place at St Peter's. Meanwhile, upstairs in the social club, other men gather in the bar to play cards, or to watch football. Women also meet, accomplishing a variety of craftwork, some of which will be sold at the annual bazaar.

St Peter's is a world of differing lives – a 'theatre of extremes', as Robert Orsi might put it (1985: 48). It is a place where the 'old' community confronts the 'new', incoming migrants. All these differing paths, that come and go, stop and depart, are key to the very meaning projected onto St Peter's church. Unlike their peers in the Centro Scalabrini, the priests of St Peter's seem secure in their knowledge of their institution as *casa nostra*, where all Italian migrants eventually pass through, if not find there an anchorage in the flow of their daily life.

St Peter's is a 'world of distances', in another of Orsi's phrases (1985: 48); the distance amongst The Hill, on one side, and Italy, Soho, the rest of London, Elsewhere, on the other. The distance between the London Italian 'community' and those from Birmingham or Gloucester; the distance between past and present, between generations. Distances that collapse in enactments of traditions that speak of the enduring presence of Italian London.

St Peter's is a place of re-membering; a place of collective memory, in which elements of the past are brought together to mould a communal body of belonging. It is where an area of London, The Hill, becomes memory in the very process of naming. Where The Hill is at once a space of living memory and the subject of recollections. This is also a place where individual lives, present and past, are called upon to inhabit the present space, to 'member' it. It is a site where individual bodies circulate, come and go, return to; where bodies are signifying actors (Gatens 1991, 1992) in claims for, and practices of, the identity of St Peter's. These bodies, in turn, are projected into a structure of meaning that precedes them and re-members them into gendered, sexualized and generational definitions of identity and becoming. The female body is elevated as the key point of suture not only between Us and Them, but also one that solves the indeterminacy of an Italian identity in contemporary London. The figure of the sacrificial 'virgin-mother' epitomizes deeply held ideas about the supremacy of womanhood, marks out and enacts the thresholds of identity and difference, while it displays the certainty of a presence. Anxieties of loss are comforted by gendered displays of generational continuity. Remembrances of The Hill work through bodies that are ethnicized and gendered at once, while the circulation of these bodies ethnicizes and genders a space in the process of claiming it as an Italian (place of) belonging.

Notes

1. In 1994 alone, 90 couples were wedded at St Peter's – more than one a week – in contrast to the Chiesa del Redentore, where less than 10 weddings took place.
2. Bryson was a pupil of Norman Shaw and W.E. Nesfield, and the chief initiator of the English Baroque revival in the 1890s.
3. *Londra Sera* is a small broadsheet that lists artistic events such as exhibitions, cinema, opera, and so on. It also has a financial page and news from Italy. The articles are predominantly in Italian. In 'community' circles, *Londra Sera* is known as the London Italian version of *Hello* magazine.
4. From a non-dated booklet published at St Peter's, *St Peter's Renovation Fund.* Capitals original.
5. 'Fagin's Den' in *Oliver Twist* was located in this area. Terri Colpi (1991a: 35–6) makes a parallel between Fagin's network of boys and the Italian padrone-run organizations of Italian children peddlers and street hawkers, which were also located in the Saffron Hill area. At the time *Oliver Twist* was published, however (1838), the Italian presence in that area was not yet significant.
6. As the following excerpt illustrates:

   > Over the years [Taddeo] developed a rheumatic condition which plagued him for the rest of his life. He vowed that his children would receive a good education and never have to work in the kind of conditions, detrimental to health and family life, that he had experienced. He clearly steered them in the right direction. Antonio . . . went into banking . . . he was a greatly respected member of the community. Annie was a brilliant seamstress. She was employed in the finest haute couture fashion houses . . . Luisa . . . although plagued by poor health, she eventually . . . became a

> linguistic secretary. Damaso was an accountant, he enjoyed life, and he could be found in the 'Coach and Horses' where he was known for his formidable skill as a card player (*Backhill*, December 1992/January 1993: 9).

For a fuller description of these aspects of Besagni's chronicle, see Fortier 1999.

7. The second work of fiction of Besagni's niece, Lilie Ferrari, is set in 'gang land Soho' of the late-1940s (Ferrari 1994). It is, to my knowledge, the only written account of the 'other' Little Italy.
8. I use a loose definition of 'diasporic moment', here, to include not only a type of diasporic consciousness – expressed in forms of longing and memory that are common to displaced people – but also actual practices that take place within transnational networks of dispersed 'communities'. These practices may circulate within a system of exchange – such as the black cultural forms within the Black Atlantic (Gilroy 1993a) – or they may be disconnected and isolated from one another, yet occur simultaneously in different places, such as the procession. More on this in the concluding chapter.
9. Bearing the three colours of the Italian flag: green, white and red.
10. This road did not exist in nineteenth century Little Italy; the church entrance was on Back Hill; for a map of the area in 1854, see Sponza 1988: 21.
11. Like the boy I witnessed grimacing at an Italian sausage his grandmother was trying to feed him. 'He is used to English food', she explained. 'It's a big shame. A good two months in Italy would do him good!'
12. For some, past relations with the Irish are characterized by geographical co-habitation and political alliances against imperialism and fascism (Sponza 1988; Ferrari 1993). Others re-member relations with the Irish as a mixture of mutual hatred, suspicion and tensions – namely within the Catholic Church hierarchy (Colpi 1991a; Marin 1975; Bottignolo 1985).
13. John Brown's book mentioned in Chapter 2 presents exactly this kind of picture with regards to West Indian families (Brown 1970).
14. Original text in English.
15. Daniel Boyarin offers a similar re-reading of Levine's argument in relation to Judaism. See D. Boyarin 1997.
16. Some define *mammismo* as Italian men's excessive attachment to their mother (Gundle 1996: 317). But I prefer to expand the definition of *mammismo* to a collective fascination for motherhood, especially for mothers' devotion, suffering and sacrifice for other human beings, namely their sons and husbands.
17. Though in the years following Mussolini, the project of an Italian liberal democratic state has also attended to women. As Leslie Caldwell (1989) demonstrates, progressive politics of post-war Italy substantially reproduced those of the fascist era when it came to the regulation of women-as-mothers.

Conclusion: Memory, Location and the Body Motions of Duration

> The question, 'When are you going home?' can be responded to in the following manner: home is here, in my migranthood.
>
> Rey Chow

Italian migrant belongings, in Britain, are generated through a group of claims about the historical, political and cultural presence of Italians. Written histories, politics of identity and popular religion are three areas where Italians create a new cultural identity grounded in memory and multilocality. At once deterritorialized and reterritorialized, Italian migrant culture combines competing definitions grouped around the central symbol of emigration.

Emigration is the basis of a new cultural terrain located between localism and transnationalism; a diasporic third space, known as 'Planet Emigration' in the pages of *La Voce*, constituted through entangled tensions that weave together new webs of belonging that trouble spatial fields of nation, 'home', and 'community': tensions between here and there; majority and minority; continuity and change.

Another tension arises *within* the idea of emigration itself. Emigration is the site of conflicting attempts to resolve the indeterminacy of the Italian presence in Britain. Elevated as an empowering experience in the constitution of a new, strong identity, emigration is also represented as the source of loss, alienation, and foreignness, which are resolved in written renditions of past and present Italian immigrant lives in Britain, narratives of transcendence, or displays of presence. The émigré culture includes multiple cultural forms configured around stories of migration; stories of beginnings (arrival and settlement); stories of alienation from and alliance with the British 'nation'; stories of continuity and stories of change. Hence the émigré culture is not homogeneous and uniform.

Key operating principles within the cultural practices, and supporting the Italian identity formation, are, as Paul Gilroy puts it, 'the social dynamics of remembrance and commemoration' (1994: 204). Indeed, memory becomes a primary ground of identity formation in the context of migration, where 'territory' is decentred and exploded into multiple settings. The thread of continuity, then, is the result of what Gilroy, following Leroy Jones, has dubbed the 'changing same', a phrase I briefly alluded to in Chapters 2 and 5. In the pages below, I reflect on how the changing same offers an alternative device for conceiving continuity and change in definitions of culture. This leads me to question the tendency, in theoretical discourses, of defining diaspora in predominantly geographical terms; to interrogate the limits of geographically-based definitions of diaspora by identifying three dualities that lie at the basis of conceptions of the empowering potency of diaspora's betweenness: here and there; homeland and hostland; indigenousness and dispersal. I propose to revisit these dualities in light of the ways in which questions of home and belonging emerge as sites of conflicted meanings in the formation of Italian émigré identity.

This is not to say that they are 'floating signifiers' which are not 'sutured': practices of migrant belongings produce 'undetermined intervals' (Butler 1993: 220) that are foreclosed in repetition. In the second section, I look back at the connection between gender, generation and ethnicity, and discuss the conclusion that may be drawn from my 'findings' whereby gender difference, in Italian émigré culture, is the emblematic statement of cultural specificity. I consider the tension that arises between everyday practices that reinstate the irreducibility of gender differences, and my concern to write an ethnographic account that does not encase these differences as foundational or universal. Also, what does this say about the position of 'ethnicity' and 'race' within the émigré identity formation? Defining the ways in which these categories are embedded, I argue, does not mean that they all operate at the same level.

Thirdly, I consider bodies as sites of mediation between social and subject, collective and individual, temporal and material. My intention is not to reduce identity to what is 'written on the body'. Nor do I posit 'the body' as nothing more than a surface of inscription, however malleable and historical, although I am fully aware that the very nature of this study – centred on representations, not individuals – invites such interpretations. For this reason, a reflection on the analytical status of the body in relation to identity formation is called for if only for purposes of clarification and refinement. By returning to the living memories of places analysed in Chapters 4 and 5, I suggest that the 'moments' of cultural reproduction are produced through body motions of duration. This conception, I argue, interrogates widely held assumptions about the stillness of space and the fluidity of time.

Running through this conclusion is a further elaboration of the notion of re-membering introduced in Chapter 5. By this I mean the processes through which spaces of belonging – imagined and physical – are inhabited, in the literal sense of dwelling, in the sense of populating or 'membering' spaces with ghosts from the past, and in the sense of manufacturing new émigré subjects.

Spaces of belonging and home

Leaders of 'ethnic organizations' are intensely aware of the task of 'creat[ing] a community', as Giuseppe Giacon stated it, which would effectively capture the imagination of its diverse segments. In other words, the issue at stake is to create a thread of continuity that will hem in the differences and resolve, even if temporarily, the indeterminacy of the Italian identity in Britain. This is what the notion of the changing same refers to: the 'logic of sameness and differentiation' which is the key defining principle of diaspora (Gilroy 1995: 26).

The changing same propels those who agree that 'we are more or less what we used to be' in a conflict about whether it is the more or the less that should be privileged in the project of identity (Gilroy 1995: 26). The changing same, then, seizes the ways in which the tension between having been, being, and becoming is negotiated, conjugated, or resolved. The Italian project of recovery is precisely juggling with these tensions, and in this respect, it is a project that is primarily about the changing same. Though some collective recollections may be lived as enduring traditions, they result, rather, from the processing and re-processing of cultural forms. Biblical stories re-told as migration narratives, or the tragedy of the *Arandora Star* repeatedly remembered as a distinguishing feature of the British Italian 'community', for instance, continually create a historical and cultural environment for the Italian population of Britain. The double process of unforgetting and remembrance stitches together elements of the past in attempts to draw lines of continuity that buttress common grounds of belonging.

The notion of the changing same as it operates in Gilroy's work concerns the ways in which sameness connects diverse black populations and cultures dispersed in different parts of the Atlantic world (1993a). In Chapter 5, I suggested that the annual procession in honour of Our Lady of Mount Carmel is a 'diasporic moment' in London Italian cultural life, for it is an event that occurs simultaneously in different parts of the world. This, however, was a deliberate construct of *prima facie* evidence of linkages between Italian diaspora communities dispersed around the globe. Few Italians I spoke with in London (and in Montreal) were aware of the synchrony of these events. For London Italians, the procession was an important moment of nostalgia, remembrance and family gathering. Hence when assessed in relation to locally specific settings, the changing same does not lose its heuristic potency, but it needs to be reconnected to 'the lived experience of locality' (Brah 1996: 192). Though memory is the primary modality of émigré identity formation, it is also tied to the creation of the identity of places: churches, chapels, neighbourhoods, or the Churchill Barriers. The changing same, here, speaks of enduring lives, and 'roots' them in local territory. In other words, it relates to the living 'memory of place' (Khan 1995: 95) without, however, reducing identity to that place. Memories of the Italian presence in Britain may be place based, but they are not necessarily place bound.

Speaking of émigré identity formation as a practice of re-membering *places* disturbs fixed notions of spatiality and territory, while it allows for considerations of memories as constituted by stationary 'moments', or intervals. Moreover, the root-term 'member' connotes some kind of physical materiality that thickens the act of memory, gives it substance. I will say more about this later. The point I wish to make at this stage is that the emphasis on re-membering is meant to suggest the extent to which the locations of culture – its origins, its beginnings, and also, more pointedly, its areas of dwellings – are not only lived in material, daily interactions, but are also imagined, multiple and moving.

In addition, the centrality of memory and of re-constituting traditions 'over here' defeats the idea that the homeland as 'home' is a constant object of longing or a permanent site of return. As Aisha Khan rightly puts it, 'the place to which one returns is not necessarily the place from which one came' (1995: 96). 'The Hill' in central London is a place where many Italians living in the UK journey back to their 'roots', as one of Olive Besagni's readers suggested. But the place of return is not necessarily a physical 'place' – for the Scalabrinians, 'where we're from' is the mythical drama of emigration, their 'migranthood' (Chow 1993: 142).

This poses the question of the place of 'space' in definitions of diaspora. In a cogent response to Clifford's mapping of diaspora as a theoretical formation, Barbara Kirshenblatt-Gimblett questions the coupling of dispersal and diaspora on the grounds that 'to think diaspora as a dispersal . . . still assumes the primacy of an earlier placement' (1994: 342). Her critique is aimed at the centrality of the trauma of displacement in definitions of diaspora, a conceptual move that, she argues, obscures other possibilities through which diaspora may be produced. By establishing the defining moment of diaspora in its inception, it is easy to reduce diaspora to its connection with a clearly bounded timespace, the 'homeland' – indeed, relations with the homeland are, for many, central in ascertaining diasporas and diasporic subjects (Safran 1991; Cohen 1997; Conner 1986; Tölölyan 1996). Hence, by making the particular conditions of dispersal diaspora's key defining principle, there is a risk of engulfing dispersed populations into culturally unified groupings across multiple and diverse locations. '[W]hat theorists of the diaspora often tend to forget', write Inderpal Grewal and Caren Kaplan, 'is that location is still an important category that influences the specific manifestations of transnational formations' (1994: 16).

More broadly, it seems to me that the association between diaspora and dispersal produces three dualities that lie at the basis of what is conceived as the constitutive betweenness of diaspora: here and there; homeland and hostland; indigenousness and dispersal. These dualities, I argue, emerge from understandings of culture that remain deeply connected to territoriality.

First, as shown in Chapter 3, the betweenness of here and there associated with diaspora is exploded in British Italian political discourses of identity that surface from a constitutive 'amongstness' where three locations, not two – Britain, Europe and Italy – are the grounds for the registration of particular claims. Though undoubtedly configured in nationalist terms, the Italian project of recovery was, from the outset, rooted in a transnational and plural terrain; it was as Europeans that Italians first began seeking integration and recognition within both the British social landscape and the Italian political sphere.

The struggle for a renewed Italian citizenship questions the position of the 'homeland' within diasporic imaginations; apart from expanding the Italian state's political constituency beyond Italy's borders, the politics of Italians abroad invert the relationship between here and there. This is not only about how 'there' is re-articulated and makes a difference 'here' (Clifford 1994), but it is also about how living 'here' could make a difference 'there'. The 'homeland', then, is perhaps the object of a myth of return, but one that challenges the status quo. Insofar as this political project expresses a will to participate in Italian national politics from 'abroad', the politics of Italians abroad are transnational in the sense developed by Basch, Glick Shiller, and Szanton Blanc (1993), who examine the political activities of immigrants in the national politics of both their country of residence and their country of origin. In contrast, Italian leaders' limited investment in UK political life, especially in the years of intense debate over new voting rights in Italy, reduces their transnationalism to a one-way street; their 'transnationalism' was primarily aimed at participating in the Italian public sphere.

Transnationalism nonetheless constitutes a horizon that some Italian leaders are turning to in their assessment of their relations with the Italian population. Scalabrinian priest Giandomenico Ziliotto, for one, embraces a transnational perspective in his view of the future of the community. In June 1997, he was involved in the formation of a new political movement – *Mani Unite* (Hands United) – in the context of the COMITES elections.[1] *Mani Unite* was founded in the wake of the defeat of the Italian Bill providing for the election of émigré representatives in the Italian parliament and the creation of four Italian constituencies abroad. As the proposed legislation did not gather much support from the émigré population, Ziliotto considers that the British Italian leadership needs to reassess its links with the grassroots and to combine struggles for political inclusion in Italy *and* in Britain. Ziliotto, like his predecessor at *La Voce*, Gaetano Parolin, believes that the present, regionally based Italian associative structure is moribund: national and transnational organizations of Italians would better serve the interests of émigrés and their descendants, and be more representative of their identities and lifestyles. Moreover, he hopes that British-born Italians will gradually participate more in émigré politics, for he thinks that they are in a better position to speak for the rights of Italians in Britain. One elected member of *Mani Unite*, Giuseppina di Silvio, born in England, deals precisely with the concerns of 'younger generations'.[2]

Hence Ziliotto and his acolytes are acknowledging that Italian émigrés are indeed 'at home' abroad. Already in 1990, Italian President Francesco Cossiga made an important distinction in his address to Italian emigrants of the world: he stated that he was not speaking to 'Italians abroad' but rather to 'Italians in their own home' *(Italiani in casa loro)*. This 'new logic', as Parolin qualified it, was about establishing new ties with a worldwide *Italofonia,* that is with Italians who potentially speak Italian. For Cossiga, such a revised definition of the Italian diaspora allowed for a better integration of the experience of the 'second generation' (LV 831, October 1990: 9). Moreover, while language is viewed as a key vector of integration, it is also conceived as a meeting place of multiple cultures. Though the notion of *Italofonia* has not gone much beyond Cossiga's declaration – either in the UK or in Italy – the recognition of the changing forms of Italian culture and identity in the face of a growing population of 'younger generations' explodes the duality of 'here' and 'there' into the multilocality of a new Italian émigré 'culture of relations'. Yet overall, British-Italian politics of identity amount to a 'deterritorialized nation-state' (Basch et al. 1993: 269). One that simultaneously undermines the idea that the reach of the state's powers is confined within the borders of a single territory, and reappropriates some of the historical narratives characteristic of nationalist discourses: origins, ancestry and genealogy.

Assuredly, this shows that nationalism still fosters an enduring appeal as a regime of knowledge that models definitions of cultural integrity (Gupta 1992; Basch et al. 1993). A creative tension arises, however, between the purchase of this model and what Richard Marienstras describes as the 'transnational modes of existence' of diasporic subjects (1975: 179). For Clifford, this is what constitutes 'the empowering paradox of diaspora', that is 'that dwelling *here* assumes a solidarity and connection *there*. But *there* is not necessarily a single place or an exclusivist nation' (1994: 322; emphasis original). Clifford pointedly argues that diaspora destabilizes nationalisms: transnational connections and multilocal networks of belonging challenge nationalist contentions about the congruence of territory and culture. Yet he still represents the constitutive betweenness of diaspora in terms of a spatial opposition between 'here' and 'there'. Moreover, as stated earlier, there is a tendency to reduce definitions of diaspora to the initial traumatic conditions of dispersal and to sustained connections with the homeland. Hence the very nationalism that James Clifford and others seek to discomfit with diaspora is reinstated within such theoretical discourses: territory and geography remain the key defining principles in definitions of diasporic subjects.

My intention is not to dismiss spatiality as constitutive of diaspora cultures, but rather to complicate the oppositional framework through which it is configured. Where or what is 'there'? Is it necessarily *not* 'here'? How long is 'there' a significant site of connection? And for whom? How far away is 'there'?[3]

Italian-British culture, to be sure, is a migrant culture where the Italian homeland remains a 'spiritual possibility' (Salvatore in Caccia 1985: 158). Historically specific conditions of the diasporization of Italians support a kind of imagining of Italy not as a mythical homeland, nor as a land of expulsion. It manifests itself in Italian émigré culture not in terms of rupture, uprooting, or discontinuity, but rather, as continuity, as a place where one *can* return. Yet the factor of time invariably alters connections to, and definitions of, 'there'. As Chapters 3 and 4 reveal, the shift in definitions of identity that is presently occurring among London Scalabrinians effectively illustrates that definitions of 'where we're from' change over time. Indeed, diasporic identification need not be solely a function of a geographical space 'out there'; as author/composer Rakim says, 'It ain't where you're *from* , it's where you're *at*' (in Gilroy 1991; my emphasis). And 'where you're at' is not necessarily a single, homogeneous or exclusivist nation, community, or home.

This ties in with a second oppositional tendency that has developed between homeland as the object of longing (in nostalgic remembrances, the myth of return, political commitment), and hostland as the object of efforts to belong (integrating, fitting in, politics of difference). By approaching institutional representations of identity as part of a longing to belong, I have raised questions about the objects and the locations of longing and belonging: *what* is longed for, and *where* is it that Italians are striving to belong? This, in my view, is not so much about the connection with a country as it is about the creation of a sense of place, which is often uttered in terms of 'home'.

Avtar Brah offers a useful distinction between 'homing desire' and 'desire for the homeland' as a way of capturing the problematic of 'belonging' and 'home' in diaspora. Brah introduces this differentiation because, she argues, 'not all diasporas sustain an ideology of "return"' (1996: 180). Brah's distinction is pertinent for it draws our attention to how claims for 'home' may vary. Italian political discourses of citizenship express a desire for the homeland that is at once reinstated and expanded to include those living outside of its borders. This political project is deeply rooted in a self-perception that Italians abroad *belong* within the public debates about the future of the Italian Republic. In contrast, re-shaping the *Chiesa del Redentore*, recollections of 'The Hill', or setting up the Italian Women's Club, may be viewed as expressions of a homing desire; that is the desire to feel at home, by physically or symbolically re-membering places as habitual spaces which provide some kind of ontological security for Italians living in a non-Italian, non-Catholic world. The problematization of home, then, invites us to interrogate the different ways it is imagined in diaspora cultures, and the different kinds of materialization this imagining nurtures. For the Scalabrinians, 'home' is the remembrance of migration and its transcendence. At St Peter's, 'home' is the re-enactment and re-processing of traditions and culture in public displays of presence. In both, temporality and spatiality, genealogy and geography, weave together in intricate webs of meanings that produce new grounds of belonging. Homing desire is connected to the creation of a sense of place, a structure of feeling that is local in its materialization, while its symbolic reach is multilocal. Indeed, the borders of Italian and English cultures blur within the new spaces of belonging. Practices of homing desire such as these are not so separate from the desire for a homeland.

They include processes through which the local is constructed to create habitual and habitable spaces grounded on different forms of remembrance, including, though not exclusively based on, remembrances of the homeland. These remembrances, in turn, take the material form of cultural artefacts or architectural replicas – importing statues of saints from Italy, for example, or modelling the interior of St Peter's on a church in Rome – that are re-imported in the church premises in order to shape it into a place to call 'home', *casa nostra* as St Peter's Father Russo puts it (Chapter 5). In this respect, desire for the homeland may be entangled with homing desire.

A third duality embedded in theoretical discourses of diaspora is one that opposes displacement and indigenousness, where the latter acquires a taken-for-granted status. Barbara Kirshenblatt-Gimblett pointedly observes that 'staying put, which having been assumed as normative for so long, no longer seems to require explanation' (1994: 342). Yet in the face of the increased movement of populations between different parts of the world, 'staying put' takes on different meanings, not only for those who do not move, but also for those who seek to establish new roots on new grounds. So much emphasis has been put on the project of return, in renditions of diaspora, that the project to stay put has been neglected. Within British-Italian historicity, for instance, the experience of settlement and the re-location of the 'origins' of Italians *in* Britain serves to delineate the specificity of an Italian presence, and to distinguish the émigrés from new Italian migrants, commonly viewed as temporary residents rather than people who will tie their destiny to the UK. Hence in many ways, the Italian émigré culture arises from and constructs a diasporic imagination where settlement becomes a defining feature. But settlement is not an end in itself. On the contrary, it constitutes a point of departure, a beginning. Settlement, in this respect, is a rhizomatic node: a site of 'intersecting movements of "lines of flight"' (Kaplan 1996: 143).

Avtar Brah introduces the notion of 'diaspora space' in order to differentiate it from the concept of diaspora. For Brah, diaspora space is a social and political space that 'is "inhabited" not only by diasporic subjects but equally by those who are constructed and represented as "indigenous". As such, the concept of diaspora space foregrounds the entanglement of genealogies of dispersion with those of "staying put"' (1996: 16). The appeal of this notion notwithstanding, the polarization of diasporic subjects and indigenous subjects can become difficult to uphold when assessed in relation to locally specific projects of identity. Who are the Italian émigrés' others? Aside from the white British 'indigene' or the 'black immigrant', 'others' are also the young Italian migrants of contemporary Europe, excluded, at times demonized, as undesirable aliens who threaten the pristine image of the Italian 'community'. This raises a number of questions about definitions of indigenousness and, more importantly, their connections with notions of migration and displacement. Does the exclusion of young migrants make the *im*migrant-settlers indigenous to England? Conversely, are they the 'indigenous-other' of the young migrants? How long does it take to become indigenous? The insistence on settlement and the ethics of sacrifice, coupled with the deep discomfort for migrancy as a way of life – the immigrant condition is one from which many of the emigrant leaders seek redemption, and one with which many London Italian residents refuse to identify – speak of the anxieties for rootings, even on the surface, as a guarantor of social and political legitimacy. The distinction between the coupled emigration/settlement on the one hand, and migration on the other, testifies to how (e)migration is the site of conflict over definitions of identity and political legitimacy within the British and Italian national contexts.

Moreover, the Italian émigré subject is constructed as *both* migrant and indigenous at once, as a result of her/his different relationships to 'others'. First, the appropriation of emigration as an empowering and creative ground of identity stands in contrast to the Italians who stayed put in Italy. Second, Italian émigrés are indigenized in the face of contemporary migrants. The Italian diasporic imagination, then, is constituted by the constant negotiation of emigration and indigenousness, each of which is plural and multi-sited.

The ambivalent relationship with sedentariness manifested in different representations of identity testifies to the tension that exists between diaspora communities and nativist discourses that support the distinction between 'original' inhabitants and subsequent immigrants (Clifford 1994: 308–9). Irredentist undertones of the politics of Italians abroad stand in contrast with claims of the historical – not natural – presence of Italians in Britain.[4] Also, we cannot overlook Terri Colpi's colonization metaphor revealed in Chapter 2, and her images of Italian settlers advancing on British territory, conquering niches within the economic landscape. Though Italians arguably do not allege any special connection to British land, the rhetoric of settlement is nonetheless woven through geographical and generational mappings that authorize the actions undertaken to produce a distinctly Italian form of belonging *in Britain*.

Gender, generations, and cultural survival

Re-membering is not only about reprocessing elements of the past or of culture, or shaping physical places and buildings to 'reflect' an identity. It is also about manufacturing 'members' who will fit in; norms of belonging are invariably deployed in practices of identity, thus arresting the flow with discursive injunctions of collective and individual selfhood. This section, then, is concerned with the moments when the movement of identity is arrested; when the compulsion to install an identity serves to foreclose the fields of possibilities and contain them in sexual and ethnic conventions. The question that I raise relates back to the embeddedness of gender, sexuality, generations and ethnicity: does simultaneity necessarily mean equivalence?

The patriarchal family trope is ubiquitous in the forms of self-representation examined in the previous chapters and, most importantly, it gains a special significance arising from its relationship with emigration and settlement. Family, here, is invested with multiple meanings: migration and supranational kinship networks, but also settlement, stability and continuity. It is a space of painful separation, and a space of comfort – Cavallaro's 'body-buffer zone' (1981: 102). For Gaetano Parolin, it is at once the corner stone of cultural continuity and renewal, and a threat to communalization. Finally, the family pushes against national borders within Fortress Europe, while its use as an emblem of Italian culture remains emphatically patriarchal, a-historical and universal.

The 'community', however, is not represented *as* a family, nor is the family the sole generator of ethnic identity/difference. As Bruno Bottignolo himself writes:

> [a]n immigrant community does not identify itself and must not be confused with the families which constitute it at any given moment. An immigrant community takes shape and defines itself in part beyond the nuclear families and the possible personal relations which branch out from them to some levels where other factors contribute to consolidate its basis and to extend its solidarities. (1985: 86)

These solidarities are indeed 'extended' within institutions such as the church, charged with the task of *preserving* and *re*producing a distinct Italian culture in London. Though defined by some as the first ethnic network and cradle of fundamental values (Tassello and Favero 1976), the family is nonetheless perceived as a necessary but insufficient condition for the realization of a collective sense of self.

The family is at once distinctly post-national – it displaces the nation as the site and frame of memory and ethnic identity – and utterly local – it is located as a crucial site for the *trial* of ethnicity – in the senses of both trying out and adjudicating. More specifically, the family is where ethnic emblems circulate, are rehearsed and deployed within a system of inter-generational responsibility that is both the emblem of 'family' and its mobilizing force. That is to say that the services of the family in the reproduction of culture are enlisted through generations: consider the ways in which 'younger generations' are enjoined to bring the Italian language back into the family rather than the community. Hence, while the connection between generations and community pass through the family, the family is *re-membered* through systems of generational responsibility – deployed, for example, in the teleology of sacrifice. In turn, the generational metaphor reaches beyond the family realm. For instance, narratives of kinship wrapped in images of generations recur in popular histories of The Hill, or in the Scalabrinian politics of identity: 'younger generations' serve as anchors that precisely secure the historical presence of Italians in British soil and validate their claims for fuller participation in cultural and political life. In short, descent is erected as a communal point of aggregation, where concerns for the continuity and survival of the 'community' congeal. This generational metaphor suggests simultaneous diversity and solidarity; it embodies the changing same that émigré leaders attempt to stabilize by calling upon the trope of kinship.

Throughout this study, I have been continually drawn back to the fundamental question of the relationship between gender, generations and ethnicity, and I have come up against the primacy of gender as a key stabilizing principle of the ebb and flow of the Italian émigré culture. Indeed, the results of my enquiry corroborate Trinh T. Min-ha's argument that, in ethnographic narratives of local cultures, 'the gender divide is always crystal clear' (Trinh 1989: 106). My concern, however, is to avoid 'the representation of a coherent cultural subject as a source of scientific knowledge to *explain* a . . . culture and [the reduction] of every gendered activity to a sex-gender stereotype' (Trinh 1989: 106; my emphasis). How can I speak of the repeated insistence and rehearsal of the 'crystal clear' difference between men and women without encasing Italian femininity and masculinity within fixed positions? In other words, am I not at risk of reproducing a set image of 'ethnic' culture as family-based and thoroughly heterosexual (and, by implication, inherently homophobic)? In the preceding chapters, I have provided a detailed understanding of the ways in which gender, kinship and belonging are produced and sutured together in particular settings. In so doing, I have sought to expose the power structures that have constituted men and women as Man and Woman (with a special focus on the latter), and which continue to do so. The aim was twofold: to challenge power structures by exposing their deployment, and to undermine claims to an original, primary Italian culture founded on timeless gender divisions and family life.[5]

The very structure of this book emphasizes how generations, gender and sexuality are stabilizing principles in mapping new meanings onto the Italian presence in Britain. *Migrant Belongings* begins with metanarratives that set out the gendered terms according to which the indeterminacy of the Italian presence may be resolved and hemmed in, to culminate in a discussion about the intersection of metaphysical and institutional practices of sex/gender in the production of particular ideas of tradition, continuity, presence and transcendence. I show that gender is the central vehicle for the mobilization of family and generations in the collective re-enactment and display of cultural continuity. It is the modality through which young Italian boys and girls participate in the communal expression of local particularity. It was the principle means of my insertion in the London Italian associative life. It frames the political inclusion of Italian men and women in the Italian national fold. Running through the different institutional practices of identity is the repeated rehearsal of generations, heterosexuality and irreducible gender differences. These, in turn, mobilize the services of the family as a crucial stage in trials of ethnicity.

In addition, the reification of family values places the relationship between men and women at a special pitch, thus crystallizing definitions of ethnic authenticity. In sum, the Italian project of identity is moulded out of deeply held ideas about gender differences and generational responsibility, all of which are products of a patriarchal regime of knowledge that reasserts the universality of male authority, and that naturalizes the different positions of men and women. Definitions of continuity are configured through systems of inter-generational responsibility, while ideas of authenticity are defined in terms of fixed gender roles and heterosexual norms.

Hence within the double process of ethnicizing and gendering spaces and bodies, the prioritization of irreducible gender differences – that also signal irreducible heterosexual complementarity – acts as a display of cultural continuity. As Judith Butler writes, '[g]ender is a project which has cultural survival as its end' (Butler 1990: 139). Gender, in Italian émigré culture, is the modality in which cultural specificity is lived and represented. This, however, remains a puzzling thought for me because I am fully aware of the conditions of continuing racism in which the Italian project of identity has developed. As explained in Chapter 1, Italians project themselves as 'invisible immigrants' which, in the British context, is best understood as the product of the racialization of immigration, where 'immigrant' means black. In addition, their project evolved in the context of new racism, where skin colour is side-stepped by positing culture as the founding principle of absolute difference. Saying that gender is the ultimate trope of difference poses the question of the position that absolutist notions of ethnicity, and racist conceptions of culture, occupy within the formation of Italian émigré belongings.

This question has been partly addressed in Chapters 2 and 3, where I show that ideas of roots and routes intersect in definitions of cultural integrity. Though the Italian project of recovery cannot be understood in terms of ethnicity alone, ethnicity is undeniably worked into British Italian belongingness. That is to say that the quest for, and location of, cultural particularity is deeply intertwined with the construction of ethnic boundaries that hem in differences and enclose them into the fold of a hegemonic 'Italianness'. Terri Colpi's applauded book consistently objectifies and normalizes what it means to be and act Italian: from *campanilismo*, to *compadrismo*, family loyalties, and first communions. Likewise, notions of a primordial culture organically rooted in Italy bleed into appeals for a 'culture of relations', which is founded on the relationship between a culture of origin and a culture of adoption, identity-as-essence and identity-as-conjuncture.

Italian constructions of identity are also racialized insofar as they are deeply embedded in the construction of a white European hegemonic identity. Though the recovery of the Italian presence in Britain is to be read as a challenge to totalizing conceptions of whiteness, it remains one that re-instates the equation between Italianness, Europeanness and whiteness. As shown in Chapter 3, this is illustrated in claims for equal status with Britons on the grounds of a shared European cultural heritage, and in the effort to be recognized as such and no longer as the 'Negroes' of Europe. Emancipation from foreignness, in British Italian politics of identity, is construed as tantamount to being accepted as white. This connects with ideals of respectability explored in Chapter 5: respectable femininity is normalized through the presumed whiteness (and heterosexuality) of Italian womanhood.

But the point is, as Vikki Bell states, that thinking gender in terms of cultural survival resists the temptation to 'regard gender and ethnicity as operating as aspects of subjectivities that can be analysed according to the same cultural and psychic processes' (1999: 5). The simultaneity of gender and ethnicity, then, is not to be read as a system of equivalence. As 'invisible immigrants', thus unmarked whites, Italians construct their specificity through the marking of gender and generational differences. In other words, whiteness constitutes the unmarked background for the construction of generational and gender differences. Culture, for its part, is accepted as inherently malleable. What I found is that Italians of London perhaps position themselves as members of an ethnic group, but that its boundaries as well as the 'cultural stuff' within them, are indeterminate and moveable. With the exception of Terri Colpi, the project of recovery put forward by historiographers and leaders seeks precisely to move beyond the reification of cultural products or behaviours as ethnic emblems. They are acutely aware that they are not, as Stuart Hall puts it, '*unified* culturally in the old sense, because they are inevitably the products of several interlocking histories and cultures, belonging at the same time to several homes' (1993: 362; italics original), and descending from different and multiple 'origins'. But the indeterminacy is resolved through the trope of kinship. Italian émigré culture results from the construction of (terrains of) belongings that are *at once* ethnicized, racialized and gendered, but where gender is the key stabilizing principle. As Paul Gilroy writes:

> definitions of authenticity are disproportionately defined by ideas about nurturance, about family, about fixed gender roles and generational responsibility. What is racially and ethnically authentic is frequently defined by ideas about sexuality and distinctive patterns of interaction between men and women, which are taken to be expressive of essential difference. (1993c: 197)

In this discursive context, re-membering addresses the shaping of individual bodies within ritualized patterns of cultural reproduction and continuity; by the same token, it concerns the ways in which collective remembrances serve to delineate the terms of membership in a collective body. In the displays of presence that occur at St Peter's, in the former *Miss Italia nel Mondo* contest, in the appeal to 'younger generations' as bearers of culture-as-essence and culture-as-conjuncture, or in the centrality of the family within the Italian cultural landscape, discourses and practices of identity *act upon*, *call upon* or indeed *appear on* individual bodies. All these events, each in their way, operate as sites of re-membrance where universal definitions of the collective body relate to multiple injunctions of individual bodies. They are performative and as such are 'sites of repetition' (Moallem forthcoming); they are part of regulatory practices that produce social categories and the norms of membership within them. And the connection between the formation of subjects and the formation of group identity is mediated through individual bodies. Male, female and generational embodiments of identity and difference – whether symbolic or material – repeatedly instantiate what it means to be a man, woman or a 'younger generation' *of* the Italian 'community'. In this respect, multiple interpellations of individual bodies by hegemonic discourses of group identity re-member them as man, woman, girl, boy, while they simultaneously member the physical and symbolic spaces of belonging with gendered and generational Italian subjects.

What, then, does this tell us about diaspora's constitutive 'amongstness'? Insofar as the Italian diasporic imagination is stabilized and sutured through gender differences and heterosexual norms, as long as cultural integrity and authenticity are configured around male and female bodies, the possibilities of amongstness are somehow brought to a halt. Gender is constructed and repeatedly rehearsed as anything but indeterminate, anything but 'among' a number of possible sexual categories. Representations of a *mouvant* Italian émigré culture are lived through linear narratives of gender and sexuality. As I watched young girls in bridal gowns walk down the aisle, the words of Maria de Marco Torgovnik resonated in my mind: 'When I think of Italian American girlhood, I think above all of being parcelled and bound' (1994: 151). Filled with my own memories of Catholic 'rites and wrongs', I could not help but feel the forces of compulsory heterosexuality and the oppressive disgust for things of the flesh closing onto my own body; to feel how the boundaries of my/their bodies have to negotiate sexual restrictions.

Given the subject matter of this enquiry, such a reaction was hardly surprising. 'Official' representations of a white, Catholic, European population residing in Britain were not likely to be subversive with regards to norms of gender and sexuality. In hindsight, however, what intrigues me are the ways in which the body is conscripted (and sublimated) to bring abstract ideas into material form. I am interested in the connection between the bodily coding of culture and individual incorporations of cultural identity. How is 'the body' put to work as a surface of mediation within wider projects of identity? Although I insist on the prioritization of gender, I would like to suggest that the modality of the embeddedness of gender, generations and ethnicity may be understood as the outcome of their deployment along similar *bodily* lines. The mutual constitution of ethnicity, gender and generation is most manifest in the sacraments examined in Chapter 5. Displays of the Italian presence work through bodies that are ethnicized, gendered and generational at once, while the circulation of these bodies ethnicizes and genders a space in the process of claiming it as an Italian (place of) belonging. Likewise, Terri Colpi's satisfaction that I would *pass* as Italian testifies that Italianness may be inscribed on the body. As argued in the opening chapter, though the body, in the formation of cultural ethnicity, may not figure as the bearer of immutable cultural or biological difference, it is conscripted to render 'visible' what is not. The embeddedness of gender, ethnicity and generations, then, bears important implications for the ways in which 'the body' may figure within conceptions of cultural identity formation.

Bodies in motion: body-images and the location of culture[6]

Migrant Belongings was partly inspired by recent feminist redefinitions of the subject premised on a new form of corporeal materialism where the body is understood as a site of inscription and performance of identity; 'a point of overlapping between the physical, the symbolic and the sociological' (Braidotti 1994: 5; Grosz 1994; Butler 1990, 1993; Probyn 1996; Grosz and Probyn 1995; Gatens 1996; Douglas 1966/1984). For Elizabeth Grosz, the body is a threshold concept: it 'hovers perilously and decidedly at the pivotal point of binary pairs', thus calling to question the very boundaries that constitute these pairs: 'the body is neither – while also being both – the private or the public; self or other; natural or cultural; psychical or social; instinctive or learned; genetically or environmentally determined' (1994: 23).

This literature is primarily concerned with the speaking and acting subject, and its emphasis on embodiment is part and parcel of an anti-essentialist critique of Western philosophical and social thought. In this respect, the concern for the body constitutes an important critique of the Cartesian mind/body split. However, as Sara Ahmed (1998a and b) rightly points out, the tendency is to conflate all forms of differentiation (sexing, gendering, racializing the body) into a system of equivalence, lining up differences onto a level playing field. The above discussion contradicts this supposition.

Another effect of the emphasis on the body is that it risks privileging the visible (what is written on the body) as a key site of construction of difference. What I have tried to suggest throughout this book, is that there is more to identity than what can be seen. Which is not to say that the empiricism of the visual field does not operate in our daily lives and have a direct effect on how we negotiate regimes of power. The reliance of practices of identity on bodily codings of culture thus begs the question of how the body becomes a site of connection between the social and the individual. Corporeal feminism is useful because it brings forth the tension between multiple interpellations of bodies and universal definitions of selfhood (collective and individual), and the difficulties that arise in attempts to stitch both poles together 'not in a dialectic manner of supersession, but, rather, as irreducibly different' (Grosz 1994: 21). Moreover, the insistence on the body as threshold allows me to think about the delicate balancing act of being/becoming of individual and collective subjects *at once*.

Drawing on from Mary Douglas's conception of the body as social text (1966/1984), Aiwha Ong and Michael Peletz suggest that 'discursive constructions of bodies are frequently plotted against divisions that maintain social order, and that women's bodies in particular are commonly used to symbolize and threaten transgressions of social boundaries' (1995: 6; see also Levine 1992; McClintock 1995). More broadly, this concerns the extent to which the performativity of gender is not only most intensive, but perhaps most imperative when the borders of communities, classes, nationalities and cultures are threatened. For Italian leaders, the issue is precisely to create a new identity at a time when the population is fragmented, dispersed, and when migration from Italy has radically changed; at a time when the 'community' is perceived as being at the threshold of indeterminacy, assimilation and cultural oblivion.

Performances and discursive constructions of identity work differently on male, female, young, middle-aged and elderly bodies. As I observed the circulation and representation of bodies in Italian émigré historicity and social life, the idea of the body as *tabula rasa*, a neutral space whereupon femaleness or maleness can be indifferently projected, could not hold. Bodies are differently re-membered into particular subject positions: brides-to-be, men-to-be, women as bearers of culture and community (*Miss Italy in the World* or girls wearing traditional dress), and men as migrant labourers, fathers and soldier-heroes. Meanings acquire a special significance as a result of the kinds of bodies that they interpellate, while at the same time bodies are shaped and reshaped into subject positions that relate back to the wider project of cultural survival. There is no single body (Grosz 1994; Gatens 1996; Braidotti 1994), nor is there a single kind of relation between bodies and thresholds.

A striking feature of Italian émigré culture is that women are (on) the thresholds of identity/difference, at once moving and fixed figures of identity and change. Firstly, the multiplicity of women's subjectivities is melted into the singular female body – the Italian 'woman' (*la donna*) – which is not only elevated as the key point of suture between Us and Them, but also one that solves the indeterminacy of an Italian identity in contemporary Britain. Deeply held ideas about gender differences that emphasize the supremacy of 'virgin-motherhood' – *mammismo* as the veneration of *mamma* as the self-sacrificing Madonna – provide some form of ontological security for an indeterminate, disparate and fragmented population for whom ethnicity has no definite appearance or determining power. The female body becomes the 'flesh' through which local particularity and collective identity are inscribed. It is offered as a guarantor of individual and collective selfhood. Secondly, the female body is not only captive or passively standing at the threshold

(Levine 1992; McClintock 1995). Women also appear as agents of change and continuity. Their circulation in beauty contests, in historical renditions of the early 'community', in processions, or between multilocal family homes, mark out the thresholds of identity *and* difference, past times *and* new times, migrancy *and* settlement, being *and* becoming. Though they are not pictured to be as physically mobile as men – women are settlers, men are migrants – they nonetheless are key actors not only in the foundation of the 'community', but in its ongoing transformations. They are also moving figures in the processes of re-membering shared belongings.

Different kinds of embodiment deployed in different forms of representation construct embodied images of stability, continuity and change. Linked to representations of spatiality and temporality, bodies are offered as images of collective and individual belongings. I am reminded of Elspeth Probyn's thoughts on the 'body-image'. Informed by the French philosopher Henri Bergson, she defines an image as an existence that is more than an idealist representation, and less than a realist thing (Probyn 1995: 14). It is not merely a product of the activity of the mind, nor can it be reduced to an object whose qualities are inherently built in. As both signified and signifier, the body absorbs and relays meanings. It circulates as part of an ensemble of other images (bodies and objects), relating to them and, in doing so, producing itself.

Beyond considerations of how body-images are producers of individual bodies and subjects – which is the main object of Bergson's *Matière et mémoire* (1939/1993) – I am interested in the connection between individual and collective bodies as it operates through bodily images of duration. For Bergson, memory is an act of duration where different states and moments have no beginning nor ending, but rather extend into one another (1939/1993: 31). As such, memory is a constitutive force of 'matter', hence of bodies. Re-membering, then, is about producing images of duration, as those of generational continuity that are performed in the church aisles, invoked in written recollections of 'The Hill', or in political discourses of cultural survival. And images of duration work through bodies in different ways – metaphorically or performatively. When deployed in performative displays of presence, they become deeply textured images, animated by the very act of re-membering: 'it reminds me of my past, of my childhood.' 'Coming here is full of nostalgia for me. I might have been born in England but my true identity is Italian; deep down I'm Italian.' In short, the performative character of rituals and commemoration is mediated through the memory work they accomplish. And spaces of belonging are meaningful insofar as they are inhabited by *living* memories. In this sense, rituals become 'the living memory of the changing same' (Gilroy 1993a: 198) and as such they are embodied and lived as expressions of an inherent, core and enduring identity that is organically linked to a larger, imagined community. Constructed through memories and duration, spaces of belonging are themselves, to some extent, continually produced as images. To be sure, the living memory of places challenge commonly held assumptions about the stillness of space and the fluidity of time.

Hence the 'moments' of cultural reproduction are lived in motions: the motions of ritualized bodily gestures, the motions of journeying in and out of Little Italy or of the Centro Scalabrini, the motions of memory. As Mark Thorpe pointed out in our written exchanges (see note 6)

> [t]his utilization of motion unleashes a paradoxical force; this is a force in which motion and stillness confound each other; where the monolith becomes a fluid conduit; where the conduit becomes momentarily trapped in 'time'. This motioning signals a 'time' where centuries are captured by moments and where moments are lived for centuries. Such motioning denies itself under a veil of permanence while the urgency of its enactment confirms its temporality.

In contrast to Bergon's refusal to think of time in spatial terms, and his refusal to accept that memory may include discrete 'moments', duration, here, combines forces of movement and attachment at once – just as, in the opening chapter, I stand aside from Probyn's emphasis on movement to also insist on the significance of dwelling and settlement in the formation of migrant belongings. In other words, this is about how people locate themselves in their environment through their lived experience of motion. The space and time when bodies 'hover perilously' between two 'moments' is lived at once as eternal and momentary, for it is inhabited by living embodiments and embodied memories of continuity, presence, and change. The sight of children dressed as 'becoming brides' and 'becoming men' – in both senses of respectability and moving from one 'stage' of selfhood to another – struck me as an intense moment where the social and the subject meet, as with my own strange (dis)comfort during my visits to St Peter's. This (dis)comfort resulted from a tension between what I was becoming, and, to paraphrase Rosi Braidotti, *who* I was, the only indicator of which were the traces of *where* I had already been – that is to say of what I had already ceased to be (Braidotti 1994: 16; emphasis original). And perhaps in 20 years time, a British-Italian woman will attend her niece's first communion and experience the same (dis)comfort. As Braidotti writes, '[i]dentity is a retrospective notion' (1994: 16). The motions of re-membering are more about interconnectedness than simple reproduction or imitation (Braidotti 1994: 5). They acquire a special significance as a result of their association not only with geographical movement and change, but also through their connection with ideas of home and continuity.

Each of these notions can be grouped together within the rubric of 'migrant belongings', which involves the process of creating momentary coherence – of place, of culture, of history – which is deemed central to the definition and duration of identities. A momentary coherence that is lived through the body motions of inhabiting, displaying and telling in order to show what cannot be seen. Migrant belongings are momentary positions that seek to 'recover' what *was* but no longer *is*, but they are also lived as expressions of an identity that *is* but may no longer *be* tomorrow. In *Migrant Belongings*, I thus seek to capture the transient thresholds of belonging; the continuous movement of being and becoming, as elements of the past are temporary references in the process of creating new terrains of belonging that will be differently re-membered. In short, understanding cultural identity as threshold is part of a research practice that accepts the quiveriness of identity and maps out the multiple points of suture and nodes that momentarily stabilize it.

Notes

1. See Chapter three for an explanation of COMITES. Four members of *Mane Unite* were elected to sit on the 12 member COMITES (Committee of Italians Abroad; *Comitato Italiani all' Estero).* Other elected members came from *Unione Associazione Cristiane* (associated with the Christian Democrats; five seats), and *Comitato Tricolore per l'Italia nel'Mondo* (fascist tendencies; three seats). Only 13 per cent of eligible voters went to the poles. This represents a drop of 13 per cent from the 1991 COMITES elections. The turn up in Britain, however, equals the European average (14.87 per cent). In was in Central and South America that voters were most numerous with an average of 31 per cent (LV 977, July 1997: 1).
2. At the time of the elections, Ms di Silvio was also member of the executive committee of the Club Donne Italiane. The other two elected members of *Mane Unite* are Padre Gabriele Bentoglio, also a Scalabrinian priest based at the Centro, and Salvatore Mancuso, professional photographer. The participation of the two priests in political life caused some controversy in the community. The leaders of St Peter's, for example, opposed what they considered as privileging politics over religion. This is the main distinction between St Peter's and the Centro: the first prioritizes religious teaching, while the second seeks to combine religion with social and political concerns. In this respect, it is worth noting that Padre Giadomenico was inspired by the theology of liberation that he encountered during a sojourn in Brazil in 1982–6.
3. In this respect, there is certainly a rich terrain of inquiry to be found in comparing Italian cultural forms in different locations of migration. Differences in geographical proximity, for instance, will influence different experiences and definitions of 'home' and connections with Italy. Italians in London live closer

to Italy than those residing in North America. Theirs is to some extent more of a border culture than that of Italians residing in Australia or in the Americas. Though they cannot be likened to Italians in southern France or Mexicans in the southern US, Italians in Britain move freely through borders, for work or leisure. Likewise, the specificity of British Italian cultural life could be further highlighted through comparison with other migrant populations, such as the Irish.

4. The connection of indigenousness and territory would merit fuller consideration if we are to further explore the issues at stake in constructions of identity based on claims of a historical presence. For Jonathan and Daniel Boyarin (1993), both indigenousness and autochthony are claims to a territory or a land, but the former is grounded history – such as conquest – while the latter is founded on the 'natural' right to a land on the grounds that those who claim autochthony have never lived anywhere else. Elsewhere, I reflect on these questions in connection to Italian-Canadian discourses on John Cabot who, for some, should be recognized as the first 'discoverer' (sic) of Canada. This is a good example of claims for indigenousness grounded in a claim to a territory. In the Canadian context, this discourse serves to separate ethnics from immigrants in the process of acquiring a special symbolic status within the Canadian social and political landscape. See Fortier 1998b.
5. I am also fully aware that Italian self-definitions exist in relation to the ways in which Italianness has been represented differently in different times, in British culture (and elsewhere). To be sure, Italian migrants have occupied an ambivalent position in relation to Europeanness – close to the edges of the Third World, yet part of the over-developed Northern Western world (Verdicchio 1997). For example, there are interesting avenues to explore in relation to the ways in which the entrenchment of Italian culture in 'traditional' values and fixed gender roles are viewed as both products of, and at odds with, Western systems of knowledge. This, in turn, may be understood as consolidating the coherence of the white West as 'modern' subject. Hence further considerations about the kind of representation my own account has produced would need to consider more closely the historical ambivalence of Italian migrants' cultural position within the British and European landscapes.
6. Elements of this section pertaining to questions of 'motion' and its connection with placement are informed by a number of conversations with Mark Thorpe. I am grateful to Mark for the invaluable hours we spent dialoguing and writing about the creativity of people's 'art of living' during the summer of 1997. I take full responsibility, however, for any shortcomings of the following argument.

Appendix 1: Methodological Considerations

I want to begin with an explanation of my decision to disclose the identity of the research settings. First, as communal spaces, these churches are part of a public realm that is independent of my research. It follows that the activities I attended and journals I read were public 'events' open to a large number of people. In addition, I want to take seriously the importance of 'authorship'. These are lived places that evolved under different conditions and that play different roles in the London Italian 'community' life. All their vitality would be lost under the veil of anonymity. Furthermore, revealing the names of the research settings opens up the possibility of other interpretations by those who are familiar with one or both locations.

In contrast, the identities of some individuals with whom I had regular contacts have been changed, while others have not. I use the real names of interviewees who are well known in the Italian community and whose biographical details would be immediately recognizable. Also, most of the information these men and women provided me with during our conversations concerned their organizations, and was thus available to the public. Likewise, their beliefs and politics are known to the readership of *La Voce degli Italiani*, which regularly publishes their views. Where I have chosen to protect the anonymity of individuals, this is in reference to private and informal conversations: the informality of the contexts from which I draw these quotations – where there is no clear understanding that I may eventually use them – prescribes that I keep the interlocutors unknown to the readers. It is worth pointing out, however, that informal conversations are only secondary sources of information in this research, and as such, have not been used extensively.

The field research was conducted between February 1993 and May 1995 and involved semi-structured interviews, participant observation and the analysis of written documents (monographs, periodicals, booklets, and so on). Subsequent interviews and observations were conducted in the summers of 1995 and 1997. From the outset, I informed all those I came in contact with that I was conducting research on Italian immigrant identity formation. During the fieldwork, I took part in a number of activities organized by the Centro Scalabrini or St Peter's church. The 'community' events I observed were open to the Italian population at large, as opposed to gatherings of regional associations, or other groups such as the football club or the Alpini association (an organization of war veterans). I spent fifteen months doing field work in order to cover all of the annual events. I attended Sunday lunches to celebrate Father's Day, Grandparent's Day, Valentine's Day, the annual picnic, the annual remembrance ceremony in Brookwood cemetery, the annual pilgrimage to the monastery of Our Lady of Mount Carmel in Aylesford (Kent), the annual Procession della Madonna del Carmine in Clerkenwell, and the annual dinner dance of the FAIE.

Apart from these yearly ceremonials and festivities, I also participated in the religious life of St Peter's. I attended Sunday masses, first communions, confirmation celebrations and, towards the end of the fieldwork, wedding ceremonies. My visits to the Centro Scalabrini revolved around the weekly meetings of the Italian Women's Club, and the weekly rehearsals of the Scalabrini choir — of which I was a member — set up especially for the celebrations of the twenty-fifth anniversary of the Centro Scalabrini in December 1993.

For the textual analysis, *Backhill* and *La Voce* provided valuable information that I have integrated into my study. I have also analysed a small body of literature on Italians in Britain, for I conceive them as textual versions of self-representation and as such, they are part of the communal project of recovery (see Chapter 2).

The semi-structured interviews were conducted with a number of 'community' leaders and intellectuals (in the Gramscian sense), in their offices or in their homes. A total of 16 men and women were interviewed, some up to three times. At the initial stages of my research, these meetings were essentially aimed at acquiring information about the London Italian organizational structure: the 'who's who' and 'what's what' of Italian associative life. In this respect, conversations with two academics and observers of the 'community' — Lucio Sponza and Arturo Tosi — were most useful. Seven other interviews were conducted with leaders, volunteers or employees of the two research settings. The rest of the interviewees included an Italian language teacher working with Italian children, the author of a book on Italians in Britain, two leaders of an organization involved in the administration of Italian language classes, two non-affiliated Italian priests, and one president of a *patronati*, also heavily involved in Italian 'community' politics. Among these sixteen individuals, only two were women, four were 'second generation' (three born in London, one in Scotland), and one 'third generation'. It was these interviews that led me to focus my attention on St Peter's and the Centro Scalabrini, for they confirmed that these socio-religious centres play a leading role in the construction of a community. Later in the course of the field research, additional conversations took place with the leaders of these institutions, usually to get an appreciation of how they formulated their notion of identity, and how they defined their role in the 'community'. Apart from the tailored questions to suit each individual's speciality, all of the interviews addressed similar themes: questions related to the structure, mandate, history, activities and membership of organisation; personal biography, including migration story, family life, and so forth.

The rationale behind this flexible methodology was to try to get a sense of what was said about the Italian presence in Britain, and of how practices of collective identity were performed within communal activities. Furthermore, I hope to render a more textured account of institutional practices by including personal observations or comments from individuals. This is meant to avoid a univocal, smoothed-out rendition of community practices that obscures the multiple meanings that may be produced through collective practices of signification. On the other hand, by gathering information from a variety of sources, contradictions and consistencies between different narratives and practices of identity may be drawn out.

Finally, a word on the use of Italian terms. As I argue in Chapter 2, the use of Italian terms may be read as an objectification of Italian culture, just like glossaries appended to monographs suggest that there is a 'key' to deciphering the language, and by extension the 'world', of an 'other' culture. This enunciative strategy installs the power of the 'knower', who at once confirms the authenticity of the 'culture' she represents, and instates her privileged access to this culture. Hence I purposefully have not included a glossary, nor do I systematically include Italian words, titles, or club names. Rather, I have use the English form when the translation was appropriate, just as I have translated passages drawn from Italian texts. In other instances, Italian terms are used for purposes of precision (*mammismo*, for instance, has no equivalent in English; see Chapter 5), or by way of illustrating and justifying the choice of a given English term (inserting *patria* in brackets, next to the English 'fatherland').

Appendix 2

Table 1. Italian-born population in Britain 1861–1991[1]

Year		England and Wales (% of total)	London (% of total)	Scotland (% of total)
1861	4,608	4,489 (97%)	2,041 (44%)	119 (3%)
1871	5,331	5,036 (95%)	2,533 (47%)	268 (5%)
1881	6,832	6,504 (95%)	3,504 (51%)	328 (5%)
1891	10,934	9,909 (91%)	5,138 (46%)	1,025 (9%)
1901	24,383	20,332 (83%)	10,889 (45%)	4,051 (17%)
1911	25,365	20,771 (81%)	11,668 (46%)	4,594 (18%)
1921	26,055	20,401 (78%)	—*	5,654 (22%)
1931	24,008	18,792 (78%)	—	5,216 (21%)
1941	—	—	—	—
1951	38,427	33,159 (86%)	—	5,268 (14%)
1961	87,250	81,330 (93%)	—	5,920 (7%)
1971	108,930	103,510 (95%)	32,530 (30%)	5,420 (5%)
1981	97,848	93,059 (95%)	30,752 (31%)	4,798 (5%)
1991	91,010	87,063 (96%)	30,052 (33%)	3,947 (4%)

* — data unavailable.

1. Compilations up to 1981 from Colpi 1991: 48, 72, 135, 167; Sponza 1988: 13; Bottignolo 1985: 165, 181, all of whom use data from the British census. Numbers for 1991 are from the British Census Bureau. For a more detailed study of the data covering the years 1851–1911, see Sponza (1988: 12–14). There is sometimes a considerable discrepancy between British and Italian official estimates of the Italian population in Britain. Bottignolo notes that the differences between British and Italian estimates are due to the fact that: 'the English census groups all residents in by birthplace [whereas] Italian data . . . is [sic] based on parentage and citizenship which, for the children of immigrants, is their parents' municipality of origin where they are registered through the Italian Consulate' (1985: 27).

Appendix 3

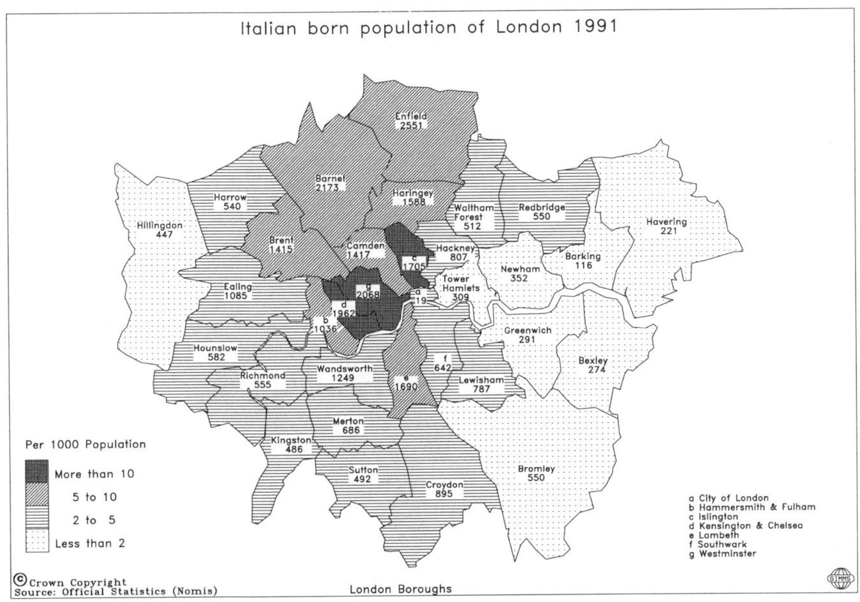

Map 1. Italian-born population in London, 1991[1]

1. The map was commissioned by Anne-Marie Fortier. It was produced by Peter Dodds, of NOMIS.

Appendix 4: Italian Associations and Committees Named in the Book

ACLI	Associazioni Cristiane Lavoratori Italiani (Associations of Christian Italian Workers)
ATI	Association of teachers of Italian
CDI	Club Donne Italiane (Italian Women's Club)
Circolo Veneto	Association for Italians from Veneto (Northern Italy)
CGIE	Consiglio Generali Italiani all'estero (General Council for Italians Abroad, Rome)
COASIT	Comitato di Assistenza Scuole Italiane (Committee for Italian Schools)
COMITES	Comitato Italiani all' Estero (Italians Abroad Committee)
CRE	Centro di Studi Emigrazione (Centre for Migration Studies, Rome)
Didattiche	Direzzione Education services, part of the Italian Consulate
ERMI	Ente regionale per i problemi dei migrante (Regional committee for problems of migrants)
FAIE	Federazione Associazioni Italiane England (Federation of Italian Associations, England)
FASFA	Federazione delle Associazioni e Comitati Scuola Famiglia (Federation of Parents' Associations and Committees)
FEDEUROPA	Federazione dei giornali italiani in Europa (Federation of Italian newspapers in Europe)
FMSI	Federazione mondiale della stampa italiana all'estero (World federation of Italian press abroad)
ICI	Italian Cultural Institute
INAS	Istituto Nazionale di Assistenza Sociale (National Institute of Social Services)
INCA	Istituto Nazionale Confederale di Assistenza (Institute of the National Confederation of Assistance)
SIE	Simbolo degli Italiani all'Estero (Symbol of Italians Abroad)
UNAIE	Unione delle associazione italiane all'estero (Union of Associations of Italians Abroad)

Appendix 5

Table 2. Result of the vote in the Italian Senate, on new voting rights for Italians abroad November 1993. (in *La Voce degli Italiani*, #899, November 1993)

Party	# Senators	For	Against	Abstentions
DC*	112	84	–	–
Pds	66	4	4	45
Psi*	50	35	2	1
Lega	25	–	6	14
Rifond.	20	–	18	–
Msi	16	15	–	–
Pri*	12	2	4	–
Psdi*	1	1	–	–
Verdi	5	1	3	1
Rete	3	1	–	1
Others	12	2	–	5

* these four parties formed the majority government coalition in 1993.

List of Parties

DC Christian Democrats (changed name to the Popular Party in 1994)

PDS Partito Democratico della Sinistra (Left Democratic Party; former Communist Party)

PSI Unità Socialista (Socialists)

Lega Northern League (right wing, alliance of secessionists parties from northern Italy including the Lega Lombardia)

Rifond. Rifondazione Comunista (hard-line communists)

MSI Neo-fascists

PRI Partito Repubblicano Italiano (Progressive on social issues, market oriented economics. Founded by Mazzini)

PSDI Social Democrats

Verdi Green Party

Rete 'The Network' (left-wing Catholic party)

Comment

Though a majority of 144 senators did vote in favour of the new legislation, 217 votes (2/3) were needed for the Bill to be adopted. The four parties in the government coalition voted in favour of the new legislation. They include centre-right, progressive and socialist parties. The MSI, the neo-fascist party also voted in favour. The new Bill thus found cross-party support, but the overall result led to its rejection.

Bibliography

Ahmed, S. (1998a) *Differences that Matter. Feminist theory and Postmodernism.* Cambridge: Cambridge University Press.

—— (1998b), 'Tanning the body: skin, colour and gender'. *New Formations* 39: 27–42.

Alba, R.D. (1990), *Ethnic Identity: The Transformation of White America*, New Haven: Yale University Press.

—— (1994), 'Identity and Ethnicity among Italians and Other Americans of European Ancestry', in L. Tomasi, P. Gastaldo, T. Row (eds), *The Columbus People. Perspectives in Italian Immigration to the Americas and Australia.* New York: Center for Migration Studies.

Anderson, B. (1983), *Imagined Communities.* London and New York: Verso.

Anthias, F. and Yuval-Davis, N. (1992), *Racialized Boundaries: Race, Nation, Gender, Colour and Class and the Anti-Racist Struggle*. London: Routledge.

Anzaldúa, G. (1987), *Borderlands/La Frontera. The New Mestiza.* San Francisco: Aunt Lute.

Appadurai, A. (1990), 'Disjuncture and Difference in the Global Cultural Economy', in Mike Featherstone (ed.), *Global Culture: Nationalism, Globalization and Modernity.* London: Sage.

Appiah, A. (1992), 'The Postcolonial and the Postmodern', in *In my Father's House. Africa and the Philosophy of Culture*. London: Methuen.

Ashcroft, B., G. Griffiths, H. Tiffin (eds) (1989), *The Empire Writes Back: Theory and Practice in Post-Colonial Literatures*. London and New York: Routledge.

Association of Teachers of Italian (1982), *Observation to the Committee of Inquiry into Education of Children from Ethnic Minority Groups*. Oxford: ATI.

Back, L. (1996), *New Ethnicities and Urban Culture. Racisms and Multiculture in Young Lives.* London: UCL Press.

—— and Nayak, A. (eds) (1993), *Invisible Europeans: Black People in the 'New Europe'.* Birmingham: AFFOR.

Baldwin, T.D., G. Carsaniga, S. Lymbery Carter, A. Lepschy, A. Moys, and R.C. Powell (1980), *Italian in Schools. Paper from the Colloquium on the Teaching of Italian in the United Kingdom 1979*. London: Centre for Information on Language Teaching and Research.

Banfield, E.C. (1958), *The Moral Basis of a Backward Society*. New York: Free Press.

Barker, M. (1981), *The New Racism*. London: Junction.

Barth, F. (1969), 'Introduction', in F. Barth (ed.), *Ethnic Groups and Boundaries*. George Allen and Unwin.

Basch, L., Glick Shiller, N., and Szanton Blanc, C. (1993), *Nations Unbound. Transnational Projects, Postcolonial Predicaments, and Deteritorialized Nation-States*. Amsterdam: Gordon and Breach Publishers.

Bell, V. (1996), 'Show and Tell: Passing and Narrative in Toni Morrison's *Jazz*', *Social Identities* 2(2): 221–36.

—— (1999), 'Performativity and Belonging: An Introduction', *Theory Culture & Society* 16(2): 1–10.

Bergson, H. (1939/1993), *Matière et mémoire*. Paris: Presses universitaires de France.

Berlant, L. (1997), *The Queen of America Goes to Washington City: Essays on Sex and Citizenship*. Durham (NC): Duke University Press.

Bhabha, H. (1993), 'Culture's in between', *Artforum*. September: 167–8, 212.

—— (1994), *The Location of Culture*. London and New York: Routledge.

Bhachu, P. (1991), 'Culture, ethnicity and class among Punjabi Sikh women in 1990s Britain', *New Community* 17(3): 401–12.

Bhatt, C. (1997), *Liberation and Purity: Race, New Religious Movements and the Ethics of Postmodernity*. London: UCL Press.

Bottignolo, B. (1985), *Without a Bell Tower. A Study of the Italian Immigrants in South-West England*. Rome: Centro Studi Emigrazione.

Boutang, P.A.and Pamart, M. (dir.) (1995) *L'abécédaire de Gilles Deleuze / entretien, Claire Parnet*. Paris. Editions Montparnasse/Sodaperaga.

Boyarin, D. (1997), 'Masada or Yavneh? Gender and the Arts of Jewish Resistance', in D. Boyarin and J. Boyarin (eds), *Jews and Other Differences. The New Jewish Cultural Studies*. Minneapolis and London: University of Minnesota Press.

—— and Boyarin, J. (1993), 'Diaspora: Generation and the Ground of Jewish Identity', *Critical Inquiry* 19 (4): 693–725.

—— and Boyarin, J. (eds) (1997), *Jews and Other Differences. The New Jewish Cultural Studies*. Minneapolis and London: University of Minnesota Press.

Boyarin, J. (1992), *Storm from Paradise. The Politics of Jewish Memory*. Minneapolis: University of Minnesota Press.

Brah, A. (1992), 'Difference, Diversity and Differentiation', in J. Donald and A. Rattansi (eds), *'Race', Culture & Difference*. London: Sage.

—— (1996), *Cartographies of Diaspora. Contesting Identities*. London and New York: Routledge.

Braidotti, R. (1994), *Nomadic Subjects. Embodiment and Sexual Difference in Contemporary Feminist Theory*. New York: Columbia University Press.

Brown, J. (1970), *The Un-Melting Pot*. London: Macmillan.

Butler, J. (1990), *Gender Trouble. Feminism and the Subversion of Identity*. New York and London: Routledge.

—— (1993), *Bodies that Matter. On the Discursive Limits of 'Sex'*. New York and London: Routledge.

—— (1994), 'Gender as Performance. An interview with Judith Butler', *Radical Philosophy* 67: 32–39.

—— (1995), 'Response to *Identities*', in K.A. Appiah, H.L. Gates Jr. (eds), *Identities*. Chicago and London: The University of Chicago Press.

Caccia, F. (1985), 'Filippo Salvatore', in *Sous le signe du Phénix. Entretiens avec 15 créateurs italo-québécois*. Montréal: Guernica.

Caldwell, L. (1986), 'Reproducers of the Nation: Women and the Family in Fascist Policy', in D. Forgacs (ed.), *Rethinking Italian Fascism*. London: Lawrence and Wishart.

—— (1989), 'Women as the Family: the Foundation of a New Italy?' in N. Yuval-Davis and F. Anthias (eds), *Woman-Nation-State*. London: Macmillan.

Calhoun, C. (1994), 'Social Theory and the Politics of Identity', in C. Calhoun (ed.), *Social Theory and the Politics of Identity*. Oxford: Blackwell.

Carroll, M.P. (1992), *Madonnas that Maim. Popular Catholicism in Italy since the Fifteenth Century*. Baltimore and London: John Hopkins University Press.

Casey, J. (1982), 'One Nation: The Politics of Race', *Salisbury Review*. Autumn: 23–9.

Cavallaro, R. (1981), *Storie senza storia. Indagine sull'emigrazione calabrese in Gran Bretagna*. Roma: Centro Studi Emigrazione.

Cavalli, C. (1973), *Ricordi di un emigrato*. London: Edizione la Voce degli Italiani.

Centro Scalabrini Di Londra (1993), *Centro Scalabrini di Londra. 25 anni di servizio. Inaugurazione della rinnovata Chiesa del Redentore*. London: Centro Scalabrini.

Cervi, B. (1991), 'The Italian Speech Community', in S. Alladina and V. Edwards (eds), *Multilingualism in the British Isles*. London: Longman.

Chistolini, S. (1986), *Donne Italo-Scozzezi; Tradizione e Cambiamento*. Rome: Centro di Studi Emigrazione.

Chow, R. (1993), *Writing Diaspora. Tactics of Intervention in Contemporary Cultural Studies*. Bloomington and Indianapolis: Indiana University Press.

Cliff, V. (1995), 'Fascism and anti-fascism', paper presented at a conference on *New Perpectives in the History of Italians in Great Britain*. Institute of Romance Studies, London: 19 May.

Clifford, J. (1986), 'Introduction: Partial Truths', in J. Clifford and G.E. Marcus (eds), *Writing Culture. The Poetics and Politics of Ethnography*. Berkeley: University of California Press.

—— (1994), 'Diasporas', *Cultural Anthropology* 9 (3): 302–38.

Cohen, A. P. (1985), *The Symbolic Construction of Community*. London: Routledge.

Cohen, P. (1992), '"It's racism what dunnit": hidden narratives in theories of racism', in James Donald and Ali Rattansi (eds), *'Race', Culture & Difference*. London: Sage.

Cohen, R. (1997), *Global Diasporas. An Introduction*. Seattle: University of Washington Press.

Colomina, B. (1992), (ed.), *Sexuality and Space*. Princeton: Princeton Architectural Press.

Colpi, T. (1979), 'The Italian community in Glasgow', in *Association of Teachers of Italian (ATI) Journal* 29, Autumn.

—— (1986), 'The Italian migration to Scotland: fact, fiction and future', in *The Italians in Scotland: Their Language and Their Culture*. Edinburgh: Italian Consulate General.

—— (1991a), *The Italian Factor. The Italian Community in Great Britain*. London: Mainstream.

—— (1991b), *Italians Forward. A Visual Hisotry of the Italian Community in Great Britain*. London: Mainstream.

Conner, W. (1986), 'The Impact of Homelands upon Diasporas', in G. Sheffer (ed.), *Modern Diasporas in International Politics*. New York: St Martin's Press.

Connerton, P. (1992), *How Societies Remember*. Cambridge: Cambridge University Press.

de Certeau, M. ((1980), 1990), *L'invention du quotidien 1. arts de faire*. Paris: Gallimard.

—— (1983), 'History: Ethics, Science, and Fiction', in N. Haan et al. (eds), *Social Science as Moral Inquiry*. New York, Columbia University Press.

—— (1984), *The Practice of Everyday Life*. Berkeley: and London: University of California Press.

de Grazia, V. (1992), *How Fascism Ruled Women*. Berkeley: University of California Press.

Deleuze, G. anl Guattari, F. (1980), *Mille Plateaux. Capitalisme et Schizophrénie*. Paris: Minuit.

de los Angeles Torres, M. (1995), 'Encuentros y Encontronazos: Homeland in the Politics and Identity of the Cuban Diaspora', *Diaspora* 4 (2), Fall: 211–38.

de Marco Torgovnick, M. (1994), *Crossing Ocean Parkway. Readings by an Italian American Daughter*. Chicago: Chicago University Press.

di Leonardo, M. (1984), *The Varieties of Ethnic Experience. Kinship, Class, and Gender among California Italian-Americans*. Ithaca and London: Cornell University Press.

—— (1991), 'Introduction. Gender, Culture and Political Economy: Feminist Anthropology in Historical Perspective', in M. di Leonardo (ed.), *Gender at the Crossroads of Knowledge: Feminist Anthropology in the Postmodern Era*. Berkeley: University of California Press.

—— (1994), 'White Ethnicities, Identity Politics, and Baby Bear's Chair', *Social Text* 41: 165–91.

Douglas, M. (1966/1984), *Purity and Danger. An Analysis of the Concepts of Pollution and Taboo*. London: Ark Paperbacks.

Dubisch, J. (1995), *In a Different Place. Pilgrimage, Gender and Politics at a Greek Island Shrine*. Princeton: Princeton University Press.

Duffield, M. (1984), 'New Racism . . . New Realism Two Sides of the Same Coin', *Radical Philosophy* 37: 29–34.

Dyer, R. (1988), 'White', *Screen* 29 (4): 44–64.

—— (1997), *White*. London and New York: Routledge.

Edwards, J. R. (1985), *Language, Society, Identity*. Oxford: Blackwell.

Eriksen, T. H. (1995), *Small Places, Large Issues. An introduction to social and cultural anthropology*. London: Pluto.

Ferrari, L. (1993), *Fortunata*. London: Michael Joseph.

—— (1994), *Angelface*. London: Signet (Penguin).

Firth, R. (ed.), (1956), *Two Studies of Kinship in London*. LSE Monographs on Social Anthropology #15.

Foerster, R. F. (1919/1968), *The Italian emigration of our time*. (Harvard Economic Studies, vol. 20) New York: Russel & Russel.

Fortier, A.-M. (1992), 'Langue et identité chez des Québécois d'ascendance italienne', *Sociologie et Sociétés* XXIV (2): 91–102.

—— (1994), 'Ethnicity'. *Paragraph. A Journal of Modern Critical Theory*. 17 (3): 213–223.

—— (1996), 'Troubles in the Field. The use of personal experiences as sources of knowledge', *Critique of Anthropology* 16 (3): 303–23.

—— (1998a), 'Gender, ethnicity and fieldwork: a case study', in C. Seale (ed.), *Researching Society and Culture*. London: Sage.

—— (1998b), 'Calling on Giovanni: Interrogating the nation through diasporic imaginations', *International Journal of Canadian Studies* 18 (Fall).

—— (1999), 'Historicity and Community: Narratives about the Origins of an Italian 'Community' in Britain', in J. Campbell and A. Rew (eds), *Identity and Affect. Experiences of Identity in a Globalising World*. London: Pluto Press.

Forty, A. (1986) *Objects of Desire: Design and Society 1750–1850*. London: Thames and Hudson.

Frankenberg, R. (1997), 'Introduction: Local Whiteness, Localizing Whiteness', in R. Frankenberg (ed.) *Displacing Whiteness. Essays in social and cultural criticism*, Durham and London: Duke University Press.

Fraser, M. (1999), 'Classing Queer. Politics in Competition', *Theory, Culture and Society* 16(2): 107–31.

Gabaccia, D. (1984), *From Sicily to Elizabeth Street: Housing and Social Change among Italians*. Albany: Albany State University of New York Press.

—— (ed.), (1992), *Seeking Common Ground. Multidisciplinary Studies of Immigrant Women in the United States*. Wesport (Conn.) and London: Greenwood Press.

—— (1994), *From the Other Side. Women, Gender, and Immigrant Life in the US 1820–1930*. Bloomington and Indianapolis: Indiana University Press.

Gans, H. (1979), 'Symbolic Ethnicity: The Future of Ethnic Groups and Cultures in America', Ethnic and Racial Studies 2(1): 1–20.

Garigue, P. and Firth, R. (1956), 'Kinship Organisation of Italianates in London', in R. Firth (ed), *Two Studies of Kinship in London*. LSE Monographs on Social Anthropology #15: 67–93.

Gatens, M. (1991), 'A critique of the sex/gender distinction', in S. Gunew (ed.), *A reader in feminist knowledge*. Routledge.

—— (1992), 'Power, Bodies and Difference', in M. Barrett and A. Phillips (eds), *Destabilizing Theory. Contemporary Feminist Debates*. Cambridge: Polity

—— (1996), *Imaginary Bodies. Ethics, power and corporeality*. London and New York: Routledge.

Gellner, E. (1983), *Nations and Nationalism*. Ithaca, Cornell University Press.

Giles, H., R.Y. Bourhis, and D.M. Taylor (1977), 'Towards a Theory of Language in Ethnic Groups Relations', in H. Giles (ed), *Language, Ethnicity and Intergroup Relations*. London: Academic Press/European Association of Experimental Social Psychology.

Gillis, J. R. (ed.), (1994a), *Commemorations. The Politics of National Identity*. Princeton: Princeton University Press.

—— (1994b), 'Memory and Identity: the History of a Relationship', in J.R. Gillis (ed.), *Commemorations. The Politics of National Identity*. Princeton: Princeton University Press.

Gillman, P., Gillman, L. (1980), *Collar The Lot!* London: Quartet.

Gilroy, P. (1987), *There Ain't no Black in the Union Jack*. London: Unwin Hyman.

—— (1991), 'It Ain't Where You're From, Its Where You're At . . . The Dialectics of Diasporic Identification', *Third Text* 13: 3–16.

—— (1993a), *The Black Atlantic. Modernity and Double Consciousness*. London: Verso.

—— (1993b), 'One nation under a groove', in *Small Acts. Thoughts on the Politics of Black Cultures*. London: Serpent's Tail.

—— (1993c), 'It's a family affair: black culture and the trope of kinship', in *Small Acts. Thoughts on the politics of black cultures*. London: Serpent's Tail

—— (1994), 'Diaspora', *Paragraph* 17 (3): 207–12.

—— (1995), 'Roots and Routes: Black Identity as an Outernational Project', in H.W. Harris et al. (eds), *Racial and Ethnic Identity. Psychological Development and Creative Expression*. London and New York: Routledge.

—— (forthcoming), *The Culture Line: Identity and Belonging in Postmodern Times*. London: Penguin.

Ginsburg, F. and Tsing, A. L. (1990), (eds), *Uncertain Terms. Negotiating Gender in American culture*. Boston, Beacon.

Giovannini, M.J. (1981), 'Woman: a dominant symbol within the cultural system of a Sicilian town', *Man* 16: 408–26.

Glissant, E. (1981), *Discours Antillais*. Paris: Seuil.

Goddard, V.A. (1996), *Gender, Family and Work in Naples*. Oxford and Washington DC: Berg.

Goffin M. (1979), *Maria Pasqua*. Oxford: Oxford University Press.

Goldberg, D.T. (1993), *Racist Culture. Philosophy and the Politics of Meaning*. Oxford: Blackwell.

Gopinath, G. (1995), 'Bombay, U.K., Yuba City: Bhangra Music and the Engendering of Diaspora', *Diaspora* 4 (3): 303–21.

Gray, B. (1997), *Locations of Irishness: Irish Women's Accounts of National Identity*. PhD dissertation, Centre for Women's Studies, Lancaster University (UK).

Grewal, I. (1996), *Home and Harem. Nation, Gender, Empire, and the Cultures of Travel*. Durham and London: Duke University Press.

—— and Kaplan, C. (eds) (1994), *Scattered Hegemonies. Postmodernity and Transnational Feminist Practices*. Minneapolis, University of Minnesota Press.

Grosz, E. (1994), *Volatile Bodies. Toward a Corporeal Feminism*. Bloomington and Indianapolis: Indiana University Press.

—— and Probyn, E. (eds), (1995), *Sexy Bodies. The strange carnalities of feminism*. London and New York: Routledge.

Gundle, S. (1996), 'Fame, Fashion and Style: The Italian Star System', in D. Forgacs and R. Lumley (eds), *Italian Cultural Studies. An Introduction*. Oxford: Oxford University Press.

Gunew, S. (1993), 'Feminism and the politics of irreducible differences: Multiculturalism/ethnicity/race', in S. Gunew and A. Yeatman (eds), *Feminism and the Politics of Difference*. St Leonards (Aus.): Allen and Unwin.

—— (1996) 'Performing Australian ethnicity: "Helen Demidenko"' in W. Ommundsen and H. Rowley (eds) *From a Distance: Australian Writers and Cultural Displacement*. Geelong: Deakin University Press.

—— and Yeatman, A. (eds), (1993), *Feminism and the Politics of Difference*. St Leonards: Allen and Unwin.

Gupta, A. (1992), 'The Song of the Nonaligned World: Transnational Identities and the Reinscription of Space in Late Capitalism', *Cultural Anthropology* 7(1): 63–77.

—— and Ferguson, J. (1992), 'Beyond 'Culture': Space, Identity, and the Politics of Difference', *Cultural Anthropology* 7(1): 6–23.

Hall, S. (1988), 'New Ethnicities', in *Black Film British Cinema*. ICA Documents #7: 27–31.

—— (1990), 'Cultural Identity and Diaspora', in J. Rutherford (ed.), *Identity. Community, Culture, Difference*. London: Lawrence & Wishart.

—— (1991), 'Old and new identities, old and new ethnicities', in A.D. King (ed.), *Culture, Globalization and the World-System.* London: Macmillan.

—— (1992), 'The Question of Cultural Identity', in S. Hall, D. Held, T. McGrew (eds), *Modernity and its Futures*. Polity and Open University Press.

—— (1993), 'Culture, community, nation', in *Cultural Studies* 7 (3): 349–63.

—— (1995), 'Fantasy, Identity, Politics', in E. Carter, J. Donals, J. Squires (eds), *Cultural Remix. Theories of Politics and the Popular.* London: Lawrence & Wishart.

—— (1996a), 'The formation of a diasporic intellectual: an interview with Stuart Hall by Kuan-Hsing Chen', in D. Morley and K. Chen (eds), *Stuart Hall. Critical dialogues in cultural studies*. London: Routledge.

—— (1996b), 'Introduction: Who Needs Identity?' in S. Hall and P. du Gay (eds), *Questions of Cultural Identity*. London: Sage.

—— and Held, D. (1989), 'Citizens and Citizenship', in S. Hall and M. Jacques (eds), *New Times: The Changing Face of Politics in the 1990s*. London: Verso.

Handler, R. (1988), *Nationalism and the Politics of Culture in Quebec.* Madison: University of Wisconsin Press.

Haraway, D. (1991), *Simians, Cyborgs, and Women. The Reinvention of Nature.* London: Free Association Books.

Harstrup, K. (1992), 'Writing Ethnography: State of the Art', in J. Okely and H. Callaway (eds), *Anthropology and Authobiography*. London and New York: Routledge.

Harney, N. (1998), *Eh, Paesan! Being Italian in Toronto.* Toronto: University of Toronto Press.

Helmreich, S.(1992), 'Kinship, Nation and Paul Gilroy's Concept of Diaspora', *Diaspora* 2 (2): 243–9.

Herrnstein, R.J. and Murray, C. (1996) *The Bell Curve: Intelligence and Class Structure in American Life.* New York: The Free Press.

Hewitt, R. (1991), 'Language, Youth and the Destabilization of Ethnicity', paper presented at the conference on *Ethnicity in Youth Culture* at the Summer University of Southern Stockholm, Fittjasgard, Botkyrka, 3–6 June 91.

Hobsbawm, E.and Ranger, T. (eds) (1983), *The Invention of Tradition.* Cambridge: Cambridge University Press.

Hoffman, E. (1989), *Lost in Translation. A Life in a New Language.* London: Minerva.

Hooks, b. (1990), *Yearning. Race, gender and cultural politics*. Toronto: Between the Lines.

Hughes, C. (1991), *Lime, Lemon and Sarsaparilla. The Italian Community in South Wales. 1881–1945,* Bridgend: Seren.

Iacovetta, F. (1992), 'Making 'New Canadians': Social Workers, Women, and the Reshaping of Immigrant Families', in F. Iacovetta and M. Valverde (eds), *Gender Conflicts. New Essays in Women's History*. Toronto: University of Toronto Press.

Jackson, J. (1990), *Italian/Italiano. Resource Guides for Teachers*. London: Centre for Information on Language Teaching and Research.

Jacobson, M. F. (1995), *Special Sorrows. The Diasporic Imagination of Irish, Polish, and Jewish Immigrants in the United States*. Cambridge (Mass) and London: Harvard University Press.

Jenkins, R. (1986), 'Social Anthropological Models of Inter-Ethnic Relations', in J. Rex and D. Mason (eds), *Theories of Race and Ethnic Relations*. Cambridge: Cambridge University Press.

Joseph, M. (1999), *Nomadic Identities. The Performance of Citizenship*. Minneapolis and London: University of Minnesota Press.

Juteau, D. (1983) 'La production de l'ethnicité ou la part réelle de l'idéel', *Sociologie et Sociétés* XV (2): 39–54.

—— (1996), 'Toward a pluralist citizenship: accounting for ethnicity', paper presented at the conference *États, nations, multi-ethnicité et citoyenneté*. Montréal, 30 May–2 June.

Kaplan, C. (1996), *Questions of Travel. Postmodern Discourses of Displacements*. Durham and London: Duke University Press.

Khan, A. (1995), 'Homeland, Motherland: Authenticity, Legitimacy, and Ideologies of Place among Muslims in Trinidad', in P. van der Veer (ed.), *Nation and Migration. The politics of space in the South Asian diaspora*. Philadelphia: University of Philadelphia Press.

Khan, V. S. (1980), 'The "Mother-Tongue" of Linguistic Minorities in Multilingual England', *Journal of Multilingual and Multicultural Development* 1 (1): 71–88.

King, R. (1977), 'Problem of Return Migration: a Case Study of Italians Returning from Britain', in *Tijdscrift voor Economische en Sociale Demografie* 68 (4): 241–6.

—— and King, P.D. (1977), 'The Spatial Evolution of the Italian Community in Bedford', *East Midland Geographer* 47 (6): 337–45.

—— Mortimer, J. Strachan, A. and Vignola, M.T. (1984), 'Emigrazione di ritorno e sviluppo di un comune rurale in Basilicata', *Studi Emigrazione/Études migrations* XXII (78): 162–97.

Kirshenblatt-Gimblett, B. (1994), 'Spaces of dispersal', *Cultural Anthropology* 9(3): 339–44.

Kristeva, J. (1983), 'Stabat Mater', in *Histoires d'amour*. Paris: Denoël.

Kukathas, C. (1992), 'Are There Any Cultural Rights?' *Political Theory* 20 (1): 105–39.

Kymlicka, Will (1992), 'The Rights of Minority Cultures. Reply to Kukathas', *Political Theory* 20 (1): 140–6.

—— (1995a), *Multicultural Citizenship. A Liberal Theory of Minority Rights.* Oxford: Clarendon.

—— (ed.), (1995b), *The Rights of Minority Cultures.* Oxford: Oxford University Press.

Lavie, S. and Swedenburg, T. (1996a), 'Between and Among Boundaries of Culture: Bridging Text and Lived Experience in the Third Timespace', *Cultural Studies* 10 (1): 154–79.

—— and Swedenburg, T. (1996b), 'Introduction', in S. Lavie and T. Swedenburg (eds), *Displacement, Diaspora, and Geographies of Identity.* Durham and London: Duke University Press.

—— and Swedenburg, T. (eds), (1996c), *Displacement, Diaspora, and Geographies of Identity.* Durham and London: Duke University Press.

Lawrence, E. (1982), 'Just plain common sense: the "roots" of racism', in Centre for Contemporary Cultural Studies (ed.), *The Empire Strikes Back.* London: Hutchinson.

Lazzari, F. (1990), 'Alcune riflessioni su cultura, lingua italiana, identità. Il caso dell'area francofona', *Studi Emigrazione/Études migrations* XXVII (99): 411–36.

Levine, A.-J. (1992), 'Diaspora as metaphor: bodies and boundaries in the Book of Tobit', in J.A. Overman and R.S. MacLennan (eds), *Diaspora Jews and Judaism. Essays in Honour of, and in Dialogue with, A. Thomas Kraabel.* Atlanta: Scholar Press.

Lloyd, G. (1984), *The Man of Reason. 'Male' and 'Female' in Western Philosophy.* London: Methuen.

Logan, O. (1994), *Bloodlines – Vite allo Specchio.* Manchester and Edinburgh: Cornerhouse and Istituto Italiano di Cultura.

Lowe, L. (1996), *Immigrant Acts.* Durham: Duke University Press.

Lury, C. (1997), *Consumer Culture.* Cambridge: Polity.

Macdonald, J. (1987), *Churchill Prisoners: Italians in Orkney 1942–1944.* Kirkwall: Orkney.

Macdonald, J.S. and Macdonald, L.D. (1972), *The Invisible Immigrants.* London: Runnymede Industrial Unit.

Mack Smith, D. (1959), *Italy. A Modern History:* Ann Arbor: University of Michigan Press.

—— (1983), *Mussolini.* London: Paladin.

Marienstras, R. (1975), *Etre un peuple en diaspora.* Paris: Maspero.

—— (1989), 'On the notion of diaspora', in G. Chaliand (ed.), *Minority Peoples in the Age of Nation-States.* London: Pluto. Trans. Tony Berrett.

Marin, U. (1975), *Italiani in Gran Bretagna.* Rome: Centro di Studi Emigrazione.

Martin, A.K. (1997), 'The Practice of Identity and an Irish Sense of Place', *Gender, Place and Culture* 14(1): 89–119.

Massey, D. (1995), 'Places and their pasts', *History Workshop Journal* #39: 182–92.

—— (1996), 'Masculinity, dualisms and high technology', in N. Duncan (ed.), *BodySpace. Destabilizing geographies of gender and sexuality*. London and New York: Routledge.

McClintock, A. (1992), 'The angel of progress: pitfalls of the term "post-colonialism"', *Social Text* 31/32: 84–98.

—— (1995), *Imperial Leather. Race, Gender and Sexuality in the Colonial Context*. London and New York: Routledge.

Mcdowell, L. (1996), 'Spatializing Feminism. Geographic perspectives', in N. Duncan (ed.), *BodySpace; destabilizing geographies of gender and sexuality*, London and New York: Routledge: 28–44.

Mcrobbie, A. (1995), 'Catholic Glasgow: a Map of the City', *History Workshop Journal* 40: 172–80

Melfi, M. (1991), *Infertility Rites*. Montreal: Guernica.

Mercer, K. (1990) 'Welcome to the Jungle: Identity and Diversity in Postmodern Politics', in J. Rutherford (ed.) *Identity. Community, Culture, Difference*. London: Lawrence & Wishart.

—— (1994) *Welcome to the Jungle*. New York and London: Routledge.

Micheals, W. B. (1992), 'Race into Culture: A Critical Genealogy of Cultural Identity', *Critical Inquiry* 18 (4): 655–85.

Migliore, S. (1988), 'Religious Symbols and Cultural Identity: A Sicilian-Canadian Example', *Canadian Ethnic Studies/Études ethniques canadiennes* 20: 78–94.

Miles, R. (1992), 'L'Europe de 1993. L'Etat, l'immigration et la restructuration de l'exclusion', *Sociologie et Sociétés* XXIV (2): 45–55.

Missionari di San Carlo Scalabrini (1987), *Di Terra in Terra . . . verso la Patria. 1887–1987, Centenario della Congregazione*. Rome: Congregazione dei Missionari di San Carlo.

Moore, H. (1994), *A Passion for Difference*. Cambridge: Polity.

Morgan, D. (1996), 'The Masculinity of Jesus in Popular Religious Art', in B. Krondorfer (ed.), *Men's Bodies Men's Gods. Male Identities in a (Post) Christian Culture*, New York and London: New York University Press.

Mosse, G. L. (1985), *Nationalism and Sexuality: Middle-Class Morality and Sexual Norms in Modern Europe*. Madison: Wisconsin University Press.

Myerhoff, B. (1979), *Number Our Days*. New York: E.P. Dutton.

Nardini, G. (1999), *Che Bella Figura! The Power of Performance in an Italian Ladies' Club in Chicago*. Albany: State University of New York Press.

O'Dochartaigh. F, (1994), *Ulster's White Negroes. From Civil Rights to Insurrection*. Edinburgh: AK Press.

Ong, A. and Peletz, M. (1995), 'Introduction', in Ong and Peletz (eds), *Bewitching*

Women, Pious Men. Gender and Body Politics in Southeast Asia. Berkeley: University of California Press.

Oriol, M. (1985), 'Appartenance linguistique, destin collectif, décision individuelle', *Cahiers internationaux de sociologie* LXXIX: 335-3471

Orsi, R. A. (1985), *The Madonna of 115th Street.* New Haven and London: Yale University Press.

Palmer, R. (1980), 'Process of Estrangement and Disengagement in an Italian Emigrant Community', *New Community* VIII (3): 277–87.

—— (1981), *The Britalians. An Anthropological Investigation*. PhD Thesis, University of Sussex.

—— (1977/1991), 'The Italians: Patterns of Migration to London', in J.L. Watson (ed.), *Between Two Cultures. Migrants and Minorities in Britain*. Oxford: Basil Blackwell.

Parker, A., M. Russo, D. Sommer, P. Yaeger (1992), 'Introduction', in A. Parker, M. Russo, D. Sommer, P. Yeager (eds), *Nationalisms and Sexualities.* New York and London: Routledge.

Parolin, G. (1979), *Foreign Catholics. The Religious Practice of the Emilian Community in London.* MA dissertation, Kent University in Canterbury.

Passerini, L. (1996), 'Gender Relations', in D. Forgacs and R. Lumley (eds), *Italian Cultural Studies. An Introduction*. Oxford: Oxford University Press.

Painchaud, C. and Poulin, R. (1988), *Les Italiens au Québec*. Hull (Qc): Asticou/ Critiques.

Pope John Paul II (1995), *Letter of Pope John Paul II to Women.* London: Catholic Truth Society.

Pratt, J. (1996), 'Analysis: Two Images of Catholicism', in D. Forgacs and R. Lumley (eds), *Italian Cultural Studies. An Introduction*. Oxford: Oxford University Press.

Primeggia, S., Varacalli, J. A. (1996), 'The Sacred and Profane Among Italian American Catholics: The Giglio Feast', *International Journal of Politics. Culture and Society* 9 (3): 423–49.

Probyn, E. (1993), *Sexing the Self: Gendered Positions in Cultural Studies.* London: Routledge.

—— (1995), 'Queer Belonging: The Politics of Departure', in E. Grosz and E. Probyn (eds), *Sexy Bodies. The strange carnalities of feminism*. London and New York: Routledge.

—— (1996), *Outside Belongings*. New York and London: Routledge.

Prosser, J. (1998), *Second Skins. The body narratives of transsexuality*. New York: Columbia University Press.

Radhakrishnan, R. (1996), *Diasporic Mediations. Between Home and Location.* Minneapolis and London: University of Minnesota Press.

Radley, A. (1990), 'Artefacts, Memory and a Sense of Past', in D. Middleton and

D. Edwards (eds), *Collective Remembering*. London: Sage: 46–59.

Ramirez, B. (1984), *Les premiers Italiens de Montréal. L'origine de la Petite Italie du Québec*. Montréal: Boréal Express.

Rodgers, M. (1982), 'Italiani in Scozia', in B. Kay (ed.), *Odyssey: The Second Collection*. (n.a.)

Rodriguez, R. (1983), *Hunger of Memory. The Education of Richard Rodriguez*. New York: Bantam.

—— (1995), 'On Borders and Belonging. A Conversation with Richard Rodriguez', in *UTNE Reader*. March-April: 76–9.

Roediger, D.R. (1991), *The Wages of Whiteness. Race and the Making of the American Working Class*. London and New York: Verso.

—— (1994), *Towards the Abolition of Whiteness. Essays on Race, Politics, and Working Class History*. London and New York: Verso.

Romano, S. (1977), *Histoire de l'Italie du Risorgimento à nos jours*. Paris: Seuil.

Rossi, G. (1991), *Memories of 1940. Impressions of Life in an Internment Camp*. Rome: Associazione culturale Scoglio di Frisio Foundation.

Rossi, M. M. (1966), 'The Italians', in D. Keir, *The Third Statistical Account of Scotland. The City of Edinburgh*. Glasgow, Collins.

Rowlands, M. (1996/97), 'Memory, Sacrifice and the Nation', *New Formations* 30: 8–17.

Safran, W. (1991), 'Diasporas in Modern Societies: Myths of Homeland and Return', *Diaspora* 1 (1): 83–99.

Sarre, P., D. Phillips, and R. Skellington (1989), *Ethnic Minority Housing: Explanations and Policies*. Aldershot: Avebury.

Savage, K. (1994), 'The Politics of Memory: Black Emancipation and the Civil War Monument', in J.R. Gillis (ed.), *Commemorations. The Politics of National Identity*. Princeton: Princeton University Press.

Shohat, E. (1992), 'Notes on the 'post-colonial', *Social Text* 31/32: 99–113.

Skeggs, B. (1997), *Formations of Class and Gender*. London: Sage.

Smith, A. (1986), *The Ethnic Origins of Nations*. Oxford: Basil Blackwell.

Sodano, T. (1995), 'Italians in Britain and their self-image', paper presented at the conference on *New Perpectives in the History of Italians in Great Britain*. Institute of Romance Studies, London: 19 May.

Sollors, W. (1986), *Beyond Ethnicity, Consent and Descent in American Culture*. Oxford: Oxford University Press.

Solomos, J. and Back, L. (1994), 'Conceptualising racisms: social theory, politics and research', in *Sociology* 28 (1): 143–61.

Spivak, G.C. (1990), *The Post-Colonial Critic. Interviews, Strategies, Dialogues*. London and New York: Routledge.

Sponza, L. (1988), *Italian Immigrants in Nineteenth-Century Britain: Realities and Images*. Leicester: Leicester University Press.

—— (1995), 'The Italian Comunity in Britain and World War II', paper presented at a conference on *New Perpectives in the History of Italians in Great Britain.* Institute of Romance Studies, London: 19 May.

St Peter's Church (1996), *St Peter's Italian Church*. Andover: Pitkin Pictorials.

Stewart, K. (1996), *A Space on the Side of the Road. Cultural Poetics in an 'Other' America*. Princeton: Princeton University Press.

Stubbs, M. (ed.), (1985), *The Other Languages of England. Linguistic Minorities Project*. London: Routledge & Kegan Paul.

Swiderski, R.M. (1986), *Voices. An Anthropologist's Dialogue with an Italian-American Festival*. Bowling Green (OH.): Bowling Green Popular Press.

Takagi, D. Y. (1996) 'Maiden Voyage: Excursion into Sexuality and Identity Politics in Asian America', in S. Seidman (ed.) *Queer Theory/Sociology*. Cambridge (Mass.) and Oxford: Blackwell.

Tassello, G. and Favero, L. (1976), *Rapporto di sintesi sulle caratteristiche, il sisteme religioso, il sisteme sociale personale della seconda generazione italiana in Gran Bretagna*. Rome: Centro di Studi Emigrazione.

Taylor, C. (1994), 'The Politics of recognition', in A. Gutmann (ed.), *Multiculturalism. Examining the Politics of Recognition*. Princeton: Princeton University Press.

Tölölyan, K. (1996), 'Rethinking Diaspora(s): Stateless Power in the Transnational Moment', *Diaspora* 5(1): 3–34.

Tomasi, S. (1986), *A Scalabrinian Mission Among Polish in Boston: 1893–1909*. Centre for Migration Studies, Occasional Papers: Pastoral Series #5, New York.

Tonkin, E., M. Mcdonald, M. Chapman (1989), 'Introduction', in E. Tonkin, M. Mcdonald, M. Chapman (eds), *History and Ethnicity*. ASA Monographs, 27. London: Routledge.

Tosi, A. (1984), *Immigration and Bilingual Education: a Case Study of Movement of Population, Language Change and Education within the EEC*. Oxford: Pergamon.

—— (1991), *L'Italiano d'oltremare. La lingua delle comunità italiane nei paesi anglofoni/Italian Overseas. The language of Italian communities in the English-speaking world*. Firenze: Giunti.

Touraine, A. (1977), *The Self-Production of Society*. Chicago: University of Chicago Press (trans. D. Coltman).

Trebay, G. (1990), 'Our Local Correspondents; The Giglio', *New Yorker* June 4: 78–89.

Trinh, T. M.-h. (1989), *Woman, Native, Other*. Bloomington and Indianapolis: Indiana University Press.

—— (1991), *When the Mood Waxes Red. Representation, Gender and Cultural Politics*. London and New York: Routledge.

Turner, V. (1969), *The Ritual Process. Structure and Anti-Structure*. London: Routledge and Kegan Paul.

Valentine, G. (1993), '(Hetero)sexing space: lesbian perceptions and experiences of everyday spaces', *Environment and Planning D: Society and Space*. vol. 11: 395–413.

Vallières, P. (1979), *Nègres blancs d'Amérique*. Montréal: Parti Pris.

Van Hear, N. (1998), *New Diasporas*. London: UCL Press.

Van der Veer, P. (1995), (ed.), *Nation and Migration. The Politics of Space in the South Asian Diaspora*. Philadelphia: University of Philadelphia Press.

Van Schendel, N. (1986), *Structure et dynamique de l'identité migrante chez des créateurs littéraires d'origine italienne et haïtienne*. Unpublished paper presented as doctoral research project to the Faculté des Études Supérieures of Montréal University.

—— (1992), 'L'Identité métisse ou l'histoire oubliée de la canadianité', paper presented in the CEFAN colloquium, Laval University, Quebec City, May.

Verdicchio, P. (1997), *Devils in Paradise: Writings on Post-Emigrant Cultures*. Toronto: Guernica.

Vignola, P., M. Bellisario, G. Bianco, W. Toscano (1983), *Aspetti e problemi occupazzionali della seconda generazione in Belgio, Lussemburgo e Inghilterra*. Roma: Istituto Fernando Santi.

Walby, S. (1994), 'Is Citizenship Gendered?', *Sociology* 28 (2): 379–95.

Wallman, S. (1978), 'Race relations or ethnic relations', *New Community* VI (3): 306–9.

Warner, M. (1976/1990), *Alone of All Her Sex. The Myth and the Cult of the Virgin Mary*. London: Picador.

Weinfeld, M. (1981/1985), 'Myth and Reality in the Canadian Mosaic: "Affective Ethnicity"', in R. M. Bienvenue and J. E. Goldstein (eds), *Ethnicity and Ethnic Relations in Canada* (2nd edition). Toronto: Butterworths: 65–86.

Westwood, S. (ed.) (1988) *Enterprising Women: Ethnicity, Economy and Gender Relations*. London: Routledge.

Young, J.E. (1993), *The Texture of Memory. Holocaust Memorials and Meaning*. New Haven: Yale University Press.

Yuval-Davis (1997) *Gender and Nation*. London: Sage.

—— and Anthias, F. (eds), (1989), *Woman-Nation-State*. London: Macmillan.

Index

Notes are indexed as 67(n20), ie note 20 on page 67